THE UNFOLDMENT

The Organic Path to Clarity, Power, and Transformation

By Neil Kramer

A division of
The Career Press, Inc.
Pompton Plains, NJ

THE UNFOLDMENT
EDITED BY JODI BRANDON
TYPESET BY DIANA GHAZZAWI
Cover design by Howard Grossman/12E Design
Printed in the U.S.A.

To order this title, please call toll-free 1-800-CAREER-1 (NJ and Canada: 201-848-0310) to order using VISA or MasterCard, or for further information on books from Career Press.

The Career Press, Inc.
220 West Parkway, Unit 12
Pompton Plains, NJ 07444
www.careerpress.com
www.newpagebooks.com

CIP Available Upon Request

Acknowledgments

I would like to express my heartfelt thanks and appreciation to the following people: David, for sharing so many adventures with so much heart. Lynda, for her love and integrity. Ronen, for the best conversations on the East Coast. Kevin, for his tremendous courage. Nate, for his honorable spirit. My folks, for their love and understanding. Mikael and Brent, for greasing the wheels. John and Arthur, for their inspiration.

Thanks to all the fine souls I've met at conferences, workshops, and conscious gatherings, for their support and insight. Thanks to everyone behind the scenes at Trident Media and New Page Books for helping to turn this into a finished product.

Finally, infinite gratitude to Maren for being an ever-luminous flame in my life.

Contents

Introduction

Spiritual Insurgence

When we pull ourselves away from the hypnotic allure of the material world and stand back from the clamor and collusion of it all, we come to the realm of philosophy. Philosophy invites us to rise above the route map of our own life and take a broader view. It is the gateway to experiences of meaning, insight, and truth. It can recalibrate the mind for contact with something of a higher order than everyday human consciousness. When approached genuinely and openly—and quite regardless of our familiarity with it—philosophy never ceases to reinvigorate our relationship with life, charging it with a vitality and a sense of adventure that many have not felt for years.

The word *philosophy* comes from the Greek *philosophia*: *philo* "love" and *sophia* "wisdom"—"love of wisdom." Considered in this light, it is a rather more natural impulse than we have been led to believe. Though scholars and academics appear to have laid claim to it from the ancient days of Babylonia, Egypt, and Greece onward, philosophy is really an abiding and essential component of everyone's life. We all know that wherever we are and whatever we are doing, the more wisdom we hold, the more fulfilling our life path.

Throughout the many journeys and realizations that have shaped my consciousness over the last few decades, I have always sought to distill my own thoughts into the most honest and lucid terms possible. This has been largely for practical purposes, so I can better understand myself, my fellow humans, and the extraordinary world in which we live. Many revelations, intrigues, and awakenings have been encountered along the way, all of them somehow interconnected at the deepest level. Though the wisdom I have come upon feels very personal and unique, I understand that, at its core, it is not. When the singular colors and textures that describe my

7

journey are set aside, what is left is universal. It is transpersonal, open, and immutable. There are seven billions paths to it—one for each of us—but the original knowing is always the same. We all feel the truth of it.

My path began with puzzlement—puzzlement at why it was that most people's lives followed a single fated formula: work, rest, eat, sleep, repeat. It was a deceptively vicious gravitation and it seemed to eventually pull everyone in. Though there were plenty of diversions available to take the edge off it, such as sport, vacations, culture, church, and parties, none of these things offered too much inspiration or insight. In a way, they made it worse. There was precious little time for anyone to think about the deeper questions and mysteries of existence. In fact, any sort of pondering on any subject was considered a rare luxury.

From all walks of life, the talk that I overhead was habitually focused on very mundane matters and was conspicuously un-magical. People shared their stories, their wishes, and their woes, but no one seemed to be really getting to the heart of things. They didn't want to talk about it. Even the most intelligent people seemed resigned to contracting the formula, as it if were a disease—quietly accepting that it would shape their lives from one year to the next. It felt wrong.

I realized that unless I took it upon myself to do things differently, I, too, would most likely fall into the same routine. I vowed that I would do my best to create my own patterns and spend as much time as I could on the things that I felt were meaningful and real. I stopped focusing on the particulars of life and instead started going to the roots. This immediately required me to regard my life as a kind of experimental art project. What I did, what I thought, and even who I was, would be painted onto a perfectly blank canvas, with absolutely no rules or restrictions. As long as I did no harm to myself or others, it was all good.

For a while, I chose to adopt the formula like everyone else. I worked, paid the bills, put bread on the table, and conducted myself in a relatively orderly manner. In parallel, I also immersed myself in the study of philosophy, spirituality, and mysticism. These seemed to be the subjects and disciplines that were best suited to the enterprise of discovery. Though they had each fallen unaccountably out of fashion, to me, there was nothing more exhilarating and consequential. I studied deeply and comprehensively. I read everything that I pulled from the shelves: the classical and the obscure, the deep and the divine, the arcane and the enigmatic. I soon realized that the wisdom our forefathers had left for us could not be absorbed in a single lifetime; perhaps not even 10. So I chose as judiciously and intuitively as I could. I put forth whatever effort was necessary to optimize my time with those texts. I read them with a great sense of pleasure and privilege.

Nevertheless, such presumptuous independence meant that I was occasionally suspected of not taking life seriously enough. I found this odd, as that was exactly the opposite of what I was trying to do. It was suggested to me that it would be better to do away with the frivolities of philosophical contemplation and instead turn my attentions to the somber responsibilities of adulthood. There were also times when I was reproached for taking it all far too seriously, accompanied by bizarre attempts to coerce me into spending my time on more acceptable leisure pursuits like football, golf, and reading spy novels.

Because I chose to pursue my studies in a non-academic fashion—instead, consciously selecting the path of the autodidact (one who is self-taught)—it had the effect of making matters even more flammable. Without a degree or a job in any of my areas of interest, it seemed that all my efforts were apparently fruitless. What I was doing was unproductive, insubstantial, and without practical value. I had embarked upon an irrational and perhaps even dangerous path. Regardless, I just got on with it and kept my nose clean, as they say. I kept my game so sharp that, despite the underlying ideological conflict, there were no real grounds for complaint.

I could not point the finger at any specific opponents, saboteurs, or individuals. My friends and family were pretty open-minded and tolerant, thank goodness. My colleagues and employers knew little or nothing of my interests. The adversity emanated from the system of social conditioning itself. All of its embedded messages, doctrines, and axioms were aimed at amplifying the old inevitable formula. Because I was rejecting that at a philosophical level, I was perpetually swimming against the tide. What was supposed to bring me pleasure did not. What was supposed to scare me did not. Yet the inertia of the whole setup weighed heavily upon me. At every turn, I was presented with solid reasons and tempting excuses to discard my conscious growth and do something else instead.

Another decade passed before I completely grasped why real philosophical and spiritual inquiry is frowned upon in the mainstream. The purpose and mechanisms of this peculiar containment are fully explored in due course. For now, let me say that the revelatory shock that ripped through my being, served only to strengthen my resolve to embrace my own sacred sovereignty as a way of life.

As I went about my studies and practices, I kept my eyes and ears open to what was happening around me. What occurred in the offices, corridors, and meeting rooms of the commercial world proved just as illuminating as the 19th-century German philosophy I was devouring in the evenings. Sometimes they even mirrored each other, if you can believe such a thing. I realized that laboring in the heart of the machine was affording me intimate knowledge of a world that I was beginning to actively deconstruct. It would be of little worth for me to sit in a comfortable study somewhere and merely speculate about the plight of the unfortunate proletariat. Before I could speak with any real passion or wisdom, I, too, had to be up to my neck in it. And I was.

It was an endless source of inspiration to me to learn that most people felt that what they were doing was somehow inauthentic. They didn't really like it and would much rather do something else. They just didn't know what or how. None of these confessions were ever prompted by me; people just told me things. In certain individuals, I noted their own private recognition that life was nothing to do with toil and reward at all. They knew something infinitely more profound and magical was occurring in the background, all the time. They felt it, secretly weaving through the panorama of reality, with only occasional glimpses and impressions to hint at its presence. Though they wanted to know more, they almost never followed it up. Time, resources, and confidence were in short supply. The overwhelming pressure to simply resume the old formula was too great to resist. Even so, I knew that the spark of truth was there.

In time, I started to understand how the formula could be dissolved. The truth of it went far deeper than I had anticipated. There were practical elements, and there were spiritual elements. It required discipline, rigorous honesty, and a big heart before a more authentic way of living could be established. It became crystal clear to me that the quality and depth of one's own consciousness was the single most important aspect of the whole equation. It contained both the problem and the solution.

Many sincere men and women have reached a point where they know they need to shift their reality—personally and collectively. There are left wingers and right wingers, pacifists and activists, fundamentalists and patriots—all striving to make the formula more equitable and fit with their vision of a civilized, thriving, and happy society. Whether reason, commerce, legislation, religion, or force is seized upon as the chosen instruments of transition, any headway that is made is invariably superficial and short-lived. The pieces on the chessboard are shuffled around, but the old game is still being played. It is not enough. We must go to the origin of all outward manifestation, the source of all ingress and egress. It is a journey of truth, consciousness, and spirit. It leads to a place of supreme equilibrium. Only from there can the game be unmade.

The purer the mind, the deeper the consciousness that passes through it. This purity naturally arises from the practice of the unfoldment: the *clarity* of the inner work, the *power* of conscious will, the *transformation* of authentic heart. Strictly speaking, such things can only ever come from experiential encounter. They rarely, if ever, can be grasped from the secure hermitage of purely theoretical study. Once more, we have to do it before we can know it. Only by getting our hands dirty can we develop the discernment necessary for true unfoldment. This introduces the concept of *gnosis*. The way I use this word is to mean a living knowledge that presents itself through direct contact, as opposed to abstract learning from books or computers.

Gnosis is closely allied to discovery. When we bring gnosis into our everyday lives—applying it to the big things and the little things—we accelerate our growth. No experience is ever a waste. No event is ever accidental. Life proves to be an endlessly supportive and enlightening phenomenon. It doesn't always feel like that, particularly when things get weird, stressful, lonely, or painful. Yet it is precisely in the midst of these challenges that the universe offers its most remarkable and precious upgrades. Fundamental realizations are often gift-wrapped in crisis. If we can fully grasp their meaning, we need not suffer their drama again.

The unfoldment teaches us how to stay centered in the eye of the storm. It reframes what it is to be a human being. Each chapter of this book explores key elements of the unfoldment: light and shadow, forthright and yielding, intimate and universal. Taken as a whole, it presents an illuminating spiritual philosophy and an empowering living practice. The deeper we go into the miraculous nature of existence, the more we realize that the unfoldment is something we are all trying to do, all the time. It is an ascendant movement of consciousness and spirit that ultimately takes us home. Along the way, life becomes a process of continual synchronistic discovery.

A life of discovery is a magical life.

Chapter 1

True Deeds

I can feel sacred truth in a smooth black pebble on the beach. I can see it in patterns of chewing gum stuck to the sidewalk. I can read it in old books and smell it in the carcass of a vulture. I can taste it in steamed broccoli. I can hear it in the voice of an old woman waiting in line at the grocery store. It is always present.

There is one universal truth from which all sacred knowledge flows. Every authentic philosophical, religious, scientific, and mystical system is attempting to rediscover the essence of that original emanation. Such is its brilliance and luminosity—that its reflection can be found in all forms, both physical and non-physical. The purer the reflection, the closer it feels. It points the way to growth and integration, and it reassures us in the adventure of separation as we live as human beings.

Truth is always a perennial discovery. Though the language and ideas that we use to articulate it are continually changing, its core resonance is constant and inviolable. It is always fundamentally the same. We can but offer our own knowing of it.

Each reflection of truth can be regarded as having three main elements to it: part wisdom, part thing, and part observer. The *wisdom* represents one strand of the original emanation of truth. It is an encoded route map back to source/the divine, lending insight and discernment to any given subject. The *thing* is the energy configuration that casts the reflection. It can be a poem, a piece of wood, a glass of water, or a memory. Anything. The more authentic and uncorrupted it is—the more organic—the clearer the reflection it will give. The *observer* is the consciousness of the person. You. Me. Your mother. The man in the coffee shop with the Salvador Dali moustache. There are countless idiosyncratic consciousnesses, each with its own customized narrative and philosophical equipment. All these things go into composing a reflection. Thus, each engagement with truth is uniquely and intimately bound to the individual experiencing it.

Depending on where we find ourselves on this planet, we are apt to perceive truth through the various social, historical, and political filters that have shaped our lands and peoples over the centuries. There are Western paradigms and there are Eastern paradigms, each with its own strengths and weaknesses. There is highbrow metaphysics and there is homespun commonsense. Scholars and mystics have grappled with the truth since time immemorial, producing enormously differing conclusions. Yet despite the singular circumstances of these men and women, were they not all looking upward to the same stars? Were their hearts not warmed by the same sun? Certainly, we each have our own personal way of approaching and interpreting truth and no single way is necessarily right or wrong—though undoubtedly, some are purer and more elegant than others.

When a small child looks into a mirror, he or she may be forgiven for thinking, "That is me!" The image behind the glass depicts a very faithful (albeit reversed) image of the child, one that is easily confused with the form of the actual child. In a similar manner, becoming confused by reflections of truth—rather than the truth itself—is not at all uncommon.

The pursuit and glorification of reflections is a game that even the brightest may inadvertently find themselves playing, sometimes for embarrassingly long periods before they finally catch themselves doing it. This wild goose chase might even be optimistically regarded as some sort of initiatory trial through which the eager spiritual student must pass. It only really becomes a problem when the reverence shifts up a gear, and the observer's consciousness becomes infatuated with the *thing* that casts the reflection. The mirror. The goblet. The person. The page. When this occurs, the vision of truth can become hopelessly distorted. Legions of well-intended souls can be seen prostrating themselves on cold floors, morosely clutching their talismans, and venerating effigies of forgetfulness. To witness the adoration of symbols, shapes, books, buildings, personages, bones, and relics is to witness the human mind falling into misapprehension. Though everyone finds their way back in the end, it can take an awfully long time in thick fog.

Whether or not we consider truth to emanate from, and lead back to, an ineffable divine source is a matter for personal contemplation. It's handy to use the word *God*, but that word is so loaded with eons of divisive religious baggage that it may confuse more than it clarifies. Regardless of the nature of that source—which remains necessarily enigmatic from our third density vantage point anyway—the observance that it is an *intelligent* source is becoming more and more self-evident. The sublime synchronistic universe, the staggeringly coherent interpenetration of all forms, and the ever-incrementing fractal hurricane of conscious evolution do not arise without an epic knowingness at their root. Whispers of this magic are everywhere. Physics and mysticism hold hands far more often than they would like anyone to know about.

Still, there are those who claim to have no interest in such fascinating expeditions of consciousness. In our everyday life, we cannot help but notice that an undeniable majority of folks do not appear in the least drawn to the enriching truths of the world. They conceal themselves from their unfoldment using all kinds of clever tricks, reasonable excuses, and encumbering diversions. They believe that if they just keep their heads down and lead a steady, productive, moral life, they'll get away with it. But deep in their hearts, they know this is a dishonest way of being. Everyone, sooner or later, must face their truth. We must all encounter that which casts its reflections into the world. Even a whole lifetime of sleek truth-dodging will simply result in a reboot incarnation—different scenery and personnel, but identical challenges and teachings, all over again. It is inevitable.

If truth is relative, might it therefore be relatively meaningless? How can it serve as a reliable guide to sacred wisdom if it's different for everyone? For example, is it true that Ernesto "Che" Guevara was a freedom fighter, or was he just a terrorist? Can both of these statements be true? Relativism holds that all criteria for judgment are relative, being variously influenced by belief, knowledge, environment, and historical precedents. If this is the case, and anything and everything could be true or untrue, then how can there be a single emanation of truth? The answer is visible only when viewed multi-dimensionally. In short, the closer our consciousness is focused upon ourselves, the more relative it is. We have our own personal truth *and* we have universal truth. When we shift perspective, we affect the universality of our truth. Zoom way out from your own concerns, and your sense of truth takes on a more universal aspect. You are compelled to know a truth that is not only valid for you, but for others, too. The further you zoom out, the more consciousness and creation that truth will have to encompass and respect. The opposite is also the case: The more you zoom in on your own personal affairs, likes, and dislikes, the more relative and less universal your experience of truth becomes.

A woman I once knew often complained that her husband would repeatedly shut down any discussion that questioned his beliefs by saying, "Well it's true for me and that's that." Despite her numerous optimistic attempts to open his mind to alternative scientific, cultural, and political outlooks, he would not budge. She used to call him a relativist Nazi. Like many people, he had established a set of easy truths as a young man and decided to stick with them. Forty years later, his stone tablets remained virtually untouched, with only rare booze-sodden self-acknowledgments of his bigotry and regret. His wife was a fan of Dorothy Parker and was the first to quote the immortal lines to me (with reference to her own dear spouse), "You can lead a horticulture, but you can't make her think."

Men are more predisposed to prematurely hardwiring their personal truths than women are. The female psyche sustains a flexible mental architecture for longer, because very wisely, women do not automatically associate their identity with their thinking, unlike men. This gives them a distinct advantage in terms of their capacity for personal transformation. It operates at both extremes however, in that the most fabulous individual unfoldments and the most spectacular psychic calamities, both consistently present themselves in the feminine aspect.

To maintain a knowingly limited set of undeveloped personal truths, with no real inclination to evolve them, is to hide under the bed. Though this may temporarily help to appease the weird convolutions of the world, it really only serves to magnify them. The monsters get bigger, the darkness gets thicker, and the truth becomes more incomprehensible. And it gets worse the longer you hide. When we recognize that our experience with truth is always changing and always refining, we can stop worrying about wrong answers. We can stop trying to identify ourselves by our collection of right answers. What we *have*, ceases to be so very important. We simply continue to live as truly as we can. We consciously allow a little more clarity and truth into our thoughts, feelings, and deeds each day.

Our truth deepens as we deepen. No experience of it will ever be repeated in quite the same way, ever again. Even on the same kind of day, with the same kind of thinking, when everything looks much the same as it ever was, truth is always created anew from one moment to the next. As Heraclitus observed, "No man ever steps in the same river twice." Though its reflections are forever moving, at its root, truth is perfectly still. It is the mind that moves. This is why it touches us so deeply when we find our own truth. We find our center, a place of inner knowing that transcends the comings and goings of life. Its stillness cuts through everything. We feel a sense of acquaintance with something greater than ourselves—something we once knew intimately. Herein lies the great romance of the unfoldment.

Chapter 2

Covenant of Amnesia

To be a human being on Earth is to undergo the toughest spiritual endurance training conceivable. To be voluntarily marooned on this singular blue orb is to be among the providential few. It is to be granted the opportunity to master the effects of consciousness in the third density by being thrown deep into the coagulum of physical pleasure and pain, arising and fading, knowing and unknowing. It is a one-of-a-kind experience. If you can do Earth as a human being, you can do anything.

We don't arrive with much. The physical vehicle of the body is the only piece of hardware we get, and we are vitally anchored to it for the duration. The tone of our relationship with the vehicle is not constant. Sometimes we recognize the ingenious gracefulness of this marvelous body, and through it we channel our unique consciousness and dream new creations into being. At other times, we feel painfully ensnared in this disintegrating meat-sack and can do little more than drag it around from one day to the next. This love-hate relationship with the body is experienced by most people at some point in their lives. Even when there is no pain or ailment, there is often some sort of awkwardness or heaviness about it. But this is all part of the training. The challenges of the body are pre-ordered especially to provide optimal growth potential for the presiding consciousness. Regardless of whether we perceive it as a biological machine or as a divine vessel, the body does a stunningly good job of transporting us around this realm.

So it is that, other than the corporeal form, we come in with absolutely nothing. No objectives, no history, no maps, no rules, no instruction manual, no evidence, no homing beacon. Like a commando parachuting naked into alien territory, we are obliged to gather and fashion whatever tools, information, and skills we can as we go along. To make matters even more interesting, the mission itself is totally unspecified. For all intents and purposes, it appears that there actually *isn't one*.

All right-thinking men and women, sooner or later in life, take a moment away from the hubbub of their day-to-day affairs and wonder: What is it all about? I mean, what is it *really* all about? In time, they may come to certain writings, both ancient and modern, that ponder this fundamental question. They are told that these writings are authored either by God, gods, prophets, or, at the very least, exceptionally clever people. In Western Europe, the Gods and prophets have become passé at the present time, so it's fallen upon the physicists to look after the secret keys of reality. Physicists like to measure things, so they present their measurements as a description of the world. How one set of measurements interacts with another set of measurements is what they call the laws of physics. Gods and prophets do the same kinds of things and produce their own laws about the world. It is notable that many of these different systems of laws disagree with each other—sometimes a little bit and sometimes a great deal. Some of the more radical devotees believe that the laws that they ascribe to are the only true laws and that those who don't believe in them have no right to be alive. Hence, it is not uncommon for people to kill each other regarding how strictly a particular set of laws should be observed.

If you happen to be born in a relatively free and enlightened country, you may find yourself in the privileged position of being able to study several different kinds of laws. Indeed, it is incumbent on those who enjoy freedom to take it upon themselves to focus their consciousness on such things; to pore over these words and ideas; to weigh them, reflect on them, and experiment with them in real life. The wisest individuals will combine the most resonant knowledge, disciplines, and practice, and formulate their own cosmology and spiritual wisdom. Even so, no matter who wrote them—quite honestly—when you place all the variables to one side, you come away with the sneaking feeling that the end result is that we get no confirmed answers while we are here. We *never* really know. Faith is all we have. Faith in God or gods, prophets, or physicists. It is up to us who gets the collective vote from our mind, body, and spirit. We can't bank on anything for sure. Nothing is going to get confirmed until later on, perhaps *much* later on. In the meantime, we are philosophically blindfolded and must fire our arrows into targets that we cannot see.

One of the most significant phases in the unfoldment is to deeply acknowledge to oneself that no one knows anything for sure. Not me, not you, no one. Ignorance is a strange thing to come to terms with in a world that pretends to know most things. Close on the heels of that realization is the further recognition that it's *okay* that we don't know anything. It is totally fine. In fact, it is a prerequisite for deep spiritual realization that we become comfortable with a state of unknowingness. Still, many people struggle with this. They think that it's better to look like you know what you're doing, even if you don't. For those who can't quite bring themselves to that level of theatrical chicanery, they instead choose to jump on someone else's bandwagon of belief, assuming that that will excuse them from the personal imperative to know. It does not. Everyone is accountable for their own choices, whether they like it or not. Just because that accountability is not necessarily hovering over our heads every day, does not mean that it's not real. Everything we do is permanently recorded in what some mystics call the akashic record, or the a-field, or the quantum vacuum. It is like a hard drive that operates at the most fundamental level, persistently chronicling every nuance of electro-magnetic energy that passes through our system. Every whisper, dream, thought, joy, pain, and creation is known. Although the forms themselves do not endure, the journey that they took—their energetic signature—is never lost.

The sooner we realize that we have assented to a covenant of amnesia, the better. Rather than constantly wondering what's going on and what it's all about, we begin to appreciate that we *can't know* what's going on, under the terms of our pledge. It would spoil the whole thing; the virtue and integrity of the teaching would be lost. The reason for coming in blank, without any sort of foreknowledge whatsoever, is to ensure that everything we attain in life is a *personal* attainment, because everything can only be arrived at through the discernment of our own freewill. The only real answers arise from within ourselves.

Those who gather all their answers from an external source—however sound, virtuous, or holy that may be—should be wary. When everything is handed over as a fait accompli, little is truly realized. If the answers, laws, and cosmologies have not been passed through the unique filters of one's own deep philosophical and spiritual inquiry, then they are ontologically precarious at best. They are borrowed investments—stakes in the marketplace. This is not a righteous path and does not constitute personal attainment.

Faith is a feeling of trueness. To have faith in a person, a deity, a thing, or an idea, is to have a sense for the truth of it. Humans are very good at this. With a little practice, we can feel the truth of a thing quite accurately in a matter of moments. The more we exercise this intuitive faculty, the better we get at it and the more reliable it becomes. We can tell how authentic something is, how constructive it is, how honorable it is, and how real it is. All of these things go into knowing truth.

Sometimes the traces of sacredness and the clues to our unfoldment come in the form of inconsistencies. Once we have a developed a keen sense for the truth of things, we can feel when something is not quite right with the world, not just on the surface, but at the very core. When the opaqueness of the consensus world fades, we can detect discrepancies between what is *supposed to be* (synthetic reality) and what *is* (organic reality). It is like living on a very high-quality film set that is an almost perfect replica of the real thing. Unless one's perceptions are finely tuned and vigilance is maintained, it may not occur to the observer that the whole thing is actually a facade—a good one, but artificial nevertheless.

The cracks are very faint at first. They can be felt well before they can be seen. Consider that a large part of spiritual ignorance is a social fabrication—a layer of mental conditioning that tells us how things are meant to be. Sometimes we have to directly experience a raging inauthenticity in our personal lives before we can appreciate its wider cultural implications.

I was once a guest at a posh dinner party in the city. It was being held at an expensive restaurant, and I had arrived early, well before my companions were due. I seated myself at the bar and enjoyed a quiet drink. An elderly woman, who was also evidently a guest, came over and took the stool next to me. We started chatting. She was very strikingly attired in a cream-colored silk gown, a pearl choker, and a black jacket. We spoke politely about our trendy surroundings and our equally stylish hosts. She asked me where I was from, what I did, and so forth. I explained where I lived and talked about my home, job, and career ambitions. We talked about our travels around Europe and compared notes. I spoke in the terms and tone that I knew she wanted to hear. I did not want to impress her, but merely offer the sort of urbane platitudes that seem to be the proper currency on such occasions. From her expression, I could tell she thought I was a thoroughly likeable young man and probably quite a catch for some nice young lady. In that moment, during a natural pause in the conversation, I *saw* myself. I spontaneously and profoundly zoomed out of my little self and witnessed the ghastliness of the whole situation. A projected vision of the evening's events rolled out before my imagination: the drinks, the sumptuous dining, the affectation, the hollowness, and the unawareness. *Why was I there? Was this the me that I wanted to create?* I excused myself from her company, explaining that I'd left my cell phone in the car. I walked out of the place. It was cold, dark, and beautiful outside. As the glass doors closed behind me, I knew I would not be going back into that particular building ever again.

The social window dressing had gone up in flames. The sort of upmarket event that smart young men in the city were supposed to take great pleasure and pride in, just horrified me. I couldn't help it. I tried to enjoy it, but it didn't work. The old circuits of civic consciousness had melted on me. Things would never be quite the same again. Back at home that evening, as I sat on the couch cradling a cup of tea, I realized that something wonderful had happened: I had gifted myself the opportunity to perceive what I should've only glimpsed 20 years later, with far fewer opportunities to do anything about it. It wasn't exactly news of the century, but it was the first time I felt it in my bones. The much-fêted, reward-driven Western capitalist paradigm was a deceit. It was not good. It was not honorable. It was no place for anyone who was trying to unfold his or her spiritual truth. Not only that, but I had temporarily *forgotten* what I was doing. I had nearly lost myself in the game.

So there I was, adrift in the same metaphysical boat as everyone else, trying to figure out what on Earth was going on. Day by day, I had been rising and falling on the interminable tides of polarity: positive and negative, promising and grim, good and bad. But now there was a stillness. I had become conscious of a definite change. I had come to the end of my dualistic courtship with the old formula. It had taken longer than I'd imagined. I had seen the believers believe and the pretenders pretend, right there in front of me. I could smell their breath and see the sweat on their collars. But now that time was over. I envisioned something fresh and potent stirring inside. Though it was undeniably a new feeling to me, I understood that it was something very old. It was an emanation of truth, and I had accepted it.

Once the cracks open up, they never close.

The problem with knowing truth is that you cannot help but perceive untruth. It glares back at you from nooks and crannies that were previously just blank spaces. When you raise the bar on your own life, your expectations of quality inevitably transform, too. There are negatives and there are positives. Situations that used to be perfectly tolerable and even quite pleasant suddenly become unhinged torture. What was once witty and cultured conversation around the dinner table shifts into a wall of white noise. Careers start to feel ludicrous really fast. It cannot be helped. There is no sense of superiority at work here, just a conscious dissonance that makes the re-capturing of past harmonies impossible. Conversely, various states of apathy, drudgery, and predictability begin to freely evaporate—both on the personal and the collective level. A renewed sense of enthusiasm for the most poignant and meaningful aspects of life begins to flood back into one's being. Passion, creativity, and mystery return.

Truth always gives more than it takes.

By not having access to the secret architecture of life, by not having any kind of prior knowledge of our overall conscious or spiritual trajectory, we are compelled to focus instead on the living truth of whatever we find before us. We watch the compass needle move and we move with it. In so doing, we exercise the divinity of our freewill and we proceed with as much honor, heart, and gracefulness as we can. This is the mission of the providential.

Chapter 3

Breaching the Narrative

Unfoldment is a multi-dimensional practice. It requires an exploration of many perspectives, disciplines, and philosophies to fully understand its power. It compels us to go deep into ourselves and far out into the world. The deeper and farther we go, the more we realize that all inward and outward journeys are, at root, one and the same. In this respect, the many different ideas explored in this book can be considered as archetypal points on the compass of unfoldment—each forming a part of the whole 360 degrees of human experience. Though there is a tremendous diversity of knowledge to be contemplated, each of the cardinal directions meet at the center of the compass. From this point of equilibrium, no terrain is too mountainous to tread, and no darkness can forbear the torch of consciousness for long. To move freely and gracefully, we must learn to distinguish between what is real and what is unreal. This begins with ourselves.

Reality cannot be perceived in a true state if the individual is too heavily invested in the dream of his or her own life script, like the actress who becomes so utterly absorbed in the character she is playing that she temporarily forgets who she really is. What lies beyond the film set is forgotten. The role becomes everything. The whole world is exclusively filtered through the lens of a single, personal narrative. Though all the associated dramas and events are ultimately fictional, it doesn't matter; it feels like the real thing.

It's easy to spot someone who has become lost in his or her own narrative. He tells lots of stories about himself and doesn't listen too well. Whatever is said to him is reflexively referenced to a previous similar event that he has experienced, without paying proper attention to what is actually being said. There is no real empathy, consideration, or contemplation—only anecdotal recoil. Not that he is instinctively self-ish; he is merely blindsided by his own inner conflict. Communication is reduced to fitting certain shapes into certain holes. Imagination and real-time thinking are absent. There is too much at stake to risk changing the program. For this reason, indignation is another common trait.

Gnosis hides from those who perpetually throw themselves into *doing*. To unconsciously push oneself along from point to point and moment to moment, consumed with all manner of duties, errands, commerce, and labor, serves only to obscure what is really occurring here on this miraculous journey. Yet are these not the very things that make the world go round? Perhaps they are. But when they are performed unconsciously and without clarity of will, they are quite arbitrary. One doing is much the same as any other doing. If this is so, why is it that we do the things we do?

Being busy rapidly fills life up by eliminating time for anything else. Regardless of what one is busying oneself with, the resulting fullness is commonly believed to constitute a good, successful, productive life. That's how it's supposed to be. The logistical engine of existence soon develops its own irresistible momentum and the individual is swept up in a whirlwind of incongruous doing. Busy people are portrayed as important people. The more doing we cram into our life, the greater our chance of fulfillment. Is this true? Walk down any street in any major city and look at people's faces. Fulfilled is the last thing they are. The startling rise in mental health problems—particularly notable across all demographics in America and Britain—suggests that aspiring to a life of state-sanctioned fullness is not quite the rewarding experience that it was cracked up to be.

For those who find themselves anchored in their narrative, however scintillating or arid that may be, it is important to recognize that it is a *choice* to be where we are. No matter how deeply we may immerse ourselves in our own performance, we are willfully positioning ourselves there. Even though the spiritual amnesia can last for years, the spark of truth will not go out. However hard one tries to smother it—by disruption or depression, love or insanity—it is quite inextinguishable. The impulse to rise up from the prosaic and connect with the divine is always with us, from first to last. It is the essence of who we are and what we are doing.

The higher will seeks to engage with a particular set of experiences, all of which are carefully situated to provide opportunities for inner growth. The little self runs with that trajectory and lives it out. We build the scenery and we write the script, then we forget all about it as we assume our leading role. That's the game. If we look closely enough, however, everything is embedded with a trace of transcendental knowledge that provides constant clues as to the real purpose of this enigmatic theater. As such, the actual material circumstances and the script itself are not to be unduly focused upon or obsessed about. It is the psychological and emotional responses that they help to stimulate that are of consequence.

If we bring the flame of pure awareness—our hand-on-heart knowing of truthfulness—close to the things and routines that we are asked to load our lives with, something curious happens. We find that, once everything is illuminated, there is only emptiness. There is nothing there. There never was anything there. The abundance was an illusion. It is a very odd feeling. Once more, it calls into question why we do the things we do. And this is the very moment—right in the midst of the mental flux—that we act. If we can resist the temptation to immediately fill the emptiness with something and instead just allow it *be*, then we create an opportunity to breach the narrative. A higher channel is opened, and we get a clearer sense of who we are and what we are doing. Instead of just following the script, we get to actually act from our own freewill. We get to direct.

Perceiving life itself as the instrument for transformation is an important step toward determining the real meaning behind the outward forms and routines around us. By regarding reality in this way, we begin to detach ourselves from the gravity of the narrative and become more consciously empowered. The story plays out, but we have more control over it and we stop dramatizing it. We see that it is the backdrop to the main event, not the main event itself. We recognize the whole organism, not just the superficial epidermis. So often, this dynamic is conceived of back-to-front. We try to change things in life to make ourselves feel better. We move things around, shake them up and wait for the inner change. Upgrade the accommodation, the vehicle, the technology, the spouse. We can change the physical forms all we like, but until we discern the root patterns that lie behind them, it is fruitless.

When a person chooses to funnel all her energy into form and doing, whatever the degree of moral industriousness, she is putting off the lightning strike of her own unfoldment for another day. Not the worst crime in the world, but certainly a self-sabotaging stunt that can so easily become a chronic habit. It happens because the ego perceives the predestined transformation that goes with unfoldment as something threatening. It imagines that the old routines will all liquefy and run down the drain. Generations of ground rules and carefully imprinted patterns gone. Then what?

I once knew a woman who tiptoed around the edges of her unfoldment for many years. Zara was intelligent, confident, and cultured. She was also attractive and had plenty of material resources. All in all, she'd been dealt a pretty good hand. What she struggled with was *meaning*. She didn't believe in any of the things she was doing. The job, the boyfriend, the nights out, the spa membership, the car, a closet full of expensive shoes—she was perfectly aware of their true nature, but didn't know how to go about bringing real substance into her life. Naturally, at first she turned to books for answers. Lots of them. Before long, the bookcase in her living room was overflowing with new age, self-help, spiritual, and mystical texts. She read them all. Though aside from a few glimpses of magic here and there, they did not contain what she wanted.

Never one to give up, Zara turned to more physical engagements for better results. She attended weekend Buddhist retreats, yoga workshops, and conspiracy conferences, and took classes in neuro-linguistic programming. She even spent two months in Tibet, consorting with lamas and trekking across the mountains. No one could ever accuse her of a lack of effort. Even so, the longed-for personal epiphanies continued to elude her. Many years passed by in this way. She juggled running her own business and being a single mother of two adult children with her unyielding quest for spiritual meaning. It was at this time, when she was nearing the end of her tether (as she later told me), that I made her acquaintance.

Unsurprisingly, our friendship was accelerated by the fact that we were both interested in spirituality and matters of self-growth. We compared notes, swapped books, and had lots of great conversations, all within the space of a few short months. One day, she asked me what I was searching for. I replied, as plainly as I could, that I wasn't really searching for anything. She frowned at me and insisted that everyone was searching for something. She said that she was searching for enlightenment. I thought for a moment. I told her that some years before, I had been looking for something, though I didn't quite know what it was. I had looked for it in books, in people, at gatherings, and in various geographical locations. In the end, I figured out that what I was looking for wasn't really outside me. Even though I'd had this wisdom spelled out to me in various texts very early on, it didn't *go in* for some reason. It seemed that I had to go through the motions of searching for this special thing before I finally realized that it wasn't out there at all. If we want to make it hard for ourselves, we are always welcome to do so.

I explained to Zara, in the best language that I could at the time, that rather than being about finding something, I felt it was more about adopting a certain kind of attitude, a sort of inner deportment. She stared at me silently, completely motionless. I looked into her brown eyes. It felt like she was either going to erupt with laughter or smash a wine bottle over my head. I couldn't tell which, so I just continued talking. I said that my most sacred experiences and meaningful personal breakthroughs had all occurred when I was in a space of emptiness. It was the exact opposite of being full of ideas, theories, and knowledge. Ironically, these things are necessary to get you to the precipice, but before you can glide off it, you have to leave them all behind. I tried to assure her that the work she had done had been enormously helpful. It was training. She was equipping herself for the moment when she could, of her own freewill, step into a deeper world and wholeheartedly begin her journey of ascendance. How exciting to let go of what is unreal and acknowledge the truth of her divine path—to make contact with ultimate reality. Isn't that what enlightenment is? She nodded.

I felt that I had shared the most appropriate wisdom that I had. I wanted nothing more than to see Zara empower her spirit to bring about the changes that she wished for herself. She had certainly demonstrated a willingness to learn and had absorbed a lot of credible knowledge. She was a good woman. Now it was time for her to apply it to her own life.

Shortly after this exchange, I moved away from the area and our paths diverged. Aside from a few e-mails, I didn't really have much further contact with her. I hoped that whatever she was doing, she was finding the fulfillment and illumination that she had so dearly desired. A couple of years later, I bumped into a mutual friend and asked about Zara. How was she doing? What was occurring in her life? Was she well? Zara had remarried, had a baby girl, and become a successful businesswoman, much admired by her peers and excelling in her chosen field. The books and the uncertainty had disappeared. The spiritual retreats were replaced with cultural voyages to the many splendid art galleries of Europe. When our friend had asked Zara about her spirituality, she had briskly replied, "Been there, done that. I'm into art now." She made it clear that the whole subject was now closed.

This resonates a very powerful and humbling teaching. I have since heard similar stories many times. It is a poignant reminder that not everybody wants to change their life. *Not really.* Some people would prefer instead to make minor edits to their narrative, so as to make it more pleasing and satisfying. They are not ready to start shaping their own destiny; they believe it is better to stay with what they have. No problem. Fundamentally, we can never know precisely where someone else is at on his or her own journey. It cannot be known, by design. All we can do is share our own knowing when the time is appropriate. If Zara did not want it at the inner level, no amount of journeying could bring it. Each time a moment of enlightenment got close to her, she ingeniously edged away from it. The time was simply not right for her, even though all the outward conditions suggested that it was.

We have to respect everybody's choice to do whatever they wish with their own narrative. All choices are relevant, however distant they may feel from our own resonance, or however strongly we might wish to support or even steer someone. In the end, there are no wrong answers. Whether someone wishes to operate from a place of honor or dishonor, consciousness or unconsciousness, truth or untruth, he or she is perfectly entitled to do so for as long as he or she sees fit. It is always an intensely personal undertaking and can seldom be understood from afar.

To prepare oneself for the unfoldment is to consciously transition from one state to another. We become something different. We know when we are ready for that and we know when we are not. This is the only judgment necessary. To switch away from a solid, well-worn life pattern that has ostensibly functioned pretty well for many years, requires a special kind of faith. To commit to the new, the fluid, and the inherently mysterious, is inviting change to become a permanent fixture in one's life. The unfoldment *does* change things—the big things and the little things; the physical and the non-physical. We learn to surf our own personal eschaton—the climax of our own history—day by day.

It is not by accident that some of the deepest and mightiest of unfoldments are often preceded by an exhilarating detonation of old patterns. Many people instinctively burn their bridges when they first feel the sovereign power of their own authority. The magnetic pull of the life script is broken. Situations that had been endured for years are promptly deconstructed and remade to more authentic designs. Revolutions arise where conventional power structures once reigned supreme. Astonished, puzzled, and delighted onlookers observe the fireworks from the other side of the river. Those who had previously always played it safe, rejuvenate themselves by taking grand magical risks. A new equilibrium is found. The universe loves risk, especially when it springs organically from empowered freewill. Change becomes an ally, not an opponent. It is no longer possible to get lost in the narrative when we ourselves take ownership of its creation.

Chapter 4

Holding Feathers

To see clearly and truthfully, we must become conscious of just how it is that we envisage our world. Why do we see things the way we see them, and how is it that we come to feel a certain way about them? Are we born feeling that wolves are wicked, or do we learn that from story books? Do we instinctively fear foreign cultures that we don't understand, or is that some outmoded deception?

Each morning when we wake up, we see the sunlight peeping through the blinds, we hear the birds singing outside, we feel the soft covers on our skin, we smell the coffee in the kitchen, and we taste the delicious, hot buttered toast. Yet it is not the senses themselves that construct this agreeable scene, but the brain. Our sense organs throw raw data into the brain, and the brain creates models of reality based on the software that it is running. Foremost among that software is the code of *belief.* Everything we comprehend passes through it and is heavily colored by it. It follows, then, that we should know precisely where our beliefs originate from, how accurate and relevant they are, and—perhaps most importantly of all—who is authoring them.

We are actively encouraged to believe in all kinds of things as we grow up: God, a certain way of life, free speech, doing well in school, telling the truth, free market economies, team sports, democracy, a balanced and nutritious diet, preparing for one's retirement. Provided that the objects of our belief are not wholly unpleasant or blatantly criminal, society whispers in our ear that what we choose to believe in is not quite as important as the process of believing itself.

Given that belief is commonly equated with confidence, drive, and vision, it is usually high on the list of defining characteristics claimed by especially triumphant businessmen, politicians, and celebrities. It is thought to nourish the very roots of personal achievement and is capable of transforming the average into the extraordinary. For society as a whole, belief serves as an important shared platform from which vast numbers of people draw their sense of community, identity, and common purpose. Few things are more troubling to those involved in educating young people, than to encounter a smart kid who believes in nothing. It is not okay to have no beliefs, because that infers that you have no ambition and no purpose.

When I was in high school, there was a rather half-hearted class called religious education (RE) that limped forlornly through the curriculum like a one-legged skunk. It was almost universally derided by students, even among the bookish and nerdy types. On paper, RE was supposed to inform and stimulate discussion about the contemporary religious landscape in Britain, Europe, and the wider world. If this were true, that would've been just fine with me. In practice, however, it was simply an occasion for the ill-fated teacher to train 30 apathetic children to memorize names and dates from a suicide-inducing textbook.

What really pins this woeful class in my memory is one incident that I can bring to mind as clearly as if it were yesterday. One gray and cloudy afternoon, the RE teacher asked the girl next to me, "Do you believe in God, do you not believe in God, or don't you know?" Without hesitation, the girl replied most sincerely, "I *feel* God. There is no belief required either way." After a brief moment of silence, the teacher ejected the girl from the classroom, seating her in the corridor where she could not disturb the rest of the class. In that absurdly tragic moment, I wondered whether *any* issues of real depth had a place in high school. It did not feel good. One might reasonably assume that epistemology and ontology had a role to play in educating 14- and 15-year-olds about religion, yet they were not mentioned at all. So I kept my mouth shut for the rest of the term and just did my porridge (an English slang term for spending time in jail).

Physics, chemistry, and biology were also enormously disappointing. Regardless of who was teaching the class—from the most effervescent tutors to the most lugubrious zombies—the curriculum was just too flat to do anything with. Put square into square-shaped hole, then put star into star-shaped hole. Bingo. You've passed the exam. And this was supposed to be one of the best schools in the whole county. Perhaps the real juicy stuff and all the associated intellectual zeal would come later? At college and university? Reports I'd heard from older friends were not encouraging. It seemed that all that separated the average student from the exceptional student were memory and organizational skills. I had a feeling that creative cerebral ingenuity wasn't really wanted at all. In fact, it might get in the way of academic performance.

It was a numbers game, pure and simple. You had to *believe* in that game to play it successfully. That didn't work for me. Though I scraped through with fairly respectable grades, I knew in my heart that what I was being asked to believe in was untrue. It wasn't really education at all; it was some kind of employment training. Woe to those who formulated the national British high school curricula of the 1980s.

Of course, it's not just Britain that suffers from a sub-standard secondary education system. American avant-garde rock musician Frank Zappa once remarked, "Drop out of school before your mind rots from exposure to our mediocre educational system. Forget about the Senior Prom and go to the library and educate yourself if you've got any guts." This may seem a little rich coming from an unconventional rock guitarist, but the reality is that Zappa was one of the most brilliant and ingenious intellects to have ever graced the creative stage, in America or anywhere else for that matter. He was a strong proponent of the autodidactic method—self-directed learning outside of a formal education. No belief systems required.

To be asked or required to believe in something that is untrue, is certainly challenging. But what about believing in something that we sincerely regard as being of real value? Something good and solid? To answer that, we need to look at what belief actually is.

A belief is something that we think might be true about the world. It is a fundamental impulse that arises in all men and women, inextricably woven into our culture, emotions, language, science, and politics.

Though philosophers and theologians have wrangled with its strange mechanisms for millennia, belief endures as a highly enigmatic phenomenon that continues to quietly dominate the way most people think, feel, and behave. For this reason alone, it has always been utilized as a powerful means of controlling people.

It is useful to consider belief as a psychological condition rather than a philosophical position. Even if a belief turns out to be true, it is wise to bear in mind that, in most cases, even so-called *true beliefs* are still simply ideas that have some form of consensus agreement and a certain level of consistency. Consider that for most of mankind's history (certainly in the mainstream historical record), it was a true belief that the Earth was flat. Everybody thought, felt, and behaved as if it were so. To imagine otherwise was lunacy, or, even worse, heresy. It was not until around 200 BC that the idea of a spherical Earth began to gain credibility. Nevertheless, many educated men still refuted the idea well into the 15th century, with some continuing to do so to this day.

As knowledge, consciousness, and the world itself shift and transform, so do our beliefs. We can therefore reasonably state that a belief is always necessarily a propositional idea, a working model, a suggestion. Even so, none of this succeeds in diluting the sheer potency of belief in any way. People remain curiously obstinate and resolute in how they cling to their beliefs, even when faced with overwhelming evidence that points to a contrary situation. At root, this arises due to a conditioned and delusional fear that without beliefs, people would begin to lose their sense of purpose and individuality. Herein lies one of the chief debilitating problems with our beliefs: We tend to personally identify with them. This is absolutely unnecessary.

When we carry a belief, it has a certain mental weight attached to it. The weight of each belief we internalize is derived from our mental and emotional investment in it. For example, if we have a modestly sized and rather casual belief, such as believing that a four-leaf clover might bring us good fortune—however subjective or insignificant that may be—it still accrues a little weight. Let us say its weight is analogous to a can of beans. We can happily throw that into our backpack and move around with no problems. It is hardly noticeable and does not impede our agility. It's not until we begin to carry a dozen or so casual beliefs that things begin to noticeably change. So, in order to avoid becoming overloaded, we naturally become more selective about what is worth believing in. What is the associated weight and what is the total amount we're capable of carrying? This is different for everyone, though the principle is the same: The weight of a belief is largely determined by the level of emotional and psychological investment we put into it. The heavier the investment—such as religious loyalty, abortion, politics, patriotism, good versus evil—the heavier the weight of belief.

Most people aren't just carrying around cans of beans in their backpacks. They're hauling anvils, rocks, and sandbags too. Strangely, the heftier the belief, the more proudly people will sometimes bear its weight. If someone has carried a belief-anvil for 40 years, she is not going to react too kindly to someone telling her that it's been totally unnecessary. All that effort and martyrdom would have been for nothing. So people hold fast to their own obstinacy, mentally staggering around under this peculiar encumbrance. Equally, carrying a *disbelief* also has weight. To firmly disbelieve a thing—often necessary to properly complement one's opposing belief—just adds to the load. Disbeliefs require the same maintenance, egoic investment, and channeled consciousness as their positive counterparts. It all starts to get a bit silly.

Certain belief systems are so potent and deep seated that those with heavy investments in their preservation will go to extraordinary lengths to defend them. A historical blink of an eye ago in 1633, Galileo was forced to stand trial for heresy by the Catholic Church for claiming that the Earth revolved around the sun. This wild whimsy directly challenged the prescribed belief that emanated from the all-powerful church, whose authority directly impacted the lives of most regular folks in Europe at the time. The sentence meted out to Galileo saw all his published works banned and required him to renounce all his heretical notions, and, worse, the 69-year-old physicist and astronomer was ordered imprisoned. The sentence was later commuted to house arrest, under which he spent the last nine years of his life, eventually going blind.

In 1947, psychoanalyst Wilhelm Reich was pursued by American authorities because they didn't like his concept of orgone energy (a form of universal life force) and the machines he built to harness its health-promoting benefits. Reich posited that all illness originated from the depletion or blockage of universal energy flow in the body. His machines accumulated atmospheric orgone energy and could focus it on an individual who would sit inside a phone booth–style box. Reich claimed his machines could help cure many common ailments, as well as more serious diseases such as cancer. Someone somewhere didn't want this research to continue. This thinking directly opposed the dominant belief in conventional allopathic medicine.

A letter to the FDA from the director of the Medical Advisory Division of the Federal Trade Commission triggered the beginning of the end for Reich. The FDA doggedly pursued Reich until finally, in May 1956, he was arrested for violating an earlier injunction when an associate transported some orgone therapy equipment across a state line. Reich got two years in jail. Meanwhile, FDA officials went to Reich's place in Maine, destroyed the accumulators, and burned his books. Later that autumn, the remaining six tons of his journals and scientific papers were burned in an incinerator in New York's Lower East Side. Reich died of heart failure in November 1957 in the federal penitentiary in Lewisburg, Pennsylvania. Not a single psychiatric or established scientific journal carried an obituary. The establishment had already buried him.

A set of data may look compelling for a long time—more than a single individual's life span, or even for entire generations. It may serve its purpose to send a man to the gallows, or to turn a speculative theory into received wisdom, but like everything else, evidence is always open to discussion and disagreement. Over time, it is usually expanded upon, reinterpreted, and in some cases completely revised. "Empirical facts proven beyond doubt" are merely good working theories—pixelated artifacts glimpsed within the undulating fractal membrane of the universe. They should be remembered as such. Everything is an individual configuration. Unreal at one level, real at another.

The contemporary prominence of scientific evangelism and technocratic atheism—apparently bent on collapsing any notions of the divine—is an illustration of what can happen when belief backfires. Disillusioned by hundreds of years of doctrinaire religious fanaticism, the scientific missionaries have swung to the polar opposite: They are proclaiming a world with no divinity and no magic—just a big, cold, galactic machine that doesn't give a damn about humans. Such distorted perceptions arise from those who have fallen foul of their own egoic fears and prejudices, self-indulgently proselytizing and aggressively chastising those who do not share their view. The Darwinian evolutionist and the Christian fundamentalist alike would do well to consider the weight of their beliefs as they continue to skate on very thin metaphysical ice.

Still, we cannot and must not claim that agnosticism is in itself any sort of destination either. The agnostic viewpoint that the true value of claims relating to God, the afterlife, and the nature of existence cannot be known is operationally curious, yet risks dismantling any inspiration for inner growth or transcendent experience. The philosophy of "I don't know so I won't bother," though once being a good excuse for setting aside one's unfoldment for another time, is fast becoming obsolete as any sort of intellectual escape route.

Can the human mind truly be content to renounce the deepest and most profound questions of existence in favor of a life of unknowingness, distraction, and frivolity? Only the frightened and the disenfranchised find consolation in such devices of psychic blackout. What's more, the universe doesn't let anyone get away with it. Sooner or later, it catches up with everyone and gives them a gentle tap on the shoulder. If that is constantly and willfully ignored, the gentle tap becomes a kick in the teeth.

Belief is often about comfort. It is reassuring to know that a thing will be the same today as it was yesterday. We set up all kinds of routines and habitual practices in our daily lives in an attempt to persuade ourselves that change is somewhere far off in the distance, only occasionally dipping in to jiggle things around. Our brains have been conditioned to favor solidity, stability, and order in everything that we observe. We *believe* that the chair exists; we can see it and touch it. It was there yesterday, and it will most likely be there tomorrow. It is a defined experience, well evidenced and self-apparent. What could be more real than the physicality of the objects in our world? Surely, we can believe in their existence? Yet this way of thinking is not accurate.

In actuality, all things are in a constant state of flux at all times. Every material form is always vibrating, shifting, and transforming. Only our brains make them look still and concrete. In Buddhism, this observance is called *annica* (impermanence) and is one of the three marks of existence that characterize the illusory world (the others being *dukkha*, unsatisfactoriness, and *anatta*, non-self). Annica teaches that all formations are impermanent and real spiritual growth begins with dispassionate experiential mindfulness of the present moment. Consciousness is in its most natural, balanced, and truthful state when brought into the center of now. This is difficult to do when constrained by beliefs of any kind. When we believe things, we create constructs that can hinder the natural flow of consciousness. We fabricate illusions of permanence to make ourselves feel better.

In the Zen tradition, impermanence is called *mujō*, indicating the transience and mutability of all compound objects. It is a vital principle in understanding the flow of the unreal. The Zen student begins to actively engage with the reality that nothing lasts, yet nothing is lost. From the *ultrasoup* of infinite energy arise all forms and patterns, and back they go to tell their story, merging with the undifferentiated whole once more. After a time, forms separate out again and go onto the next voyage. Belief only slows this realization down.

In 1980, David Bohm published his book *Wholeness and the Implicate Order*, articulating the same ancient wisdom but in the modern language of quantum physics. His view of the enfolded implicate order and the unfolded explicate order was radically different from the prevailing mechanistic physics of the time. Today, his ideas are still deeply antithetical to the reductionist fetishes of mainstream science. In Bohm's model, primacy is given to the undivided whole and the enfolded implicate order within the whole, rather than particles, quantum states, and continua. What this suggests is that forms arise from a wholeness of energy; they are a result of particular formations that are bound by consciousness. He shows that the universe is not a vast machine made up of atomic building blocks. Indeed, there is no sustainable distinction between manifest reality and consciousness. For Bohm, the whole encompasses all things, entities, structures, abstractions, and processes. Nothing is entirely separate or autonomous; it is all part of a unified and extremely cohesive whole.

It has to be said that the impermanence of all things can be an unsettling notion for even the most elastic of human minds. We can't help but value an element of constancy and predictability as foundations for a well-ordered life. This is why we fashion beliefs—in the hope that they will serve as mental life rafts that will help keep us afloat. But there really is nothing to worry about. We must contemplate that it is consciousness itself that molds the objects around us. There is no physical boundary between oneself and that which is outside oneself. It is only our brain that proposes a gap, in order that we can navigate around our world more easily. But in the business of unfoldment, we can reduce or even dissolve that gap by realizing that our consciousness *is* the chair, just in the same way that our consciousness *is* our dreams. It is the intelligent holographic fabric of reality itself, an emanation from the divine. As the great alchemical sages put it, "the all is mind, the universe is mental." Belief plays a key role in either opening or closing that flow of potential energy.

It certainly seems that there are helpful beliefs and unhelpful beliefs. A helpful belief is "I believe that by drinking this glass of water, my thirst will be quenched," whereas an unhelpful belief might be "I believe that the nasty disease that I have just been diagnosed with is going to kill me." They are both working models, though one has a positive aspect and one has a negative aspect. So why on Earth would anyone ever sustain a negative working model that does not benefit them? Why believe what might not be true and could well contribute to his or her own undoing?

People believe because of consensus. They believe because of the compelling gravitation of all the other people who believe the same thing. There are so many abiding beliefs that tell us that the body is just a machine, that hospitals are the best place for biological machines to get fixed, and that the system of Western medicine is the most advanced in the world. Such powerful and well-established beliefs—with such irresistible group blessing—soon overwhelm any individual conception of the body's own innate capacity to heal itself. That is merely a wishful fantasy that promptly evaporates in the hard light of someone else's manufactured reality.

The *placebo effect* is where a positive therapeutic effect is experienced by a patient, physically and/or psychologically, after receiving an inert treatment (such as an inactive sugar pill) that is believed by the patient to be an active and effective drug. Certain sections of the medical establishment have long sought to rubbish and discredit this whole phenomenon as it presents some worrying philosophical dilemmas for conventional medicine. Curiously, the placebo effect is not just limited to the patient's physical and mental responses; the doctor's attitude can play a role, too. In 1961, Henry K. Beecher, an influential figure in the history of anesthesiology and medical ethics, observed that surgeons he categorized as *enthusiastic* succeeded in relieving their patients' chest pain and heart problems more than *skeptical* surgeons. Is consciousness once more being caught entangled in form?

In July 2011, the ABC Medical News Unit reported on a pilot study published in *The New England Journal of Medicine*. The report suggests that we should:

Never underestimate the power of the mind when it comes to feeling better. In the newest demonstration of how healing can be triggered by patients' expectations of what medical attention can do for them, placebo treatments were as good as real medication in making asthmatic patients feel they were breathing more easily. Thirty-nine asthma patients reported about as much perceived relief from a placebo inhaler or from sham acupuncture as from an inhaled dose of the steroid albuterol.

Coauthor of the study Dr. Michael E. Wechsler, an asthma specialist at Brigham and Women's Hospital and Harvard Medical School in Boston, writes, "Placebo effects can be clinically meaningful and can rival the effects of active medication in patients with asthma." Predictably, the study later goes on to say that "patient self-reports can be unreliable." However, in an accompanying editorial in the same issue of the journal, Dr. Daniel E. Moerman, an expert on the placebo effect from the University of Michigan–Dearborn, called into question the idea that patients' self-reports were unreliable because their perceived improvements from treatment were not necessarily corroborated by lung capacity tests. He stated, "It is the subjective symptoms that brought these patients to medical care in the first place. They came because they were wheezing and felt suffocated, not because they had a reduced [lung capacity]."

Not all doctors are swept up in the pressure to conform to the norm. In their 2005 paper, "Making Space for the Placebo Effect in Pain Medicine," Dr. Daniel Moerman and Dr. Anne Harrington detail some fascinating mental effects of *brand marketing* on the administering of active drugs and placebos:

> In one study, 835 women who regularly used over-the-counter analgesics for headaches were placed randomly into four groups: one group received unlabeled placebo; one received placebo marked with a widely advertised and widely-available brand name, "one of the most popular...analgesics in the United Kingdom and supported by extensive advertising"; one received unbranded true aspirin, and one received branded true aspirin. Each subject was asked to note the amount of headache pain relief experienced an hour after taking the pills. The results showed, unsurprisingly, that aspirin was more effective than placebo. More surprising, perhaps, was the finding that brand-name aspirin was more effective than generic aspirin, and brand-name placebo was more effective than generic placebo. Aspirin relieves headaches, but so does the knowledge that one is taking pills whose efficacy one has learned to trust from television advertisements. In this study,

a brand name itself turned out to have independent active properties, enhancing the effects of both placebos and true aspirin.

Concluding their paper, Moerman and Harrington note:

What we know, understand, think, and feel; what we are told and believe; the relationships we have with our clinicians—our doctors, nurses, and probably receptionists and parking lot attendants—can very directly affect our response to medical treatment, and, in particular, analgesic treatment. These matters are, these days, largely left to chance, or to ideology, or to market forces, but are still rarely subject to robust science. There is much to be learned here that is not only of enormous intellectual interest but that also might lead to material improvements of the quality of medical care for pain and other disorders; making room for the placebo in pain studies may complicate matters, but there is too much at stake to do anything else.

The marketing of belief has a physical effect on the body. Whenever we detect that fear is being marketed, particularly through mainstream television, we should be on our guard. If fear is present in the propagation of a belief system—whatever that may be—there is always disempowerment. The dominant human tendency to identify with the biological shell of the body is a fundamental piece of fear conditioning. If people believe that they *are* their physical shell, then they will remain subservient and deferential to those who are apparently capable of looking after it. It is an old trick and one that has been used for a long time by those who desire to manipulate. Simply put, if your belief is being controlled, your mind and body are being controlled.

Questions arise. Is belief required for one's authentic unfoldment? Does it have a role to play in the attainment of gnosis and the process of conscious individual growth? Is belief even necessary at all? With reason and honesty, these questions have remarkably straightforward answers.

Do we need to believe in God to have a relationship with God? No. We just have a relationship with God. Do we need to believe that we can cook a fabulous Thanksgiving dinner to actually succeed in cooking one? No. We just cook one. What about believing in ourselves? Or believing that we can play the piano beautifully? What we are really saying is that we would like to focus more conscious energy into these things. The more we do that, the better they will turn out. The belief associated with them is just an extraneous mental construct that gets in the way of the smooth flow of consciousness. It is not needed.

Our beliefs tend to be *binary*. They are either yes or no, black or white, 0 or 1. Popular consensus strongly affects that result, whether we like it or not. To believe that we cannot levitate the coin in the air because the overwhelming majority of people would say that that is impossible, means that the programmed subconscious mind will not permit it. The common mistake is then to immediately charge the opposite belief: that we can do it. This, too, gets in the way because it creates a paradigm-cracking conflict that the mind would rather not have to deal with. Paradoxes are not allowed in belief-laden minds. The wise move is to believe nothing. To carefully, but willfully, remove belief from the operating system altogether. To let consciousness flow without hindrance. This is the secret of the physics-bending adepts of Europe and Asia. They have learned to jettison belief and just get out of their own way.

We do not need to believe. We can operate with integrity, fine conduct, and honor without any beliefs at all. We can create, inspire, grow, and love without believing a thing. We can feel free to formulate striking and elaborate theories about the world, as many as we wish, but we need not become attached to them. We can let them come and go, transform, and evolve, in a much more organic way.

I propose that we replace the concept of internalizing beliefs with the concept of holding ideas. It is hard to dig out of a heavy belief, but it is not hard to let go of an idea that you are merely holding. Beliefs require ongoing energetic maintenance and a fixed narrative to sustain them. In contrast, something that is just being lightly held, without internalizing it as belief or disbelief, remains as light as a feather. It requires no safeguarding of any kind, and there is no weight to it. We can hold many ideas without feeling any weight at all. If any given idea proves to be useless or untrue, we simply let go of it. If it proves to be useful and true, we keep it. Over time, these ideas gain higher and higher fidelity as they continue to refine themselves, until they become totally weightless. No investment is required either way. No investment = no weight.

Don Juan Matus said, "A warrior is never under siege. To be under siege implies that one has personal possessions that could be blockaded. A warrior has nothing in the world except his impeccability, and impeccability cannot be threatened." This applies equally to possessions of the non-physical kind. With no beliefs to carry, the speed, fluidity, and expansion of the spiritual warrior is greatly enhanced.

Chapter 5

Russian Dolls

To engage in the process of unfoldment is to walk in a much larger world. The customary realm of objects, people, and places—which we have been taught constitutes "everything"—proves to be one small part of something else. The rules are rewritten. The purpose of the game changes. Some people are excited by this, and others feel uneasy. But once we grasp that the quaint logic of our world is not the be all and end all, a lot of things start to make a lot more sense. The randomness and separation that make life so taxing are replaced by a beautiful coherence and a deep interconnectedness. Things do not move interminably to their end; they move to their beginning. Energy refines itself and moves homeward. Human consciousness is part of that movement. Therefore, in contemplating the structure of the universe, we are actually looking into the most intimate aspects of ourselves. This is the real value of metaphysics and the secret alchemy behind the numbers.

Mystics of old referred to the different realms of existence as *planes* or *spheres*. Hindus, Buddhists, and early Christians sometimes call them *heavens*. Physicists might call them *dimensions*. In recent decades, many popular new age writers have adopted this scientific dialect, with the result that the word *dimension* is currently in vogue as the preferred term for states or spaces that transcend the known physical universe. Despite the occasional disgruntled physicist or two, it is a broadly useful term for thinking about a distinct energetic movement—physical or otherwise—from one condition to another.

There is a further way of describing the various layers of reality that I feel is even more serviceable—that is, in terms of *density*. Straight away, we must acknowledge that there are many different types of density, such as the classical "mass per volume" type, but also area density, linear density, bulk density, particle density, vapor density, Planck density, charge density, current density, tensor density, and many others. Particular fields of scientific specialization will understandably have loyal adherents laying claim to their own preferred definitions. Some do so with rigorous integrity and a desire for accuracy, others from a place of zealous fundamentalism, which can be unhelpful. It is wise to be mindful of such things in one's communications and thinking. Regardless, the esoteric perspective of densities nicely places the emphasis on raw consciousness, rather than any sort of spatial dimension. It also removes any confusion about time (or lack of it) and how that might influence space.

Everything can be thought of as a configuration of energy, be it a human being, a tiger, a tree, or a rock. All these configurations have a unique experience of consciousness, though not necessarily in the way that human beings like to lay claim to what that is. It is more effective to consider consciousness as sentient participation in the unfoldment of the universe. That participation looks and works differently depending on *what* you are. We know, for example, that many types of plants communicate with each other. Willow trees will emit a specific chemical when attacked by caterpillars that alerts all nearby willows of the danger. They can then respond by secreting tannins that modify the leaf proteins and make digestion troublesome for would-be attackers. Other kinds of trees can produce defensive alkaloids (nitrogen based chemicals that alter consciousness) to confuse the attacking insects' nervous system and make normal scavenging activities impossible. Imitation amino acids can even be pumped out that produce defective proteins within the insect's own physical biology—a form of organic chemical warfare.

Whether it is the human brain using complex electro-chemical signaling or plants using pheromone chemical signaling, the principle is surprisingly similar. Though a plant's modality for organizing and expressing sentience is different than a human's (they don't use one particular organ as the central processing unit), it does not mean that they cannot know things about the world. Any gardener will tell you that plants know a whole lot more than they let on.

What is special about human consciousness is that it can *conceptualize* to a degree that few other conscious entities can (at least, that we are commonly aware of). Humans can not only perceive and respond to things in their physical environment, but they can form mental pictures of objects, scenarios, and ideas in an entirely abstract manner. A man can dream up a bridge in a virtual mental space. He can then sit down and make a technical drawing of it, plan the construction, and finally go out and actually build the thing into physical existence. What is it that is occurring here? The human mind is changing the vibratory rate of a thought-form and moving it from a low density state (personal imaginal realm) to a high density state (consensus physical realm). As the vibratory rates changes, so does the density. The faster it vibrates, the lower its density and the less physical it is. The slower it vibrates, the higher its density and the more physical it is. For example, as the vibratory rate of low density water decreases, it turns into higher density ice. The fluid becomes hard.

In the ordinary world, not everyone is prepared to accept the authentic existence of a thing that has no physical form. Most people want to see it, touch it, and smell it before they can comfortably classify it as real. In the absence of a tangible structure, therefore, there is a reliance on instrumentation for measuring the various effects that a force has on the physical world, such as with electricity, magnetism, or radiation. In circumstances where a thing has no verifiable physical form and cannot demonstrate any measurable interface with the physical world, it is usually deemed to be unreal. In other words, when the density of a thing decreases beyond a certain threshold, it essentially disappears off the radar of reality altogether. Poof! Gone.

Some quantum physicists might say that they've been looking at similar issues in terms of studying *wave-particle duality*. This is the idea that quantum scale objects exhibit both wave and particle characteristics. In other words, they can be either little balls of energy or dispersed membranes of energy. One perspective on resolving this duality suggests that energy is actually always in both states at the same time, but we can only observe one at a time from our limited dimensional perspective.

My formulation of the nested layers of reality posits a number of enfolded densities. Each form that enters the theater of existence arrives in a first density state. It then slowly ascends through each density sequentially, over many millennia and through many singular perspectives and modes of being. Finally, after fully experiencing and comprehending each of the various densities, the entity may choose to return to source, to the divine. Or, it can return to any realm that it has mastered through experiential attainments and explore further. However, such is the spectacular amount of energy expended in the grand voyage of ascendancy, that a merging with the ineffable unity of the divine is a welcome prospect indeed. In a very real sense, it is *going home*.

Let us begin with first density on Earth.

The first density is characterized by *pure, undifferentiated being*. It is being as radiation emanating from blackest interstellar space. Being as a vast swelling ocean on a beautiful planet. Being as a tornado moving across the plains of Nebraska. It is the base solids, liquids, gases, and chemical compounds that give expression to this primal layer.

The second density is characterized by *differentiated being*. In short, one could say that the animal, mineral, and vegetable kingdoms largely embody this density. The innate virtue of their experience and the spontaneous purity of their consciousness form the root of an evolving intelligence that arises from the very core of the planet.

The third density is characterized by *self-aware being*. Self-awareness represents an important plateau of attainment on the journey of consciousness and marks a considerable accomplishment for any soul vehicle. Reaching third density signifies that an unambiguously epic venture is already underway, incorporating several enormous prior density transitions. The human mind is synonymous with this distinctive quality of self-aware, conceptualizing consciousness. When properly calibrated, it constitutes the perfect mental staging area from which to shift into the first non-physical layer.

To fully appreciate the elegant and holistic nature of reality, it is essential to grasp that each layer of density enfolds all previous layers, rather like Russian dolls. The third encompasses all aspects of the second and first, even though from their perspective, the third density is entirely unknowable and largely invisible. None of the densities are separated by space or distance; they interpenetrate one another completely. They are each a critical constituent element within a single cosmic ecology. What happens in one density affects all the others. The very greatest and oldest of entities residing in the seventh density are intimately present in our own right now, in this very moment, just as we abide in theirs. If a single divine source emanated the entire seven densities from within itself, then we are all permanently and intimately enfolded in its majestic creation. As proclaimed in Acts 17:28, "in Him we live and move and have our being."

The fourth density is characterized by *non-physical energetic being*. Without the need for the anchor of physical form, entities in this realm can move, evolve, and transmute themselves in a more unrestricted manner. Form is still available, though it is infinitely more pliable and molds to conscious emanations instantaneously. This is the last density where negative conduct and the conflict of war are operational.

The fifth density is characterized by *multi-dimensional being*, where consciousness can operate across multiple selves and densities, with simultaneous awareness. Polarity almost entirely recedes as a teaching mechanism. The reliance on self as a vehicle for identity is no longer necessary. Parallel harmonious selves, narratives, and identity patterns begin to fuse together to form a *consonance*.

The sixth density is characterized by *creational being*. This is the first realm where creation can emanate from sovereign being and does not require transformation from another energy source. This requires the ultimate responsibility and breadth of experience, thus obligating mastery of the previous five densities. No polarity at all. The consonance acts with sublime and effortless accord.

The seventh density is characterized by *wholeness and divinity*. It is the realm of so-called angelic entities, with awesome creational powers, complete mastery of all dimensions, and profound lineage of experiential soul threads. From here, a consonance may choose to return to source, or dive back into the adventure of separation and exploratory growth in the lower densities.

These are the functional layers of reality through which we can map consciousness, understand the advancement of sentient life, and trace our own personal arc of unfoldment. The number of densities is somewhat arbitrary. I can give good reasons to posit nine dimensions, 12, or 13. But I have focused on seven divisions to map the core principles of conscious evolution, partly through the teaching of my own higher self, and partly through establishing a composite picture from what I feel are the most credible esoteric sources on the subject. It is the principle of ascendant transformation that is valuable. To grasp how energy and consciousness shift and refine, is more important than attempting to establish something that is ultimately variable.

Many mystical traditions go into great detail with regard to the seven aspects of man and the seven fundamental journeys through reality, particularly Sufism, esoteric Judaism, Gnosticism, Hermeticism, and Rosicrucianism. There is no harmonic concurrence however. Others talk of 11, 12, or 13 spheres, planes, and densities. Physicists conceive 10, 11, or 26 dimensions, these being required for standard string theory variations. What does this tell us about our knowledge base? It tells us that humans are funny creatures. Ultimately, we know what we know *personally*—and little else. Theories are useful, but *knowing* is where the unfoldment focuses consciousness.

From time to time, we take it upon ourselves to conceptualize, calculate, and inquire. We seek to devise the best working model of how this place hangs together and how we might subsequently move through it with a little more style. This is the human impulse. What matters is that we bring this endeavor into our felt experience, not just our conceptual understanding. We make our conscious ascendancy—from one density of being to another—part of our everyday lives. It is why we are here. Walking this sacred path is never restricted to any particular type of man or woman. It is not the private dominion of scientists, mathematicians, clerics, priests, bishops, mystics, philosophers, or (heaven forbid) politicians. It is a terrain that is *free and open to everyone at all times*. Indeed, in the end, we are each destined to engage with our own unfoldment and compelled to traverse the gloriously unknowable densities in all their richness and mystery. It is the one and only obligation we have. Let us take to it with heart, wonderment, and fortitude.

Chapter 6

Knowing the Field

There are no hard divisions between the different densities and dimensions. They merge at the edges, like the spectrum of colors in a rainbow. Red bleeds into orange, and orange into yellow. The only thing that anchors us in the third density is our state of consciousness. When we conduct our thinking in a mechanical and rigid manner, we keep our consciousness coarse. This prevents it from interacting with the other densities. The natural bleed-through cannot be perceived or integrated. Fortunately, there is an abundance of teachings available on one particular aspect of the fourth density that offers many personal and practical openings for transcendental experience.

The field is the first experiential layer of ultimate reality. It is the first thing we come into contact with when we get outside of ourselves.

The field is well documented in the teachings of many mystical, spiritual, and shamanic traditions, arising from every continent and spanning multiple time lines. Whether Christian, Islamic, Buddhist, Celtic, druidic, shamanic, Zoroastrian, Bon, Hindu, or Gnostic, many core observations are shared regarding this enigmatic phenomenon. Though such knowledge is routinely excised from the exoteric public texts, the inner teachings clearly show the parallels. We may summarize them as follows:

1. Nothing is discretely separate from anything else; the field unites everything.
2. All forms manifest out from, and into, the field, with conveyance over any distance instantly.
3. The experience of human consciousness represents one particular vibration of this field.

4. Techniques exist to move the mind from its ordinary state into a field state, which, once attained, renders various magical abilities commonplace.

In modern terms, the field can be thought of as a quantum medium that transmits energy through the universe. It increasingly presents itself as the solution to many previously perplexing mysteries, such as how objects can affect each other over a distance with no known mediator (so-called spooky action), how a single object can appear to be located in two distinct places simultaneously (bi-location), and how consciousness affects matter. Most classical psychic phenomena fit into one or more of these categories.

As we begin to unpack these precepts, many of the apparently supernatural or unscientific aspects of extrasensory and physics-bending wizardry become quite reasonable and explicable. Indeed, an increasing number of free-thinking progressive physicists have been obliged to concede that the ancient mystics were accurate in their esoteric knowledge of the underlying mechanics of the universe. The sages and seers were correct in positing that the everyday physical world of the 3D is but a narrow reflection of a more majestic and multi-dimensional reality that functions as one flowing system. Crucially, consciousness was understood to be an integral part of the universal dynamic and quite inseparable from all its manifestations. It is the living intelligence of the field itself.

Hungarian philosopher and systems theorist Ervin László fuses science and mysticism by calling the field the *akashic field*. Highlighting new discoveries in vacuum physics, he lucidly explains how the field produces all material forms, serves as a universal storage system for recording all events, and is intimately tied to consciousness. He openly and plainly acknowledges that contemporary physics is essentially rediscovering and rearticulating a key component of ancient spiritual philosophy.

Five thousand years ago, the sages of ancient India proposed that the universe was formed from a primary element that they called akasha, an imperceptible substance that permeates all space. *Akasha* is a Sanskrit word that means "aether." It is the same aether that was contemplated by Victorian mystics who, in precisely the same way, put forward aether as the fundamental medium of the universe. What we think of as magic is the result of consciously interacting with it.

In part, this mystical cosmology was a deliberate reaction against the strict reductionism of the preceding century, which vehemently denied the reality of anything that wasn't founded on concrete reason and physical evidence. Then, as now, the human mind was so enamored with the five-sense reality matrix of electro-chemical signal processing that any perceptual shift away from the "if I can see it and touch it—it's real" mentality, proved extremely uncomfortable.

In discerning circles of the ethno-botanical community (focused on studying the relationship between humans and plants), it is thought that psychoactive substances like *dimethyltryptamine, psilocybin,* and *salvinorin A,* rather than simply creating aberrational visual distortions, actually permit us to see an unfiltered version of reality—one that is absolutely foreign to the Western mind. This represents an extreme example of uninstalling the consensus reality program and going into totally uncharted waters. An adventure for some, a nightmare for others.

For me, there is no doubt that "sacred plant medicine" offers direct personal experience with the field. However, due to th legally ambiguous nature of many psychoactive substances and an almost-complete absence of officially approved research (though this situation is slowly improving), any well-intended psychic explorations must be approached very sensitively indeed. Such explorers—or *psychonauts,* as they are sometimes known—are required to exercise tremendous levels of intelligence, judgment, and discipline in any such potentially paradigm-cracking undertakings. Writer and philosophical stunt man Terence McKenna did much to elevate the profile of these incredible compounds in his time, shifting them away from the damaging, CIA-sponsored propaganda of the 1960s into a more enlightened and truthful space.

The field can be talked about in many different ways. When Zen Master Shunryu Suzuki spoke of little mind and big mind, he was proposing a clear distinction between the conditioned individual mental sphere and what, perhaps, we might now call *field knowing*. Using scriptural dharmic teachings and meditation, such Zen practice, offers a way for the mind to reach beyond the constraints of self and connect with the primary consciousness of the field itself. From big mind, the Zen student learns to recognize the differences between the brain's construction of a thing and the thing itself. This removes a dense layer of mental abstraction that affords the percipient a much more lucid and resonant encounter with any object. First-time experiences of this nature routinely take one's breath away and can bring tears to the eyes, such is their exquisite beauty.

Big mind connection can sometimes happen quite spontaneously. When an unsuspecting patient is given the shock news that she only has two months to live, upon exiting the doctors examination room, the flowers outside appear devastatingly gorgeous. The smiling eyes of her 5-year-old niece are simply perfect. What is true and meaningful is amplified. Previous frustrations and annoyances melt away. When the customary circuits of the little mind are temporarily suspended, the barriers to the field knowing of big mind are removed. It flows into us. Our insight naturally deepens.

Everything that is, vibrates. Each different type of vibration creates a form, and we give names to those forms. They are the stuff of the world. They are what the Taoist philosopher Lao Tzu called the ten thousand things. There are many other things in our world that do not have a physical aspect, yet they are things all the same—things like humor, friendship, melancholy, arousal, bewilderment, and bliss. We have conceptual notions, too, like the weather, economics, freedom of speech, and holistic medicine. They are configurations of energy— patterns of electro-chemical signals firing across our neural pathways. They are vibrations.

Is there anything that does not vibrate? Rationally, we could say that only what is not, does not vibrate. This is pointed at in the emptiness of Zen and the not-doing of Toltec shamanism. It is all a very strange business, is it not, when everything we have ever been taught is geared toward interfacing with things, doing things, achieving things, making things? Only in the unconsciousness of sleep do we have any sort of contact with something that is a not an ordinary doing. Though the brain certainly invokes its own scrapbook of nocturnal montages—memories, fears, and desires—it is acknowledged in mystical circles that there is another order of visionary experience that is quite separate from the everyday dreams we have. These can occur spontaneously or they can be intentionally brought about.

In this other realm, we may encounter peoples, lands, and experiences of such supreme trueness that they seem more actual than our waking reality. Color is more brilliant, nature is more organic, music is more melodic. The whole thing seems hyper-real. When we are in this "place," when our consciousness is moving in this fourth density state, we are not interfacing with energy in the ordinary way. There is no distinctly separate self to bear witness, no additional layer of interpretation at all—hence the heightened perceptions. Something else is happening. Such is the *otherness* of experience in this realm, that it is virtually impossible to render any of it into normal language. It is in this sense "state-specific" in that it can only be properly understood from within its own domain.

Expect strangeness.

If we get right down to it, all forms everywhere in the universe are really vibrating blobs of energy embedded in the creational mesh of the field. The most direct experience of any given object—let's say a flower—would therefore involve not describing the particular vibration of the flower at all. This would merely add another separate mental layer between you and the flower. The purest experience of flower would be to actually merge with it, to *become* the flower. This is the central principle of field knowing: a merging of object and subject. Unlike the linear process of learning representational information about a thing (watching videos, listening to lectures, reading books), instead we seek a direct experiential encounter with it. We intentionally blur the boundaries. In so doing, we transcend the vantage point of self and go into the field. The flower is of the field and in the field, as are we ourselves. If we remove the conceptual perimeter fences of the mind, we can be, and know, whatever we turn our attention to.

How can the field know everything? Simple. It is everything. The field not only describes creation; it is the stuff of creation itself. It is the music, the score, the conductor, the orchestra, the instruments, the audience, the auditorium, the cocktails in the bar, the silver earrings, the cement between the bricks, the rain on the sidewalk. It is everything.

To understand the mechanics of field knowing, it helps to understand how it is that we ordinarily comprehend the world around us. As many people know, the brain conjures millions of moment-by-moment sensory inputs into our perception of the world. However, the vast majority of these are screened out because the ego considers them irrelevant to the survival of the body, which, arguably, they are. We cannot help but filter incoming information every time we survey the world around us. The single basic survival filter is this: Will this thing harm me or not? This key physiological safeguard keeps the body out of harm's way and runs automatically in the background all the time. From here upward, the remaining filters are within our control. We are free to create, erase, tweak, or re-design them to our heart's content.

Even for the data that does get through, it is immediately translated into symbolic mental images from the raw electrical signals themselves. That is to say, the things that exist, as we ordinarily understand them, exist purely in our mind as virtual constructs. We rarely, if ever, see them as they are: vibrating blobs of energy, connected to all the other vibrating blobs through the field in which they sit. It is for this very reason, as the old spiritual adage goes, that we are all one. Nevertheless, we have formed a very persuasive consensus to the contrary.

We cannot help but perceive ourselves as separate entities in a world of discretely differentiated objects. We have reached agreement on what they look like, what we call them, and what they mean to us—be they people, freight trains, hedgehogs, or cottage cheese. It is purely a conceptual agreement. In no way does it represent an accurate interpretation of the vibrating blobs of energy themselves. But we have made it our world. Thus, to engage with the truth of ultimate reality is to change the world itself. At least our version of it.

Timothy Leary, former assistant professor at Berkeley and Harvard psychology lecturer, coined the term *reality tunnel*. This was further popularized by philosopher and author Robert Anton Wilson, who really helped to seed this handy metaphysical shorthand into progressive philosophical and countercultural circles. In essence, the idea of reality tunnels implies *representative realism*—the notion that we can never perceive the world as it really is, because all we have to go on are our own sensory inputs and mental interpretations. So we each have our own personal versions of reality, all of them subjective and utterly unique. This echoes ancient Indian philosophy, which posits that the phenomenal world that we commonly perceive is actually Maya, a lesser, illusory realm of mental abstraction that is merely superimposed upon the ultimate reality (Brahman).

In addition to the billions of personal reality tunnels, there are also group reality tunnels that characterize particularly belief-laden mindsets. These are prevalent in many religious, philosophical, scientific, and political organizations. Specifically, amid groups where fundamental beliefs are critical to membership (whether in Christianity, Islam, Judaism, empiricism, rationalism, socialism, capitalism, and so forth), there is a temptation to uphold and augment one's reality tunnel by retaining proximity to others who share the same tunnel dynamics. Similarly, it can be said that in the act of attacking those who belong to group tunnels that are antithetical to one's own, there is a form of inverted corroboration occurring. For example, when the atheist gleefully pours scorn on the beliefs of a fundamentalist Christian, he is in fact covertly seeking to affirm and preserve his own reality tunnel. And vice versa.

Every human being has a reality tunnel. What we do with it is up to us. If we choose to do nothing, then before long, we inevitably find ourselves gravitating into a group tunnel. Eventually, as the years go by, we awaken one portentous morning to realize that we've spent our whole lives living in someone else's version of reality. This is called a mid-life crisis. It used to occur at 50, but that age is getting lower all the time. In terms of the unfoldment, it is simply an opportunity. For the soul that values the alchemical adventure of authentic being, such dramatic existential cataclysms can be prevented altogether by simply keeping one's reality tunnel flexible, empathic, and open to upgrades. When we stand at the center of our being, we are far less likely to be taken out of orbit.

Does the idea of reality tunnels imply that absolutely everything is subjective? Or is there an absolute objective reality—a solid, definitive platform that we can all empirically refer to? Various prominent thinkers have explored this, in recent times, most notably Descartes, Hume, Kant, Hegel, Marx, Freud, and Heidegger—each offering his own unique perspectives on how to collapse, combine, or reframe such dynamics. In contemplation of these abstract philosophies, the issue can be most effectively de-pressurized by invoking the idea of a *metaverse*, in which all reality tunnels constitute a *composite* reality. All polarities of texture, color, form, and movement are included. Everything that is, simply is. Personal truth is part of universal truth. Even so, on closer inspection, there does appear to be a guiding principle of elegance, or divine ordinance, to all manifest phenomena. There is a magic to creation. It is this very observance that inspires the mystical impulse for deeper movement into the field of ultimate reality.

The process of linking our mind to the field—what we might call *field uplink*—requires a certain configuration of energy before it can operate effectively. You can't really make it happen; you have to allow it to happen. Just as you can't make yourself go to sleep, you have to allow it to occur naturally, by itself. Though in a similar way, there are certain things you can do to make it easier to achieve the state you desire.

Normal, everyday beta brainwaves are too noisy for the mind to receive a clear signal from the field. It's like listening to a very weak radio station that you can't quite hear through all the static. You hear a few words here and there maybe, if you listen very attentively, but it's really just too fuzzy to make out. If you could remove the static of all the other radio signals however, you'd be able to hear the target signal much better. Once that is the *only* signal being intentionally channeled, you could then safely amplify it by turning the volume up (giving it conscious focus). This is not possible with all the usual hiss and crackle of static, as it would be far too much to bear.

To have psychic power is to be able to consistently demonstrate the capacity to reduce mental static, identify a particular frequency of signal, and then consciously amplify it. It is a matter of influencing one's own frequency of brainwaves, quieting down from beta (14–30 Hz, cycles per second), to alpha (9–13 Hz), to theta (4–8 Hz) and finally to delta waves (1–3 Hz). Usually we only produce delta waves when we are asleep, but with practice, this state can be achieved in a conscious, wakeful state.

The word *psychic* derives from the Greek *psykhikos*, "of the soul, spirit, or mind." The flexibility of meaning is complicated by its usage in the varying fields of philosophy, psychology, and mythology. If we strip away any unnecessary cultural baggage, it simply means "of the mind." As we know full well, in mainstream society, the word *psychic* usually denotes someone who professes an ability to perceive information hidden from the normal senses through his or her capacity for extrasensory perception (ESP). Fair enough. It is very common. If you call someone on the telephone who was thinking about you in those preceding few moments, he or she will invariably answer with the response: "You must be psychic. I was just thinking about you!" On many occasions, this is technically accurate, even though the reductionist reality tunnel insists on calling it coincidence. In the unfoldment, there are no coincidences. How could there be in a universe of seamless energetic super-coherence? What happens in one part of the field is known in all other parts of the field. If we can tune into it that is.

The mind's naturally tendency is to connect with the field. If a connection is possible, it will make it. Contact with the field is therefore far more common that one might think. However, because many of these connections are non-visual and non-symbolic, we don't necessarily notice them. The transfer of energy is more direct. For example, our personal sense of perspective, our level of optimism, and our natural compassion are greatly enhanced by field connection. The field helps us bring the gift of the "two months to live" perspective into our everyday life. We need not necessarily sit beneath the sword of Damocles to enjoy such a vivid mental shift.

The strength and potential of our field knowing ebbs and flows as we go about our various physical and mental activities. Over time, we have undoubtedly conditioned ourselves to willfully detach from the field in many of our everyday tasks. We are taught from an early age that we are at our most effective when we're operating in local brain mode only. Much more significant than our actions themselves, however, is our state of mind. Fear, stress, anger, and sadness cut the connection immediately. Though such emotive impulses naturally arise from time to time, they need not become habitual states unless we allow them to be. Our attitude powerfully influences our relationship with the field. The more we bring equilibrium, confidence, heart, and wisdom into our daily being, the more field uplink organically establishes itself as part of our regular mental flow.

Strange to think that there are those who choose to purposefully live in a state of separation and psychic corrosion. To willfully consign oneself to the narrow ruminations of ego-dominated brain churn is to live in the unreal dream of the distortion. Regular consumption of mainstream media broadcasts—particularly news, politics, business, and entertainment—only serves to augment this condition. This form of persistent field severance is endemic in society today and is accepted as the norm. Without the harmonizing unity of the field, it all seems a bit unruly. One day is good; the next day is bad. We feel happy and then we feel sad, for no apparent reason. The stream of incoming vectors feels wholly indiscriminate. We blindly throw ourselves onto the mysterious roulette wheel of fate, with fortunes won and lost in a totally random manner.

The more we filter the outer world exclusively through our personality and ego, the more separated we become from it. Narratives are chaotic. People, objects, events, and emotions seem to bubble up from a complex set of de-coherent and unfriendly occurrences. As materialist science would have it, the universe is a vast frozen territory with no interest in the termite mound of homo sapiens. We might just flicker in and out of existence without ever being noticed. This is the reality for those who choose not to determine their own dynamic participation in the unfoldment and live disconnected from the field.

To truly know a thing, we need to become it. This kind of knowing is set apart from ordinary knowledge in that it is a primary contact rather than a secondary informational artifact. What is it to be a wolf? We can examine the human acquired data on wolves and determine their appearance, how they hunt, their habitat, their social structure, their eyesight and hearing, their reproductive cycles, the adaptation of their coat to different environments. But this does not tell us what it is to be a wolf. It gives us human data about the wolf. A shamanic field knowing would involve a movement of consciousness to actually become "wolf." All forms are expressed, maintained, and manifested within the field. Wolf resonance is no different. The shapeshifting abilities of the shaman are accomplished maneuvers of consciousness. For those able to consciously perceive the field, they would physically see the transformation. For those unable to do so, they would see nothing.

Knowing can be envisaged as a circle. The size of the circle is determined by one's capacity for contact with the field. A large circle of knowing indicates a deep, harmonic resonance. A small circle reflects a discordant resonance or even total disconnection. Regardless, we can become destabilized from the natural center point of our circle, whatever its radius and influence. Ego-centric responses, stress, and inauthentic behavior can knock us off-center very easily. It happens to all of us from time to time. Mainstream media reinforces these destructive behavioral patterns in the promulgation of its lewd cultural narratives and restrictive social norms. To counter this disorientation, we need only be mindful of our knowing. Whatever we bring into our consciousness—in order to discern the truth and relevance of it—we simply ask ourselves do we have a knowing of this thing, or just information about it.

Standing at the center of a small circle is better than being off-center in a large circle. The circle of knowing in a typical 5-year-old is stronger than that of a typical 50-year-old. Balance and flow naturally emanate from the center point of knowing. From an off-center position, it is much harder to see anything clearly. In many martial art forms, a man is easily thrown to the ground when his center of gravity is not properly held. When he is owning and maintaining his own center, not only is he more resilient, but all his affirmative actions are hugely more powerful. From the center, a single strike can penetrate a brick wall. Off-center, the exact same force is relatively innocuous.

Quiet the mind. Stand at the center. Know the field. Become the other.

When we initially bring the living reality of the field into our felt experience, we get an eerie sense that there is something terribly wrong with the mainstream view of things. It is as if the contemporary social paradigm is deliberately set up to separate human consciousness from the field. Not only is there a distinct absence of accessible information on the field itself (other than in esoteric mystical writings and dense scientific ruminations), but even the way we apparently define ourselves—through our culture, media, politics, and economics—seems opposed to the whole organic flow of nature. It is conspicuously disempowering. Why would anyone want to block the ascendancy of the human spirit?

Chapter 7

Imperial Secrets

Reality is a dangerous concept. The *control system* exists to regulate access to it.

Envisage reality as a three-dimensional sphere, full of creativity, power, growth, and magnificence. Now collapse that down into just two dimensions, making it a flat circle, like a disc-shaped piece of paper. Finally, out of the 360 degrees of that circle, remove 359 of those degrees, so you are left with a single, thin, two-dimensional sliver of reality. This is what the control system puts forth as the whole of reality.

The control system is a hierarchical network of entities, philosophies, and mechanisms that manufactures and broadcasts a distorted version of reality that it likes to market as the only game in town. It is a very narrow world and not very true. The main consequence of imbibing this *distortion* is that it impedes the natural ascendant flow of consciousness; it puts it into suspended animation and people live their lives like bugs in amber. Though this encasement might feel protective at times, it is first and foremost a tomb.

The control system distortion deeply affects the human mind, making people easier to influence at the physical level and enabling their consciousness to be carefully regulated at the non-physical level. In the same way that we need water to stay below 0°C/32°F if we are to utilize it as ice, consciousness must be kept to a lower vibrational level if it is to be kept operationally immobile. Everything is a configuration of energy. From a radish to a radio wave, it is all energy vibrating at various rates and manifesting at different densities. Consciousness can be considered in just the same manner, as indeed it can also be regarded as an energy source like oil, gas, copper, tin, wind, or sunlight. What flows through our heads is a very particular vibration of energy—no less usable, no less harvestable, and no less precious.

It is an old game. The control system has been around for a very long time and has been administered by every empire that has ever sought to dominate people. From the Egyptians to the Romans, from the Mongols to the Qing Dynasty, from the British to the Americans, wherever there is empire, there is the control system. It is a totally apolitical, invisible, and unaccountable entity. It is not something that is ever talked about, acknowledged, or referenced in any way. Under normal circumstances, well-behaved citizens will have absolutely no clue as to the existence of it, despite the fact that it tells them what to think, what to do, what is okay, and what is not okay. Their whole lives come and go without them ever perceiving the very thing that has led them by the nose every step of the way.

The brilliance of the control system is that its tyranny does not compromise the law of freewill. It tells its subjects what it is going to do to them, and they give their consent—silent yet willful. The boot in the face or the gun pointed at the head is rarely needed, at least in the Western world. Instead, the distortion plies its unseemly magic through an enormous containment zone that is so curiously comfortable and accommodating that few would ever wish to leave it, even if they were conscious of its existence.

The control system can be likened to a so-called *black project*, a term used in America and Britain to denote a highly classified military project that is publicly denied by governments, military personnel, and defense contractors. For a senior elected political official to deny the existence of something that he or she knows exists to Congress—in other words, to lie—is illegal. Instead, political protocol provides specialist training in how to leave an issue *unacknowledged*. The more important and technologically advanced a black project is, the heavier and longer the duration of the accompanying unacknowledgment. Strong evidence for government-sponsored assassinations, false flag operations, stealth aircraft, molecular weapons, networks of underground bases, space propulsion systems, and weather manipulation is all over the place, should one care to look. It is a busy time for those who like to draw back the veil of conspiratorial misconduct.

In recent decades, many independent thinkers and researchers have specifically analyzed the control system by way of its political machinations, its military-industrial aspects, and its esoteric entanglements in what we call secret societies. This has brought predictably derisory reactions from the old guard and an uninformed populace who cannot imagine anything outside the 2D sliver of their containment. Still, it is rather sobering to witness the sheer penetration of the control system in the minds of our fellow brothers and sisters, however unpleasant they may sometimes be.

For a highly instructive allegorical study of the control system, one could do a lot worse than sit back and watch Patrick McGoohan's visionary masterpiece, *The Prisoner*, a 17-part television show that ran in Britain from 1967 to 1968. The premise was a simple one: A former secret service agent, referred to as "Number Six" (played by McGoohan), is held prisoner in a small village located on a remote island, where his congenial captors constantly attempt to trick and coerce him into revealing why he resigned from his job. "The Village" is very comfortable indeed. Six has his own well-appointed, private home, with all manner of food, drink, female company, socializing, and leisure activities on hand. The only problem is *you can't leave*. Six makes many elaborate bids for freedom, but they are all thwarted, despite his remarkable ingenuity. Yet, the controllers also fall short of the mark, as they repeatedly fail to win his obedience; they fail to take ownership of his mind. There, he remains absolutely free and sovereign. At last, in the final inspired episode, the true nature of the control is revealed and everything changes.

The Prisoner beautifully illustrates one of the key strategies that the real life control system employs to manipulate consciousness—that is, the promulgation of *hive mentality*.

Regard the hive as a medieval city within defensive stone walls. What goes in and what goes out are strictly controlled by official guards operating under very explicit orders. All access to information, goods, and services is meticulously regulated by the rulers of the city. As a citizen living within the hive, all the knowledge that is available to you has already been edited, spliced, and sanitized before you get anywhere near it. Consequently, you have no real idea about what goes on outside the hive. The rulers of the hive sometimes tell its citizens that those who dwell outside the hive are plotting its downfall. Hive patriotism is highly encouraged. After a few generations of living in the hive, the general citizenship have become habituated to unquestioningly obey hive law, cannot remember what came before the hive, and cannot imagine what might be a better alternative to life in the hive.

If all this seems a bit drastic, consider that up until the end of the 17th century, the hive was a literal and physical reality for most regular folks in Europe. *Feudal society*, characterized by the legal subjection of the majority of the population to a hereditary landholding elite, reigned supreme for many hundreds of years, until it was finally brought down by the peasant class who decided that a lifetime of enforced slavery to the elites was unfair and inhuman. Stories of bloody revolts and uprisings (by no means limited to just peasants) fill the history books. It was a long and bitter struggle to change society, with 330 years of separate revolts over England, France, Germany, Sweden, Estonia, Catalonia, Hungary, Slovenia, Croatia, Finland, and Russia, officially ending with the Swiss Peasant War of 1653.

In the face of this massive social disintegration, the control system realized that a shrewder system of subjugation was required to keep man from realizing that he can govern himself. Not for the first time, a subtle shift from overt to covert control was manifested through the sanctified dominion of religion. The brilliance of this strategy was that it would take the laws out of the hands of man and seemingly pass them to God himself. The deranged controllers of the Christian church (not the church authorities themselves), having ordered the systematic extermination of countless souls in a series of military campaigns that lasted hundreds o. ears (the Crusades), were now set to become the new standard bearers of the hive's sociological, moral, and spiritual edicts.

The church austerely decreed and upheld hive principles, on every issue under the sun, from commerce to sexuality, from art to science, from taxation to war. The state was inextricably linked to the church, and failure to give allegiance to God (the church) and the King was punishable by death. These were the good old days for the control system. If they didn't like what you said they'd take you away, chop off your head, and stick it on a spike at the city gates. Individuals, groups, countries, and whole continents were subject to the rampant domination of a single belief system. This had nothing to do with spirituality, religion, God, or consciousness; it was imperialism, plain and simple.

A central tenet in the philosophical model of the hive is *group think*. This is a system of thought within which group members reach consensus without critically analyzing or evaluating specific ideas and concepts. Group think can be manipulated to produce everything from infernal Kafka-esque bureaucracies to rampaging mobs, depending on the desired outcome.

Psychologist Irving Janis determined eight symptoms that are indicative of group think:

1. Illusions of invulnerability.
2. Rationalizing warnings that challenge group assumptions.
3. Unquestioned belief in the morality of the group.
4. Stereotyping those who are opposed to the group as weak, evil, disfigured, impotent, or stupid.
5. Direct pressure to conform.
6. Self-censorship.
7. Illusions of unanimity.
8. Mindguards, self-appointed members who shield the group from dissenting information.

Every major capitalist, communist, and totalitarian regime demonstrates these characteristics. Group think is not an Orwellian fiction; it is a day-to-day reality. Carefully implanted group think memes are used over and over again to accelerate and heighten public opinion and social trends—Problem–Reaction–Solution as it has become known. As a perfect and perennial illustration, in order to manufacture civil unrest, the control system uses an inflammatory formulation of nationalism, negligent immigration controls, and the mixing of discordant racial groups to assemble a ready-made time bomb. This is further augmented by establishing parallel segregated communities (slums), exploiting working class tensions over jobs, housing, and culture, and highly sensationalist and irresponsible reporting of inter-racial violence.

With the European Super State now encouraging movement from poverty-stricken Eastern Europe to the more highly technocratic West, there has been a massive influx of Polish and Ukrainian people into England. They are simply economic migrants seeking a better way of life for themselves and their families, though the gentle English middle classes are often secretly disgruntled to hear a Polish accent at the supermarket checkout or the gas station. This is precisely the reaction the control system seeks to induce. It is the precursor to the radical social solution that they would love to roll out: an enormous all-encompassing surveillance and tracking system. The requisite infrastructure is already present in every major UK city, from London to Birmingham, from Manchester to Edinburgh. Nowhere else on the planet has so much surveillance.

Alongside group think, the control system uses another powerful mind trick to impose its will: It binds the concept of *normality* to hive behavior. Do what everyone else does, and you'll be all right. Thus it swells the ranks of the lowest common denominator who so obediently and diligently uphold the values of the mainstream. When ignorance overwhelms honor, the outcome is disintegration.

In behavioral psychology, *normal* means a lack of significant deviation from the average. It is considered good to be normal, and anything else is either a bit weird or just plain bad. One only has to take a look at the explosion of talent/reality TV shows that encourage viewers to ridicule the unusual and feel relief at their own bloated normality. This is an amusing concept for those who value creativity, genius, eccentricity, passion, and vision. None of these things ever spring from that which is normal. Yet the hive vigorously champions the normal and rewards those who infect themselves with its vile conformity with guarantees of group acceptance and pleasurable distraction.

Let us turn our attention to the organizational structure of the control system. The control system is a master of concealment. It uses every trick in the book to achieve optimal resilience against penetration from an outside agency. It employs the classical covert command structures of clandestine cell, phantom cell, and lone wolf to keep its core intact and unobserved, while remaining highly effective in the field. Basic organizational, deployment, and communications tactics can be further articulated by studying the inner workings of modern intelligence and terrorist groups operating in America, Europe, China, South America, and the Middle East.

There are several key layers to the system, which can be broken down in order, as follows:

1. *Enforcement.* Military, police, private security.
2. *Government.* Superficial policy administration.
3. *Realpolitik.* Practical, power-based politics as opposed to principled, ethical politics.
4. *Think tanks.* Managed social, economic, and cultural change; formulated by globalist foundations and institutions.
5. *Esoteric groups.* A synthesis of sequestered ancient world sacred knowledge.
6. *Ultra-terrestrials.* Terrestrial, non-terrestrial and extra dimensional/density consciousness.

From layer six down, each layer passes its instruction down only to the immediate lower layer. From layers one to five, each layer has only minimal upward communication with its immediate superior layer. Layer one has no contact with layer three, layer three has no contact with layer five, and so forth. With the in-built fault-tolerance of the clandestine cell system (distributed hierarchical and organizational structure), if any elements within lower layers become compromised, they can easily be denied, deactivated, or terminated.

Clearly, once we move beyond layer four, we run into the sort of unfamiliar territory that lies well beyond the control system's sliver of reality. Nevertheless, however unfamiliar it may be, if one studies the evidence—filtering out political bias, discerning truth from untruth, taking into account official, unofficial, and esoteric historical records, as well as the lore and cosmologies of the people—the trail consistently leads back to highly esoteric and ancient sources that challenge even the most flexible of belief systems. Private and honest contemplation is needed.

The primary role of the esoteric groups is as gatekeepers of specific strata of knowledge from the ancient world—a world totally unknown to the general public. There is a primary understanding amid these groups that not only do human civilizations cyclically rise and fall according to galactic principles, but that some of those civilizations were not spiritually, technologically, socially, and culturally inferior to us. Some were massively superior. Neither were they all exclusively terrestrial. Filtered through the control system distortion, this knowledge is literally incredible. Remove the distortion filter and it flips to become both credible and completely matter of fact. Once more, only a committed level of personal research allied with direct experiential encounter will afford any sort of practical knowing. One cannot expect to believe it secondhand.

Some of the esoteric groups are known and can be studied. Some groups operate through the main monotheistic religions. This is a shrewd move, as it very effectively protects against probing and criticism, as religion is so close to many people's hearts. To accuse the church of skullduggery (though this has become increasingly popular even in the mainstream news in recent years) is to risk losing your credibility altogether. Hollywood films that dramatize and fictionalize secret orders also serve to dissuade serious scholarly esoteric inquiry and sober intellectual conversation.

Other esoteric groups remain entirely unknown. Induction comes only through loyal and committed membership of the public-facing groups. Through the rigorous initiatory structure enforced by these mysterious groups, only the most advanced adepts receive meaningful passage from the outer exoteric shell of broad symbolism, to the inner esoteric core of precise gnosis. Note that not all of these groups are necessarily negative in and of themselves. It is their covert sequestering/requisitioning by outside agencies that affects the integrity of their constitution and principles. The study of esoteric group histories is beyond the scope of this book, but suffice it to say that they are absolutely existent, and their significance and influence are becoming more transparent by the day.

To approach the ultra-terrestrial layer, let us take an example of a well known ultra-terrestrial entity. From a Christian perspective, Jesus Christ is a being who descended from a higher realm through God's love and wish to save the spirit and consciousness of man. Though he was also a man, Jesus was operating at a completely different density of consciousness, emanating from a higher realm. Yet, of his own volition, he remained bound to the Earth and the plight of its inhabitants, as a symbol of how ascendance is achieved through divine transpersonal gnosis. Though Jesus is now no longer physically present on Earth, his spiritual presence interpenetrates the consciousness of millions of third density beings who have cultivated a relationship with him. In this respect, Jesus can be fairly considered as an ultra-terrestrial being.

Naturally, if Jesus was of divine origin and his consciousness was supremely pure, he is unlikely to have anything to do with the control system. Yet there are many other ultra-terrestrial intelligences that have not yet risen beyond the polarization of positive and negative, and are far from the divine. Particularly those who have manifested without the harmonic balance of the male/female unity of the original spirit remain distorted by the inversions of self-conceit and destruction. They are still very much trapped in the attraction/repulsion of the good versus evil game. To be fenced in by a realm that is still subject to entropy means that some form of power source is required, just as humans need food and plants need sunlight. Lower density consciousness is a prime target for this fourth density sustenance. It must, however, be of the same resonance (albeit it an *octave* lower) as the consciousness that it is being channeled into, so self-conceit and destruction must run through it. Hence the apparent state of pandemonium in the world is not quite so uncoordinated as it might seem.

Gnostic and pre-Christian scholars had no problem with such things. In the Nag Hammadi Library (NHL) tractate *The Hypostasis of the Archons*, the very first paragraph states that the great apostle Paul tells us that "our contest is not against flesh and [blood]; rather, the authorities of the universe and the spirits of wickedness." *Authorities* is a well-understood term for *archons*, supernatural ruling entities that are deeply involved with worldly affairs and its original creation. Roger Bullard's introduction to *The Hypostasis of the Archons* (in the James Robinson edition of the NHL) draws our attention to the proclamations of this text as regards "the reality of the archontic rulers: far from being merely fictitious, imaginary powers, the archons are all too real. These rulers indeed exist. This is a grim reality for the Christian Gnostics, who define their own spiritual nature in opposition to that of the ruling and enslaving authorities."

We learn more about these supernatural adversaries in the NHL's *Authoritative Teaching*:

> For man-eaters will seize us and swallow us, rejoicing like a fisherman casting a hook into the water. For he casts many kinds of food into the water because each one of the fish has his own food. He smells it and pursues its odor. But when he eats it, the hook hidden within the food seizes him and brings him up by force out of the deep waters. No man is able, then, to catch that fish down in the deep waters, except for the trap that the fisherman sets. By the ruse of food he brought the fish up on the hook. In this very way we exist in this world, like fish. The adversary spies on us, lying in wait for us like a fisherman, wishing to seize us, rejoicing that he might swallow us. For he places many foods before our eyes (things) which belong to this world. He wishes to make us desire one of them and to taste only a little, so that he may seize us with his hidden poison and bring us out of freedom and take us into slavery. For whenever he catches us with a single

food, it is indeed necessary for us to desire the rest. Finally, then, such things become the food of death.

We must swiftly counterbalance any potential consternation upon absorbing this information by understanding that *it's not personal.* The supernatural ultra-terrestrial/inorganic beings need low resonance human consciousness in the same way that whales need the plankton that drift through the Atlantic ocean. Inorganic beings identify a certain energy oscillation to locate emanations of low consciousness.

These adversaries are by no means limited to the Gnostics. Many spiritual traditions speak of supernatural beings that stalk men and lay claim to their ownership and creation. They are the dragons, the Annunaki, the Orions, the flyers, the predators, the holes, and the blackwings of countless European, Middle Eastern, South American, and African cosmologies. Whatever names we give to them, they certainly seem to share some important characteristics.

In his 1980 book, *The Way of the Shaman,* author Michael Harner tells of his exchange with a wise Conibo shaman, with whom Harner recounts his vision of mysterious creatures that he'd seen descending from the sky:

> I went to his hut, taking my notebook with me, and described my visions to him segment by segment. At first I told him only the highlights; thus, when I came to the dragon-like creatures, I skipped their arrival from space and only said, "There were these giant black animals, something like great bats, longer than the length of this house, who said that they were the true masters of the world." There is no word for dragon in Conibo, so "giant bat" was the closest I could come to describe what I had seen. He stared up toward me with his sightless eyes, and said with a grin, "Oh, they're always saying that. But they are only the Masters of Outer Darkness." He waved his hand casually toward the sky. I felt a chill along the lower part of my spine, for I had not yet told him that I had seen them, in my trance, coming from outer space. I was stunned. What I had experienced was already familiar to this barefoot, blind shaman. Known to him from his own explorations of the same hidden world into which I had

ventured. From that moment on I decided to learn everything I could about shamanism.

I love how the Peruvian shaman diffuses the drama and the conceit of the "masters" with a touch of humor—though his observation could not be more significant. He unveils another principal strategy of control system power (and the consciousness that created it): to promote itself as infinitely more powerful than it actually is.

Evidently, it is absolutely necessary to suspend all belief systems when analyzing the control system. Fundamental concepts, erroneously implanted in us from infancy, must be un-learned and disengaged before we can see what is real. Only a clear consciousness can perceive and comprehend each layer of the control system. In this vein, it is not constructive (or advisable) to take a person who has remained firmly at government layer two all his life and attempt to elevate his knowing straight up to layer five. His own conditioning will not allow that jump. A burst of revelatory information may indeed shock, but it is unlikely to advantage or enlighten those who are wholly unprepared.

Information alone is of neutral value. Information, when fused with critical judgment and intuitive correlation, becomes knowledge. Knowledge, with deep absorption and spiritual insight, becomes wisdom. Wisdom with direct experiential encounter becomes gnosis.

information > knowledge > wisdom > gnosis

All attainments of gnosis become permanent artifacts in the field. They shift densities, moving outside the constraints of individual consciousness and into a non-local quantum field. From here they are instantly accessible for future reference and teaching to anyone who possesses the codex of personal spiritual accomplishment.

Psychic equilibrium is an indispensable tool on the path of unfoldment. It is a mistake, for example, to concentrate all of one's energies exclusively on the unveiling process. To specialize solely in matters of exposing conspiracies is tantamount to spiritual *seppuku*. Endless conspiratorial digging serves only to repeatedly confirm the existence of the control system. No solutions, just problems. Many powerful minds have had their spiritual advancement hindered, and in some cases terminated, by succumbing to this negative vortex. Equally, ignoring the unveiling altogether can lead to the hugely worrying *space bunny syndrome*, where previously evolving minds liquefy into self-contained escapist fantasy worlds where everything is always bouncy.

As consciousness is moved to focus on one's own evolution and therefore naturally reaches out to higher densities of being, it has the agreeable side effect of automatically vaporizing the psychic restraints of the control system. Their mindjobs and imaginal seeding no longer function. Their solemn sliver of reality morphs into a ludicrous parody. It becomes hard to take their propaganda and disinformation seriously anymore. By concentrating on the path of sacred unfoldment, we free ourselves, expand our consciousness, benefit others, and dis-empower the control system.

The biggest secret of the control system is that it requires our consciousness to function. If we stop believing in it, it falters. If we stop channeling our consciousness into it altogether, it breaks down. Herein lies the mental transfer from the gross to the subtle. We are not helpless objects inside the control system. We uphold it; we make it. The solution is simple. By recognizing and claiming our own sovereign power to create reality—and actually exercising it—we disconnect from that which is unreal. Knowing this makes the mind infinitely harder to influence and returns the power of creation back to the real masters of reality—us.

We are the music-makers,

And we are the dreamers of dreams,

Wandering by lone sea-breakers,

And sitting by desolate streams;

World-losers and world-forsakers,

On whom the pale moon gleams:

Yet we are the movers and shakers

Of the world for ever, it seems.

—"Ode" by Arthur O'Shaughnessy

Chapter 8

The Distortion

Billions of people spend their whole lives residing not in a world, but in a mental model of a world—a construct. This construct is at once a description, a simulation, and a set of laws. It is a representational idea about the world, specifically designed to displace the real thing. Because it is so supremely articulated and sensually substantive, it does not normally occur to people that there is any other way of being. Yet, when our perceptions are filtered through this mental model, a subtle yet fundamental error is perpetuated in day-to-day living: The map is mistaken for the actual territory. Consequently, the multi-dimensional splendor of the real world is occluded.

Contrary to what many believe, human beings inhabit concepts just as readily as they inhabit houses. Indeed, these two seemingly divergent things are almost identical at their root; only the form is different. One is represented by energy condensed into a form that we call brick, the other into a form that we call thought. The distinction is subtle. It is merely a question of density and oscillation. A dream, a whisper, a zebra, a universe—they are all derived from the same energetic building material.

The control system has fabricated a sanitized and reduced version of reality that it broadcasts as the whole of reality. It is *the distortion*. Popular consent is required for this sliver of ordinariness to properly function as a complete world. Consent is given by willfully feeding one's own consciousness into it. The more consciousness it amasses, the more real it appears.

To properly understand what the distortion is, we have to know how it works.

The distortion is a map that is given to everyone when they first arrive on Earth. Unlike a normal map that just shows pictures of where things are and how we get to them, the distortion is a deeply immersive virtual-reality experience that connects directly into the mind. It is widely believed that the distortion offers the best way to understand and navigate the world around us. It tells us what things are, how they work, how we interact with them, and what they mean.

Babies, children, and adults alike are repeatedly told what a thing is until they no longer question what they've been told. *This is this; it isn't something else.* Politicians, movie stars, doctors, businessmen, plumbers, scientists, teachers, students, mothers, and fathers all agree that the distortion is the way things are. They consent to the idea that the distortion *is* reality. It is this way; it is not some other way. As infants, quite naturally, we follow suit. We continually observe distortion rules, routines, parameters, beliefs, and traditions. Repetition is a very important part of this teaching. By age 14, the foundational conditioning is usually complete. From then on, whenever we see a thing, or hear a thing, or touch a thing, we are seeing, hearing, and touching the distortion.

What makes the distortion so utterly compelling and persuasive is that almost everyone on the planet agrees with it. It is the norm. It's just the way things are. It is the real world. We all see things the same way, and that way is the distortion. So potent is this consensus reality, that the tiny minority of folks who don't operate within its parameters are considered to be very strange individuals indeed. They might even be thought of as undesirable or dangerous. If the regular institutions of schools, colleges, and workplaces fail to instill the reality of the distortion into these oddballs, they are taken away to special institutions where they are tutored in the way of righteous conformity, so they can function normally within distortion society. One could say that normality is the religion of the distortion. To move away from normality is to risk being shunned.

The massive weight of collective human accord with which we imbue the distortion gives it such an awesome degree of power, credibility, and concreteness, that it becomes more real than anything else.

Everywhere we look, the distortion is king. It is raccoons and teapots, just as it is orchids and skyscrapers. It is what the Taoists call the ten thousand things. To question the reality of the distortion is to question existence itself. Surely, it is only eccentric, old philosophers and disheveled, wandering mystics who would even wish to ponder such things.

Most people simply don't have the time, inclination, or awareness to contemplate the nature of the distortion. For someone who has dwelled in the distortion for his or her whole life, the idea of probing it, clarifying it, playing with it, or even leaving it behind, is downright disturbing. This dissonance arises because the questions addressed to the distortion become mirrored back into the heart of the questioner. For the distortion-dweller who is entirely unacquainted with his or her own inner landscape, the prospect of profound philosophical revelation is not particularly inviting. The thundering emptiness perceived in his or her own psyche is simply too much to handle. The knee-jerk impulse is to immediately fill the void with distortion media—voices, images, news, entertainment, anything. The distortion abhors a vacuum. So it's just better to stay put. Stay within the distortion hive. This is precisely what the distortion relies upon for its structural integrity. It needs high volumes of immobile consciousness to flourish.

So, then, why would anyone question what is commonly considered to be the best possible mode of reality—potentially walking away from the received wisdom of thousands of years of human history? There are three answers on three different levels.

1. On a collective level, the mainstream historical record of human endeavor has not been a very peaceful or sane narrative. It is full of violence, pain, and hardship. Indeed, such things have become so commonplace that we are tempted to think that's just how the cookie crumbles so far as the gross ineptitude of humanity goes.

2. On an individual level, we are obliged to acknowledge that the distortion is not our personal model; it is someone else's. It may not therefore be best suited to our own individual journey.

3. On a metaphysical level, with a little contemplation, it is clear that we have habitually come to confuse one description of reality (the distortion) with reality itself. Hindu spiritual philosophy refers to the fake map as maya, a "beguiling concealment." The genius of the distortion is that it hacks into the organic element of the illusory world—which exists to teach us about spiritual ascendance—and annexes it for its own purposes. What was once a vast and glorious playground for unfoldment has been transformed into a shroud of ignorance.

Although we can intellectually debate these points and offer various persuasive counter arguments for further deliberation, at the inner level, when we are completely authentic with ourselves, we know full well that the human story has gone off track. This is what is important. The system under which we labor does not serve us; we serve it. Once more, it has been this way for millennia. But now, that paradigm is shifting. The seasons are changing. The territory of the familiar has become uncertain. The old hierarchies of our governments and institutions are losing their authority as people stop believing in them. It is time to do things differently. It is time to move away from the distortion. This opportunity comes around every 25,000 years, and we are at one of those reboot points again now.

A key realization in learning how to detach our perceptions from the erroneous gravitation of the distortion is to understand the origin of it. Like a bank robber who seeks to bypass a complex security system, the secret to successful penetration is in knowing who created the system, how it was created, and what precisely it is designed to protect. It is perhaps this latter point that proves to be the most revealing, as we shall come to see.

Humans have a definite left-brain impulse to categorize, label, and file the entire world into a single huge taxonomy—a hierarchical system of classification. The distortion plays directly into this propensity by instilling its world taxonomy into us from birth. We are trained in its homogeneous apparatus, its descriptions, procedures, resolutions, and policies. We are persuaded to consent to its science, religion, education, legalities, pressures, and demands. The conditioning is ceaselessly broadcast through all distortion hubs: through parents, friends, and family; schools and universities; homes and workplaces; institutions and corporations; and every screen and page of the media.

The distortion puts a straightforward deal on the table: If you accept the taxonomy, you get to choose anything from its colossal pre-defined shopping list of material gratification. Name your poison; it's all there. You can drive your convertible, live in the city, drink beer, eat lobster, play sports, vote in elections, have sex, read the newspaper, join the army, join the masons, listen to Wagner, and bungee jump off the Victoria Falls Bridge. Whatever. Herein lies the guile of the distortion. It sure feels like freedom when you can select from such a vast catalogue of stuff. Indeed, the overwhelming degree of choice actually deters almost everyone from any further contemplation of what true liberation actually looks like.

The distortion is not reality. It is a description of it, and we have decided to inhabit that description. Over time, this de-spiritualizes both one's personal world and the collective world, reducing everything down to biological machines, nuts and bolts, clockwork. The play, the creation, the depth, and the mystery of existence vanish. People live lives they do not want to live. Their families, relationships, jobs, finances, plans, and imaginings become artificial and dysfunctional. Whether on-track or off the rails, they do not satisfy. The distortion breeds this profound disappointment, because it is not a natural formation.

As has been laid out in innumerable classic spiritual texts, it is an explicit observance that if one does not know oneself, then everything on the outside is also essentially unknowable. This is because the outside is misconstrued as a depersonalized realm with no accountable connection to the individual. This is untrue. Outside is mind. It is a direct projection of the inside and is no less ours than our own self. The distortion therefore, like all clouds, has a silver lining. Liberating oneself from the distortion and moving into the real world compels everyone—male and female, young and old—to dive into their own spiritual journey. This is where the solution lies. From a higher perspective, we can even say that the distortion is actually a gift concealed as a threat—one that actually accelerates our conscious and spiritual evolution.

The pragmatist might reasonably think that this is all very well, but given the colossal and all-encompassing nature of the distortion, how do we move away from that which is everywhere? What can you possibly do to change something that is our whole world, rightly or wrongly?

By design, the distortion normalizes the perception of everything and everybody. It is the default gravitation for those who choose not to generate reality from themselves. The reason most people choose not to generate their own reality is because they do not realize that they can. The information and techniques have not been made freely available. In fact, they have been deliberately hidden. The shards of knowledge that do filter into the public domain are far too oblique and fragile for a mainstream distortion-saturated mind to take hold of, let alone understand. The first step therefore is to begin decontaminating the mind from the chief broadcasting edifice of the distortion: the mainstream media.

To move away from the noise of the distortion is to permit the human mind to find its own natural state of equilibrium. The mix of creation, harmony, spontaneity, and depth differs from moment to moment, from one person to the next. So whether we are sitting in silence by a lake, or hurtling across it on a jet ski, what is most appropriate for the time and best aligned with unfoldment will arise of its own accord and find its own expression. None of this is possible, however, if the mind is being willfully force-fed the info-sludge of gossip, deceit, and dishonor that characterize the mainstream media. So we must stop feeding it such things. We turn off the television. We cancel the newspaper subscription. We do not go to see the latest blockbuster movie, which we know is rubbish anyway. We don't follow the mainstream fictional narratives that are presented as the hot topic of the moment. We disregard untruth.

Most people you will ever walk past in the street, for the entire duration of their lives, never proactively question the distortion. They do not feel the defiant impulse to vault its ramparts or spelunk its hidden caverns. And if, as occasionally happens, one noble heart does dare prod the dragon's tail, there is a tidal upwelling of such perilous psychic discomposure that the inquiry is immediately dropped and rarely, if ever, returned to in any meaningful way. Too weird and too hard. No thank you. Go back to the previous page. This ingenuous failsafe deters nearly all human souls from walking the ascendant path of conscious spiritual evolution.

People can *feel* the distortion, even though they may not know what it is. Their inner sonar pings the surrounding reality and when the echo returns, even though all the instrumentation returns a normal reading, it still doesn't seem quite right. Not infrequently, people will reach the halfway mark of their lives, after they've been immersed in the 9-to-5 distortion game for a good long while, and instead of feeling deeply fulfilled by all their marvelous achievements and realizations, there is a faint but definite suspicion that they are still somehow off course. On paper, everything may look okay and be proceeding very much according to the plan of what grown-ups are supposed to being doing with their lives. But the feeling remains: Something is wrong. There has to be *more*.

Should one feel guilty about this? Is it ungrateful? Is it wrong? Is it important? The knee-jerk response is often to upgrade one's resources and see if that helps. Get a bigger house, a new car, a better-paid job, some new clothes. Lose 20 pounds, redecorate the spare room, go on vacation. Though these diversions take the edge off things for a short time, they do nothing to address the root of the problem. It is a seemingly insoluble predicament, and there is usually very little effective help from friends, family, or medical professionals, because they don't understand the root either. All the while, the mind continues to struggle for freedom and clarity. The result? People go a bit crazy and do impulsive things.

This state constitutes a psychic moratorium on untruth and a special occasion for honesty, re-evaluation, and course correction. At this time, there is often a strong accompanying desire to throw oneself into *real experience*, as opposed to running through the same old predictable tasks and neurotic calculations of everyday life. It is a desire so potent that it can displace all other aspirations and suspend standard operating procedure. Vividness of experience rapidly becomes more valuable than anything else.

In the middle of such an opening, all the normal chaotic traffic of humanity suddenly changes its aspect, as if a heavy snow has descended to quiet the whole landscape. All customary routines and regulations go off-line. There are then two paths forward. The first path leads to the root and faces the inauthenticity head on. To look around, take stock and say to oneself, "This is all unreal." To realize that life has been lived on a film set. To look at the deliberations and scurrying of one's compatriots and realize that they are oblivious and all of their endeavors succeed only in distancing themselves from their unfold. To know that one's own toys, constructs, and fabrications are transitory rubbish. Despite the initial pain of this naked observance, it is a sacred act of regeneration and something truly powerful begins to arise within. At last, life and self start to transform. Old things break up, and new things blossom. In contrast, the second path avoids the root and chooses to press the self-destruct button. This takes the form of either sensory inversion or mental shutdown, or both. When the crash comes, the evasive maneuvers are forgotten, and exactly the same inauthentic prior course is dutifully resumed.

If normality is the religion of the distortion, to oppose it is not only to gamble with excommunication, but it also places the individual in a position where he is obliged to figure out how he's going to replace the unreal with the real. To dig out untruth and start over. Few have the requisite humility for such a feat. The distortion is hugely uncooperative in this regard. One has to seek out real support, real knowledge, and real healing for oneself. Many refuse to give up and succeed in pushing through, even though it all looks so vague and imprudent. They are the noble spirits who think for themselves, question authority, and direct their energies to real philosophy and real spirituality. They intuit that the most significant and sublime attunement is to explore the nature of existence itself through personal encounter—through unfoldment. In acknowledging this, one can't go far wrong, regardless of the eventual outcome. Such intractable autonomy is frequently branded as eccentric, weird, or hazardous. The strong-hearted spiritual adventurer is never concerned about such things.

Detaching oneself from the untruths of the distortion begins with brutal honesty. Cool, lucid, transparent inquiry into oneself. One question: *What are you doing?* If the answer to this is not agreeable and affirmative, then it is an echo of the distortion. That's the bad news. The good news is that changing the answer to that question is completely within one's own realm of total sovereign power. No one and nothing can stop the will that has decided to free itself and become true. As with all subtle but profound powers, this has to be claimed for oneself. It has to be firmly grasped and clearly declared to oneself before any outward action can be relied upon as being true.

The conveyor belt of endless productivity that the distortion uses to captivate its subjects is slowing down, day by day. It is slowing down because a critical mass of conscious humans is discovering that what is being producing is not beneficial to humankind. In fact, what rolls off the production line is entirely arbitrary; it is a hollow negativity that diminishes the human spirit. All the blood, sweat, and tears that go into this flaccid industriousness need not be spilled. Honor is as valid a tool in this forswearing as is wrath. All ideas of deriving self-worth from the workplace must be abandoned. It is notable that men and women of high spiritual attainment are never seen in positions of traditional power. They are not in the White House or Downing Street, nor are they investment bankers, media moguls, or visionary businessmen.

The impulse to say no must be backed up by *not doing*. To not believe a thing is to not put consciousness into it. To not do a thing is to reroute consciousness back into one's own pool of knowing. Where dishonor and untruth are encountered, no further belief or deeds need go there, should we so wish. The damaging protestant work ethic that ties labor to godliness is counterfeit. The divine creator of the universe does not require anything from anyone. A gift of *returning* is freely given and elegantly woven into our engagement with spiritual growth. We need only graciously accept it. What we learn on the journey back is our gift to the divine.

The origin of truth is divine; it can only be known through spiritual endeavor. There is no meaningful success outside the unfoldment of one's own being and the joy of the ascendant journey. The only measure of value—in oneself, in others, or in anything—is truth. How true are we to who we are and what we know we are capable of? Are we healing old deceitful patterns? Are we creating new harmonious ones? Do we consistently move with integrity and honor? Are growth and discovery part of our everyday experience?

It is never too late to begin the journey, no matter how long a mind has slumbered in the distortion. Some people become conscious early on, some mid-way, some toward the end. Some do not become conscious at all, at least not this time around. Awakenings occur at precisely the right time, when the most favorable energies are aligned. We can only know when that is for ourselves. When we do, it is time to act.

In realizing that we are our own authority, we permanently free the mind from the delusion of servitude. We bring more and more consciousness into everything we do and accept nothing within the distortion at face value. We discern. We choose. We determine what is fit for our conscious attention and what is not. To not engage—to content oneself with watching others go about the business of running reality—is not an option. There is nobody acting on our behalf and with our best interests at heart. There cannot be. It is something we can only do for ourselves. Indeed, to be content to do nothing is to consign oneself to a state of conscious limbo and forfeit the most precious and powerful gift in the universe.

Chapter 9

Silent Consent

The universal principle of freewill naturally ordains that no entity can impose on the will of any other entity without its consent. Moreover, the higher the level of consciousness, the more precisely this mechanism has to be observed. At first glance, this concept can seem a little odd, especially when one considers how frequently it appears to be contravened by some of the more shadowy agencies and hostile individuals of the world. Yet the deeper one probes beneath the husk of visible appearances, the stronger the equation of freewill resonates.

Within the more esoteric branches of geopolitical research, the phrase *predictive programming* often arises. This is a technique formulated by globalist think tanks to acclimatize the collective public consciousness to certain ideas, perspectives, and technologies that are specifically designed to steer the course of a society. Both the factual media networks and the entertainment industry are leveraged as conduits for this highly influential conditioning, more often than not remaining entirely unconscious of their own complicity in this propaganda.

It is the trends themselves that are controlled, not the legions of media professionals who follow them. No grand conspiracy is necessary. The think tanks design social trends that smooth the passage for the desired political, economic, and military strategies. Proportionately, only a tiny number of people need be involved. They are the ones who decide what gets hyped and what gets buried, from one culture to the next. By the time this invisibly filters down to the executives, producers, and directors, it is virtually indistinguishable from organic social evolution. Besides, in the frenzied world of the modern mediaplex, not many people have the time to trace the esoteric roots of the prevailing vogues and appetites that shape New York, Los Angeles, Tokyo, Paris, Berlin, and London.

Who would've thought 20 years ago that more than a billion Europeans and Americans would choose to publicly share the most intimate details of their personal lives with strangers online? Or that everyone would carry a little plastic rectangle in their pocket that would track and log their exact whereabouts 24/7? Or that modern, democratic governments would publicly announce that they lift people off the streets—without charge or hearing—to confine, torture, and murder them? Do these social developments spring from the hearts and minds of honorable men and women? Do they have integrity? Are they good things?

Long-term strategies are frequently disguised as natural reactions to the needs and wants of a modern world. Key social changes are seeded at least a generation before they appear in the consensus reality tunnel. The little things are brought in through the mainstream news networks; the big things are brought in through the entertainment industry. Apparently imaginal scenarios are dipped into the hive mind and then withdrawn again. Then they are reintroduced from what look like unconnected sources. The same message is re-worded, re-colored, re-imagined, and re-broadcast over and over until it looks like spontaneous, organic social development. It looks like it comes from the people. But it does not.

The more controversial a particular predetermined social shift is, the more it is filtered through fiction. In introducing the associated themes and images in this way, not only are dramatic paradigm-changing events presented to the public consciousness in a seemingly *safe* context, but critically, the associated moral and ethical questions are effectively removed from the conversation. No one is interested in examining the virtue of a fictional maverick CIA operative who, in his mission to bring terrorists to justice, breaks international laws and disregards universal human rights. It's just television. It's just fantasy. When real-life operatives are then reported to behave in a similar way, the psychological payload is less shocking. "We've already seen that on TV. I guess that's the way the world works." This also averts any unprofitable social panic or rioting, or, even worse, mass revolt and organized rebellion. Not part of the predictive programming agenda at all.

Though we can safely say that the integrity of senior policy-makers within the globalist think tanks is undoubtedly low, they are nevertheless operating with a very high level of cerebral processing. They represent the pinnacle of what can be achieved using the biological computer of the brain alone. As detached as they are from the spiritual unity of human empathy and true-heartedness, they still have to observe the natural order of freewill. They cannot simply enforce their will upon an unknowing populace; they require their consent. So they ask for it.

This functions in a very similar manner to the more domestic laws that one finds in civil proceedings. In law, there are two typical ways of giving notice of something. The first is called *actual notice*, where information is conveyed directly to the person in question. For example, with the notification of a divorce, the papers are physically served to the recipient. The second type of notice is called *constructive notice*. This is where notice is posted or published in a public space, such as on a building, on a notice board, or in a newspaper. Though the relevant parties may not have this notice immediately brought to their personal attention, they are nonetheless considered to have had fair warning of any intended proceedings. This is how predictive programming tackles the rule of sovereign freewill: It gives constructive notice to all concerned parties. The deafening silence with which such notices are usually greeted is consent enough.

To help crystallize the mechanics of predictive programming, it is enlightening to reflect on an old legal maxim: "Ignorance of the law does not excuse." This is from the Latin *ignorantia juris non excusat*. This principle holds that just because one is unaware of a law, does not mean that one can claim exemption from liability. Whether it is *fair* in honorable human terms is irrelevant. (Any overseas visitors who may have innocently driven a rental car through central London and later received a surprise "congestion charge" fine can attest to this principle.)

Irish philosopher Edmund Burke, whose works would later help to form the basis of modern Conservatism, warned of the dangers of a ruling system that wasn't necessarily operating illegally, but was nevertheless set against man. In his 1770 publication, *Thoughts on the Cause of the Present Discontents*, Burke stated, "The discretionary power of the Crown in the formation of Ministry, abused by bad or weak men, has given rise to a system, which, without directly violating the letter of any law, operates against the spirit of the whole constitution." This radical observation prepared the way for him to make one of his more insightful and oft-quoted observations later on in the same document: "When bad men combine, the good must associate; else they will fall one by one, an unpitied sacrifice in a contemptible struggle."

People actually have to *do* something if they want to live in a more natural, equitable, and spiritually vibrant world. It's not enough to just donate to charities that are doing supportive things, or volunteer at a soup kitchen now and again, or walk around holding up signs of protest. They are all very good and have their own relevance, but by totally occupying oneself with such external causes, the root internal issue is subconsciously circumvented.

It begins with having the confidence to take oneself seriously—to perceive and treat oneself as a powerful, consequential, and unique conscious being that has been given the opportunity to do something of tremendous value. It's a two-way thing. The more we grow, heal, and stay true to our spiritual ascendancy, the more the planet grows, heals, and steers its own organic path of beautiful evolution.

Part of the healing is to no longer consent to what is dishonorable. Wherever that is seen and at whatever level, withdrawing consent stops fueling the fire. It requires a strong and true heart—something that all humans have, should they care to take ownership of it. The sheer weight of public acceptance of what is untrue and deceitful does not matter. In fact, it serves to test the veracity of one's own freewill and self-assurance as a sovereign being. That freedom is immutable. The problem is: Do people actually want freedom?

In a moment of remarkable lucidity, Jim Morrison, the singer from The Doors said:

> How can I set free anyone who doesn't have the guts to stand up alone and declare his own freedom? I think it's a lie—people claim they want to be free—everybody insists that freedom is what they want the most, the most sacred and precious thing a man can possess. But that's bullshit! People are terrified to be set free—they hold on to their chains. They fight anyone who tries to break those chains. It's their security.... How can they expect me or anyone else to set them free if they don't really want to be free?

To be free, one has to make decisions for oneself. A surprising number of people don't really want to do that, because they associate decision-making with risk. The outcome of making a wrong decision is often portrayed in the mainstream media as a life-shattering failure. It is a very binary equation in the unreality of the distortion: win or lose; black or white. But reality is not like that. There is no failure on the spiritual path, other than the temporary postponement of not walking it.

A conscious decision to *not* do something is as valid as choosing to do something. One must consider the personal relevance of a thing from one's own inner core before exercising will. Contemplate removing *should* from the process. There is doing, and there is not doing. *Should* doesn't come into it. If I feel that it would be good to go and visit my elderly neighbor and help her chop firewood, then I do it. If I don't feel that, then I won't do it. No should is required.

Should compels people to act from imbalance—from outside their truth. It is closely allied with public expectation and social standing, which are habitually flawed, as they are mired in the distortion. It is rather like behaving with super fine conduct, but not recognizing morality. There are many people on this planet who have no concept of holding fast to social expectations of ethics, morality, or law—yet they treat each other right, with compassion, with equanimity and courteousness. Everyone has a sense inside of what is right and wrong. This perception can be deepened and clarified by equating right with truth and wrong with untruth. The more that spirit is allowed to present itself in day-to-day life, the easier it is to tell what is true and untrue, both personally and universally. So whether hunting in the primeval forests of Oregon or eating a peanut butter sandwich on a park bench in Manhattan, it is spirit that serves to resonate the truth of a thing.

Thinking differently begets behaving differently. Even those who genuinely want to redesign the way they live—to resonate more sincerity and depth—often attempt this process in reverse, with predictably regrettable results. It takes time to figure this out. Doing hours of sitting meditation, following ceremonies and rituals, or even just watching endless online videos, yields little more than mere rumors of illumination. To get to the real thing, it is necessary to first stop everything. Everything. Only by holding still can we go deep beneath the calm of the surface and actually look into the darkness. Whatever is there is you. Blemishes, conquests, beauty, mortification, bafflement, and longing—all of it has to be first *seen* as just what it is. Our personal history is a series of energy exchanges, implemented with various degrees of consciousness. There is no judgment. There is only receding and progressing.

Spirit can be thought of as that part of ourselves that is in the immediate higher density of being. It is *above* us in the sense that its perspective means that it can see and appreciate the effect of one's energy exchanges on all the other configurations around us. People, places, things, ideas, dreams. To some extent, one characteristic that differentiates the spirit from the self is elegance. Without discipline and gnosis, the self will ordinarily remain rather ungainly in terms of how it conducts itself in the world. This doesn't mean that it's bad. It is just like the child tottering around an expensive glassware store, risking knocking things over with every inexperienced step he takes. The spirit, on the other hand, sees all the shelves, aisles, corners, shadows, and distances, and comprehends the overall interplay of cause and effect. Because of this elevated point of view, it can plot a safe and pleasing course, should we care to acknowledge its wisdom. Though it resides at another density of being, the spirit is not separate from the self; it encompasses it completely, as water encompasses the goldfish in the bowl.

Consent is a conscious act. To do nothing and stay silent when our spirit tells us that such inactivity is untrue, is to willfully relinquish control. No one has the right to complain when they have shackled themselves and handed over the keys to another. On the other hand, to do something and speak up when we know it is true—even in the face of overwhelming opposition—immediately detaches the individual from the authority of the distortion. The more we exercise our sovereign authority to decide every action and inaction for ourselves, the more authentic and powerful we become. The more natural we become.

When Burke said, "when bad men combine, the good must associate," he was speaking both practically and philosophically. Perhaps now we can draw a further level of insight from his words. We can reasonably say that the control system and the distortion represent the first half of the statement. As for the second half, how exactly are the good to associate? How do we go about that? Do people get together, link arms, and chant anti-government slogans? Do they throw sticks of dynamite through the windows of gangster capitalist bankers? No. This is doing it back to front. The association is one of truth. With that truth comes the power to negate the untruth of the distortion.

Only when you know what is true, can you know what is false. Practically, it means detaching oneself from the infrastructure of the control system, beginning with limiting one's exposure to it. It means treading confidently yet lightly through the minefields of unreality, with as little investment and indebtedness as possible. It means shouting loudly when the time is right, with honor, strength, and spirit. It means exploring the phenomenal terrain of the real world, in all its abundance, mysteriousness, and brilliance. The energetic movements of the yielding and the steadfast are wholly complementary. We make as many exits as we do entrances. We demolish as much as we create. We give our conscious consent only to what is true.

Chapter 10

Touchstones

By making truth a significant and operational part of our everyday experience, the impulse for philosophical inquiry draws us necessarily closer to the big questions of life. How can we *not* be inspired by our own true origins, our purpose, and our final destination? What has happened to the consciousness that prefers not to ponder such things? It is natural to wonder. It is natural to plunge into the luscious depths of this sacred existence. Wisdom is our eternal sister. To suppose that we might be content with obliviousness is to conceive of a universe that has forsaken its own progeny. This is not so. The universe wants us to engage with it, question it, know it—to regard ourselves as an integral part of it. Yet these things are only of value if they are recognized by our own freewill.

Need we bow our heads or bend our knees to anyone in this engagement? Does the divine emanation of truth require veneration? Why would it? Yet there are those who are quite determined to worship that which is ostensibly unknowable, just as there are those who are resolute in their denouncement of anything that is obviously unknowable. As has been the case many times before, the schism between the godly and the godless is widening again. Is this a natural process? Do we need to choose one or the other? How are we to best approach that which is unknowable? We can begin by considering what we do know.

We are born unto this world. We grow. We wander. We talk to people, read some books, observe the terrain, contemplate the situation. After a while, one way or another, we are obliged to concede that nobody *really* knows what is going on. Where do we come from? What are we supposed to be doing here? Where are we going next? Unknown.

Unknown. Unknown. These foundational questions, upon which all human endeavor is ultimately assembled, lie permanently in shadow. What's more, there is an unspoken rule that to even inquire after them is the height of social impropriety.

For those who disregard the secret statute to cleave not to the big questions of life, there are two conventional ways to proceed: the secular approach and the faith-based approach.

Britain is now principally a secular nation (secular meaning "relating to the worldly, rather than the religious"). This is very obvious if one spends a little time there, walking through the villages, towns, and cities, and sitting at the dinner tables of working class and middle class families. The influence of organized religion, as represented by signed membership and the number of active churchgoers, has been in steady decline since the end of World War I in 1918. Visiting Americans are often surprised to learn how the once-buoyant cultural interface with religion has been reduced to ashes in little under a century. Though mainstream television and newspaper coverage obscures this fact with gallons of romanticized fiction, it is getting harder and harder to disguise the giant paradigm shift that is underway.

The first half of the 20th century was spent preparing for, executing, and recovering from two devastating world wars. The second half was spent laboring under the aggressive polarization of domestic politics, culminating in the industrial misery of the shambolic Wilson-Callaghan governments and the vile hyper-materialism of Thatcher. Between these three prime ministers, 16 consecutive years of *scorched earth* policy brought the consciousness of the British people to a new low. There was precious little bandwidth left for sincere spiritual discovery.

Today, the percentage of the UK population defining themselves as Christian in the official 2011 UK Census is 55 percent. This figure drops to 43 percent when formulated by the respected 2010 British Social Attitudes Survey. In practice, that figure is again much lower, as the majority of those who tick the Christian box on surveys know next to nothing about Christianity, let alone have any experiential awareness of its doctrines, ceremonies, or theology. Perhaps the most useful benchmark for religious participation is physical church attendance. This figure is a mere 17 percent, from the 2010 British Social Attitudes Survey, and an even more subdued 6 percent, as projected in the 2005 Brierley Census of Churchgoing survey, with an expected dip to 4.4 percent in 2020. Will it reach zero by 2050?

This jettisoning of organized religion has significantly changed the way the world is commonly perceived in Britain. It is the secular, data-based perspective that informs the mainstream conception of reality, essentially regarding the universe as a huge cosmic machine that is satisfactorily articulated by science. Humankind lives inside the machine and is in fact made from the same raw materials. In continuing to examine the elaborate mechanisms in finer and finer detail, a point will be reached where most things will be adequately charted and explained. All the salient laws, principles, particles, and particulars will be conveyed and arranged in neat hierarchies. From this secular standpoint, the big answers are currently given thus: Where do we come from? *An accidental mix of chemicals that produced a primordial slime that gradually evolved into homo sapiens.* What are we doing here? *Passing on genetic material to our progeny.* Where are we going? *Into the galactic recycle bin.*

So we may say that the secular approach to understanding and exploring the world is not inevitably derived from simple arrogant atheism. Neither is it the natural heir to the rational enlightenment of the 18th century. No amount of social corrosion, personal apathy, or shared ignorance can account for such acute and massive despiritualization, even at the surface level of religious observance. No. It is a century of sustained mass trauma programming that has disconnected millions of Britons from their unfoldment.

America is much more belief-orientated than Britain. It is also a radically younger nation. Consequently, religion is still bound into the highest governance of its constitutional republic, much more so than many would care to admit. It is quietly understood that no one can take senior political office without demonstrating an active faith. No God = no vote.

The significance of religious adherence, whether actual or contrived, cannot be overestimated in the public-facing world of American political life. To the impartial spectator, this might seem like a strange anachronism, especially considering the mega-corporations' obvious dominion over all things political. It would seem easier to simply replace religion with science—surely a much more suitable bedfellow for the totalitarian industrialist? Yet science does not have the power to capture the same quantity of imaginations that religion does. It cannot inspire hearts in quite the same way. Religion can speak to any segment of the population at any time: rich or poor, bright or dim, left or right. It can effortlessly traverse the kinds of racial, cultural, and educational barriers that leave science stranded. For this reason, religion is an important weapon in the political armory.

It is my observation that religion in America serves as much as a moral touchstone as it does a system of spiritual belief. Morals are perceived as somehow more *immediate* than beliefs; they show us right and wrong, and provide a template for acceptable behavior. In uncertain times, a good proportion of the population will vote for the most morally virtuous men and women to represent them. People are more liable to give their power away to someone who they perceive as more moral than themselves. It resonates a deep submissive impulse in many humans beings who *want to be told what to do.* They want the problem to go away and things to get better, and they want mommy or daddy to do it for them.

If I were an immoral tyrant masquerading as a credible American presidential candidate, the first thing I would do is create a version of myself that was exceedingly moral and devoutly religious. The next thing I would do is hire a covert intelligence team to go out and erase any of my prior indiscretions, be they minor transgressions or major felonies. At the same time, they would be tasked with digging up the dirt on my challengers and handing it over to carefully chosen media people. If no dirt could be found, then they could fabricate some. This is exactly what real political campaigners do year in, year out.

Religious participation in America is appreciably more evident in family life, politics, business, the media, and education than anywhere in Europe. Seventy-six percent of Americans identify themselves as Christian, according to Aris in 2009, with a generous 41.6 percent attending church regularly, according to a 2009 Gallup poll. In my own travels through the byways and backwaters of more than 40 American states in the last few years, I have noted an unexpectedly high number of churches—far more than I would've reasonably envisioned. Not only were they mostly well maintained (hugely surprising to this Anglo-American traveler), they were also well populated, both on Sundays and throughout the week. I observed this particularly in multiple counties of upstate New York, where I resided for a year.

Though I have been intermittently alarmed at the church's cynical absorption of the more underprivileged members of society, it is hard to dismiss the many accounts I've heard (including several firsthand) of these very same lives being saved from certain tragedy, were it not for pious intercession. As one British humorist noted, "They always get you when you're down." This may be so, but if I'm in a cardboard box under a bridge and the deal is *come to church and consider our religion, and in return we will put a roof over your head and food in your belly*, then it's a good deal for a desperate man. Someone in a sketchy part of Louisiana once said to me, "In this town, you either go to church or you go to jail." When times are hard and physical and psychological resources are scarce, this is quite true for communities who lie far from the privileged froth of smartphones, suede boots, and maturing 401Ks.

The churches of America, be they Baptist, Lutheran, Pentecostal, Presbyterian, Jehovah's Witness, or Mormon, have absolutely no problems with directly addressing the big questions. Where do we come from? *God*. What are we doing here? *God's work*. Where are we going? *Back to God* (as long as you qualify).

As an infant, I was baptized a Methodist and later attended a Church of England primary school. By age 10, I had already participated in hundreds of Christian rituals, ceremonies, prayers, hymns, and oaths. None of this behavior was at all uncommon in the North West of England in the 1970s. It's just *what people did*. At the time, I had no conception of what my religious deeds meant. It would be another 15 years before I began to study their ancient origins and mystical function, which dated back at least 6,000 years.

Every autumn, on the occasion of Harvest Festival, all the local schoolchildren would walk in procession to the parish church, carrying boxes of fruit, vegetables, and canned goods. I can still see the bananas, carrots, and canned peaches now. These would then be solemnly transported inside the building and left as a bountiful offering at the steps of the altar. Hushed tones of approval wafted from pews full of ruddy-cheeked old ladies, as squadrons of slightly baffled children trundled up and down the nave. The food would later be distributed among the *poor and needy* (to use the old politically incorrect term) within the community. Everyone taking part could feel jolly good about themselves, even though few of the children had a clue what was going on. I have an abiding memory of my good friend at the time asking me, "Why are we bringing cabbages and cauliflowers here?" I said I didn't know. He tugged at the teacher's sleeve to ask her about it, but she just told him to be quiet.

Despite any unappetizing conceit emanating from either the faith-based or secular approach, it would be imprudent to totally discard either of them. Both have wisdom at their core. They each bring their own skills of analysis, intuition, and devotion. They offer legitimate *departure lounges* for those who feel too overwhelmed by the big questions to arrange their own philosophical passage. The faith-based approach offers a yielding experience with the unknowable. The secular approach gives steadfast experience with data. We need both to attain real penetration and crystal-clear vision. To be always yielding or always steadfast is to create imbalance. The way of unfoldment is to move gracefully between the two as the flow of consciousness moves through us.

The other common approach to the profound inquiries of life is that of the agnostic. Agnosticism is basically the idea that, as we can never know the big spiritual and metaphysical answers, there's little point in pursuing them. Only human experience and empirical data can be trusted to determine whether something is valuable or not. Everything else is to be necessarily regarded with the utmost skepticism. Is this wise? Does it feel true? Is there a temptation for the agnostic to presuppose that all existence is only happening on the third density? How soon would this change with a profound individual felt experience of direct fourth density being? About 10 seconds typically. The bottom-up philosophy quickly disintegrates in the face of the beating heart of one's own genuine unfoldment.

So do the technicalities of science and the faith of religion help move us closer to truth and knowingness? Yes. They are tools of perception, and as such, they help us to evolve. However, if they are our *only* tools, then we move slowly—*very* slowly. To disregard the perfection of our own unfoldment and simply expect to run with someone else's program is to have one's journey marked in inches rather than light years. No less sacred, but much less invigorating.

Does the conscious equation balance? To expect to only ever move forward based on verifiable data is to always have one's weight on the back foot; to stockpile consciousness at the rear. Such a leaning means that any sort of graceful onward momentum is unlikely. On the other hand, to lunge pompously into the unknown, without discipline or focus, is to gamble on a drastically foreshortened journey. Too much weight at the stern or the bow makes all movement wearying.

Although it can be disheartening to witness lapses of critical reason and spiritual stagnation in our kinfolk, to see good men and women at least *making an attempt* to explore ascendancy—however unrefined that may sometimes appear—is better than doing nothing. In truth, our life circumstances are always configured to provide us with optimal growth, be they rough, smooth, simple, or complex. When we start to acknowledge this at the inner level, our engagement with reality takes on a more reciprocal aspect. The old filters that want to tag everything as either profitable or unprofitable begin to fade. We recognize that conditions are just conditions—perfectly neutral and devoid of any agenda. Only *self* charges the scenery with giving and taking. The true vision of reality is always serenely detached. Cool as a cucumber, as it were.

Unfoldment champions individuality and the freewill to go one's own way. Strictly speaking, there can be no dead ends on such a journey. Even so, now and again, we might come across a welcome shortcut that hastens our advancement, just as at other times we will find ourselves hiking along a lengthy diversion upon which we may temporarily lose our bearings. Perhaps the worst misdeed in life is merely to drift for a while. Yet in any misadventure, all we need ever do is to make contact with what we know is true. This is the alignment of true North, from which we can establish all other possible directions.

When we touch this truth, we see that it is also an immaculate mirror. Though we may have looked into it to behold the beauty of the universe, we might be surprised to see the most intimate reflections of our own self staring back at us. In so doing, we quickly come to observe not only the metaphysical aspect of self, but also its simple, day-to-day conduct—how we use our self to go about the world, and how we interact with other selves, both within and without.

Chapter 11

School Bus of Selves

Many people find themselves behaving in ways that they don't really want to. Despite their educated, mature, and rational minds, they continue to say and do regrettable things—to themselves and to other people. Sometimes they are little things and sometimes they are big things. How is it that an otherwise lovely day can be suddenly transformed into a warzone? The very smallest seepage of discord can rapidly balloon into something of spectacular unpleasantness. Just where exactly do these things come from and how do they assume power so quickly?

Humans do have a peculiar capacity for acts of self-sabotage, aggression, and fear. When the spiteful finger is pointed and mouths distort with fury and pain, all good sense is temporarily thrown out of the window. Following such outbursts, we often hear explanations such as "something just snapped inside and I lost it." These words spring as easily from the mouths of those living on park benches as they do from those living in penthouse apartments. It is exactly the same mechanism regardless of background or circumstances. The question is: What is it that was lost? As one might expect, the short answer is *control*. Yet if that is so, then how is it that control can be surrendered by oneself, and, more importantly, to whom is it being transferred? There's no one else in there, is there?

Imagine that your psyche—your entire mental superstructure—is in fact a yellow school bus. It is a bright yellow American-style school bus with two rows of seats, an aisle down the middle and a big driver's seat up front. The bus is nearly always in motion because it is on a very long journey that will last for many years. Inside the bus, there are three types of people:

1. *The composite self,* who is the driver.
2. *Character selves,* who represent particularly prominent aspects of the personality, each with their own seat.
3. *The survivalist ego,* whose job it is to look after the bus itself.

When the journey is smooth and there's plenty of open road, everyone is happy and gets along just fine with each other. The composite self drives along whistling a cheerful tune, the specialist selves chat among themselves or snooze, and the survivalist ego quietly wanders around making sure everything is ticking over okay.

The composite self, as the name suggests, is a synthesis of all the character selves fused into one entity. It represents the most balanced combination of knowledge and life experience. It is therefore the most appropriate choice for being the driver. The character selves are different for every bus, though there are some common types found on most buses, such as warrior, baby, actor, doomer, tyrant, mouse, comedian, and explorer. The survivalist ego is there to make sure the bus is properly maintained and doesn't go over a cliff. It can be a bit of a worrier, but has a good heart.

It is only when the road becomes a little more challenging, and the journey is rather less certain, that things can begin to change. Taking a wrong turn, going too fast or too slow, getting lost, going into the city, reversing into tight spots, getting a flat tire—all of these occurrences can elicit powerful responses from the character selves and the survivalist ego. Depending on the situation, the warrior will shout, the baby will cry, the actor will dramatize everything, the doomer will spread doom, the tyrant will seek vengeance, the mouse will hide, the comedian will crack jokes, and the explorer will get all excited. It can get pretty chaotic. All the while, the poor survivalist ego runs around like a lunatic, frantically trying to regain the control that appears to have been so hopelessly lost.

To make matters worse, every now and again, one of the character selves or the ego will make a dash up the aisle and try to commandeer the whole vehicle. The composite self, aware of the commotion but absorbed in trying to keep the bus on the road, can be caught off guard and unceremoniously hauled out of the driver's seat altogether. Usually the ego is there first and grabs the wheel. It has a strong urge to take over. Though it thinks it is doing the best thing and acting from good intent, in actual fact, it does not have the proper skills and experience for safe driving, and is therefore putting the whole vehicle and its passengers in considerable jeopardy. You can imagine what might happen with each of the various character selves in the driver's seat.

This figurative model demonstrates how different elements of our psyche can unexpectedly leap to the fore in challenging situations. If the mind is slumbering and we allow ourselves to behave *reflexively* rather than reflectively, we can end up relinquishing our natural command to a naïve part of ourselves that is only capable of acting from the perspective of its own very limited life lens. The actor, for example, simply loves to transform everything into a drama. Making mountains out of molehills is its raison d'être. When a situation requires a wise and measured response, the actor is the last person you want at the wheel, yet this is precisely what we invite if we are startled into negligence by our own emotions.

Being aware of the different aspects of our own character is the first step toward responding in a more composed and effective manner to the demanding conditions that we often encounter in life. Take a moment to identify and contemplate what powerful characters you have inside you. What facets of your personality do you frequently find yourself giving voice to? Is the baby prominent when the going gets tough? Is it the mouse? Or is it the tyrant? If we are honest with ourselves, we know full well who it is that likes to go for the wheel in any given crisis.

Be mindful that the character selves are neither good nor bad in themselves. They are simply those areas of our psyche that we choose to give a little more consciousness to than others. They arise gradually as we go through life, representing the development of our wider personality. What's more, the cast of characters changes over time: Some roles are with us only for a short period; others stay for the whole journey. Frankly, it's a good thing to have some of them with us on the bus. The comedian is almost always a very useful ally, as is the warrior when acting in a disciplined and honorable manner. As for the characters that we don't think are helping us to grow—perhaps the tyrant or the mouse—when they have served their purpose, we can choose to stop sustaining them with our consciousness. When we consciously reclaim the will that gave them form, they begin to dissolve.

Of course, these character selves are not actual separate selves as might be presented in a mental diagnosis such as multiple personality disorder. That is something quite distinctly different. We are speaking here in strictly metaphorical terms for the purposes of elucidating the process of inner control.

In times of stress, it's not difficult to perceive that some part of our psyche is hurtling down the aisle toward the driver's seat. Most people can catch that happening. The problem is that, without understanding the principles behind the composite self, the character selves, and the ego, they have no idea what to do about it. Do you stop it or let it happen? To simply blockade the energy outburst—to attempt to somehow keep it suppressed or even quash it—is not a healthy or realistic option. Neither is it good to amplify the upsurge and let it go wherever it might. Emotions arise to tell us important things. If we persistently shut them down or falsely elevate them, then over time they begin to distort and give us misleading information. They are best handled with subtlety. Acknowledge them, understand their purpose, and act on them appropriately as the multi-dimensional composite self. That is where our deepest wisdom lies.

The ego is a special passenger on the bus and warrants a little further consideration. As the ego is totally committed to the welfare of the vehicle, it can be forgiven for impulsively wanting to take the wheel every time things get a bit weird. It just wants everything to be okay and often feels that that is best achieved by taking over. This is rarely, if ever, true. When in a natural disposition, however, the ego plays a crucial role, and it would be very short-sighted to eject it from the bus altogether. If it weren't there at all, many of the inner workings of the vehicle (which no one else really knows much about) would quickly begin to go awry.

The ego simply wants to feel that it is heard. If the ego knows that it can calmly speak to the driver and appropriate measures will be taken when necessary, then it will panic far less, and there will be fewer false alarms. Moreover, it is important to acknowledge that the ego can spot things that the composite self misses. It has keen instincts and a natural flair for navigating safely through real perils. Authentic communication is therefore far better than petty conflict where the ego is concerned.

The composite self is almost always in the best position to drive, because not only does it enjoy the experiential knowledge of all the character selves and the instincts of the ego, but it is also in communication with a wise source that lies entirely outside the bus. Some call that source the higher self, or the spirit. It is able to see the whole terrain, far ahead of the bus and far behind. It takes a deep and broad view, capable of remaining utterly serene, even in the most trying circumstances. Occasionally, this can be a lifesaver.

So we may say with some conviction that the composite self is the most capable all-round performer on the bus. The ego and the character selves all agree (when they are seated comfortably and feeling suitably acknowledged). For a rewarding and harmonious experience, the composite self is wise to develop three key skills: vigilance, communication, and composure. Consider each of them as an ongoing exercise in becoming sharper, smoother, and cooler with every mile that is covered.

When the composite self has found a degree of balance and realized that it can safely integrate all the apparently separate character selves, it achieves a more natural state of wholeness. Once this has occurred, we immediately wield a far greater degree of authority and integrity in our communications with our friends, our family, our communities, and the wider world. Our words have power. We have earned it. It becomes clear that the influence of our spoken and written language is directly proportionate to the amount of inner work that we have done. Though our words remain purely figurative (they are not meanings in themselves), when we do communicate, people can see that *we mean it*. They can feel that we walk the talk. If we are living our truth in our own lives 24/7, all our expressions are tangibly infused with it.

Language certainly takes on a special significance as our unfoldment deepens—not just in how we employ our words to share wisdom,
love, and fellowship, but also in understanding how words themselves
have become the very bricks and mortar of reality itself. In becoming consciously conversant with our chosen language, we learn how
to construct and deconstruct things at the most profound level. We
gain an appreciation of the secrets of design and destruction in this
media-drenched world of the 21st century. To liberate ourselves from
the constrictions of language is to move closer to its true value: that
of evocation.

Chapter 12

Word Bondage

Words create images. When we intone certain words, either mentally or out loud, we evoke an image. Encountering the word *lemon*, the brain instantly images that singular yellow fruit, with all the associated sensations of taste, smell, and touch. It is an almost automatic impulse. The spoken and written word are thus *image triggers*, capable of modeling considerable chunks of reality from a single word, a brief conversation, or a few paragraphs. In this way, language doesn't just help us to share information; it actually affects the felt experience of our everyday life. Try thinking about any object in your immediate environment, without using or hearing a single word in your mind. It is quite a feat.

The brain likes to chatter about what's going on, from one event to the next, from one moment to another—like a sports commentator watching a game. We cannot help but narrate our own daily affairs. Whether drinking a glass of milk or planning a mission to Mars, we are compelled to describe what we are doing, as we are doing it. The mental narration that accompanies drinking a glass of milk might go something like this: "A glass of milk would be nice. Walk to fridge. Colorful postcard from Italy on door. Open door. Familiar milk carton in door compartment. Is it fresh? Open carton. Sniff, sniff. Yes, seems fine. Another few days on that yet. Go to cupboard, get tall glass, pour milk into it. Reseal carton and return to fridge. Close door. Drink milk. Look out of window while drinking milk. Cool sensation down throat. Refreshing. Wipe top lip. Put empty glass in dishwasher."

As we move through the world, mentally and physically, we describe it. We share these descriptions, filter them, refine them, regard them as true, and codify them into law. As the leading language for international discourse, English is used as one of the foundational materials for the ongoing construction and maintenance of a colossal *world description*—a life-sized, real-time virtual narrative that tells us what everything is and what we should be doing with it. Such is the gratifying and highly wrought sumptuousness of this description that many people have chosen to live in the description, rather than the world that it is describing. It is like living in a museum dedicated to New York City, rather than living in the actual city itself. Why would people do that? Many reasons. The museum is safer than the city, it is easier to understand, and someone else is managing the narrative for you. All the charts, maps, pictures, and texts explaining city life are there for you to peruse at your convenience, should you care to. In truth, most people don't bother. They may occasionally read a few names, dates, and bullet points, but that's about it. It's just nice to have everything looked after by someone else.

Many of those who find themselves living in these descriptive museums have been known to develop a peculiar mental fetish called *word bondage*. This is the practice of deriving pleasure from tying oneself down with words. It is most often performed upon one's own person, though it can operate quite pleasingly in group situations, too. This fascinating linguistic masochism is especially prevalent among those who strongly associate their identity with their intellect (which, ironically, is a very dumb thing to do). As well as using words for pleasurable restraint, the fetishist also exhibits an exaggerated protectiveness over certain words and surprising violence in attacking others. He or she finds it annoying and disconcerting when someone suggests a different connotation to a word or term. The fact that words and their meanings naturally evolve over time is simply ignored. Such is the ideological smog of the fetishist.

Back to clean living wordage.

To keep language as a natural ally, we must learn to handle it smoothly and deftly, as one would a delicate bird in one's hands. Hold it too hard, and you will crush it to death. Hold it too lightly, and it will escape and fly away. Knowing that language is a living organism is the first step to treating it properly. The realization then arises that to become vigilant of the way we use our language, is to become more independent and powerful in our own thinking. We take control of our own images.

Naturally, we endeavor to articulate our perceptions and ideas into the most functional and precise language we can. The more eloquent we can be, the better we understand things. Whether discussing culture, medicine, science, art, or politics, each field has its own lexicon from which to draw, with specialist jargon and phraseology to really help pin things down. Yet it is this very process of pinning things down (which we all like to do) that presents unique challenges in the realms of spiritual philosophy and metaphysics. This is chiefly because the concepts we are dealing with seem to lie far beyond the ordinary, tangible world. Not only are they remarkable in this sense, but they also address matters that we cannot empirically determine using reason alone. We begin to comprehend that reason is not the only instrument for determining valuable knowledge.

Epistemology is the branch of philosophy that focuses on the nature and scope of knowledge, within which knowledge is often divided into two broad categories: *a priori* (prior to, or before the fact) and *a posteriori* (posterior to, or after the fact). A priori knowledge functions independent of experience, as in saying that "Queen Elizabeth II will reign for a finite period of time." A posteriori knowledge requires experience or empirical evidence to function, as in saying that "there are often bees in my garden."

When we move into the realm of spiritual philosophy, the usefulness and precision of these classifications begins to wobble. For example, many spiritual teachers from both Eastern and Western traditions will affirm that it is mind that creates "table." No mind, no table. This calls into question the received a priori assertion that tables exist independently of our experience or evidence of them. The fact that we've spent our whole lives believing that tables exist quite happily on their own without us takes some undoing. It is so very strange to entertain such an overwhelmingly uncommon notion. People get an uneasy feeling in their chest when they realize that commonsense is not quite as loyal and bulletproof as they thought it was. Yet the discomfort derives as much from our stubborn clinging to language as it does from the thoughts themselves.

To avoid being misled by language or, worse, being tightly bound by it, we have to keep it fluid. It there are words that stick in our throat, switch them out for something else. This is especially valuable in studying concepts outside one's customary field of expertise. When a piece of disagreeable terminology is encountered, simply substitute a more suitable wording that carries a parallel meaning. This allows disentanglement from any unkind thorns of nomenclature, focusing the mind not on the appearance of the envelope, but on the meaning of the letter inside it. Many diverse disciplines and foreign paradigms can be profitably explored in this way.

The Eastern proverb of the finger pointing at the moon highlights this beautifully: "All instruction is but a finger pointing to the moon; and those whose gaze is fixed upon the pointer will never see beyond." If you confuse the pointer with the thing that it is actually pointing to, your perception is short-circuited and unsound. You're looking at the wrong thing.

If we ignore a concept just because it is clothed in language that we find a little abstruse, then we catch ourselves indulging in the fantasy of our own self-importance: My words are better than your words. My meanings are more authoritative than your meanings. This is not the way of spiritual growth; it is the way of intellectual snobbery. No defenses whatsoever are required on the path of transformation. No words are too important or too trivial.

Chapter 13

Projected Images

Control the language and you control the thinking. Control the images and you control the imagination. By influencing the meaning of words and images, by constraining the available vocabulary, and by infusing certain symbols with predetermined beliefs, it is possible to shape how the common man thinks about the world.

The word *conspiracy* derives from the Latin *conspiratio*, which means "union or agreement." For a long time, conspiracy simply meant "concurrence in action"—people agreeing to do something together. It was the later legal usage that began the switch into something a little more sinister, that being "an agreement between two or more persons to commit in concert something reprehensible, injurious, or illegal." That is now the regular dictionary definition. Yet the word has today taken on an additional meaning in the collective consciousness, largely due to its unavoidable association with another word. Exactly how this came to be can be traced back to the 1960s, and a very pivotal event in American political history.

In 1963, American intelligence operatives successfully orchestrated a mass manipulation of public perception by forcing a gross polarization of any discussion regarding the assassination of President John F. Kennedy. After Friday, November 22, 1963, the only possible conversation regarding the murder of JFK was either (a) the official story, or (b) nonsense. There was nothing in between. To achieve this, the intelligence operatives took a leaf out of Britain's Psychological Operations (PSYOPS) division, which had been conducting perception management exercises since 1899. British PSYOPS strategists had noted that in addition to physically controlling an event, it was possible to regulate how people could discuss and even think about an event, thereby drastically reducing the visibility and significance of any information that might leak into the public domain. In short, if a thing cannot be coherently talked about, it soon fades from the memory.

The intelligence community JFK PSYOPS hinged on sequestering the previously little-used word *conspiracy* and binding it to the word *theory*. This had the subtle yet potent effect of resonating "collusion and insubstantiality" in the same breath. This new terminology quickly deflected the questions and hypotheses of any serious investigators at the time, diverting them into a black hole of incredulity. Though one of the earliest recorded uses of the phrase *conspiracy theory* dates back to 1909, it was not until JFK's assassination that it entered popular usage.

In the days, weeks, and months following JFK's death, at every opportunity of media/press exposure, any version of events that wasn't the official government version was labeled as *conspiracy theory*. The suggestion was clear: Conspiracy theories—being entirely unapproved and without official endorsement—are inherently dubious, unreliable, and maybe just plain nuts. This message was underlined by the persistently scornful, mocking, and arrogant attitudes of interviewed government representatives toward any alternative theories.

The goal was to control and lock down the issue for the longest time possible. The records collected as part of the Warren Commission's investigation into the assassination of JFK were submitted to the National Archives in 1964 to be sealed for 75 years (until 2039). This was overturned by the Freedom of Information Act of 1966 and the JFK Records Act of 1992. By 1992, most of the data was available for release to the public, with only minor redactions. The remaining documents are scheduled to be released to the public around 2017. Still, many key pieces of evidence and documentation are lost, cleaned, or missing from the original chain of evidence. In addition, the Kennedy autopsy photographs and X-rays were never part of the Warren Commission records, and were dealt with separately via the National Archives by the Kennedy family in 1966 under restricted conditions. Despite polls suggesting that as many as 80 percent of the American public do not buy the official story, the objective was nevertheless achieved: With the passage of time, most people no longer care what happened to JFK.

The intelligence operation had worked.

This old linguistic trick was evoked once more on September 20, 2001, by George W. Bush as he addressed a joint session of Congress following the 9/11 attacks, where he stated, "Either you are with us, or you are with the terrorists"—the desired effect being to shut down any further discussion. Any alternative investigations into the murder of 3,000 people on September 11, 2001, were deemed mere conspiracy theories and not to be taken seriously. Only government-sponsored investigations had credibility and weight.

After the 1960s, the derisory connotations of conspiracy theory would forever more induce notions of anti-establishment whackos, strange cults, and half-baked obsessive fantasies. Look up the JFK assassination on Wikipedia and you get more than a dozen pages of official story and one paragraph on "assassination conspiracy theories." The juxtaposition of this against the rest of the entry, together with the preloaded terminology itself, erodes the value of any alternative scenarios, analysis, or consideration—well before the average reader even begins to engage his or her own apparatus of perception.

Such is the enduring power of the term *conspiracy theory* that many alternative researchers (particularly those examining politics, corporatism, and the military) have, of their own volition, dropped the term altogether so as to avoid limiting the acceptance of their work.

PSYOPS derives from what used to be called propaganda. Its origins, certainly in modern English history, can be traced back to the Second Boer War in 1899 and later to World War I (1914–1918) when the British Government officially created the Ministry of Information (MOI) to control the spread of information during international conflicts. Of course, the use of propaganda per se stretches back to the most ancient records of human conflict and can be observed in the historical documents of early Persian and Roman military campaigns.

The contemporary use of the word *propaganda* originates from the Vatican. In 1422, Pope Gregory V founded a group called the *Congregatio de Propaganda Fide* (Congregation for the Spreading of the Faith) tasked with the job of spreading Catholic doctrines as far and wide as possible. The group continues its work to this day, although it has since undergone one or two marketing makeovers in order to make it appear more palatable to a modern audience.

Shortly after World War I, the word *propaganda* really began to take on negative connotations. People were beginning to understand that propaganda was not just a weapon that their government used against *the enemy*; it was something they frequently used against their own people. At the outbreak of World War II in 1939, Britain resurrected the MOI to once more regulate and manipulate news flow. It was while working for the MOI that a certain Mr. Eric Blair, aka George Orwell, was inspired to create the terrifying vision of the Ministry of Truth in his dystopian novel *1984*.

Orwell had grown increasingly disillusioned with the MOI's warped news coverage and eventually resigned in disgust. The fascist ideals and practices of a Britain that claimed to be open and democratic were to become a powerful theme in Orwell's written works. In 1946, Orwell said, "Political language—and with variations this is true of all political parties, from Conservatives to Anarchists—is designed to make lies sound truthful and murder respectable, and to give an appearance of solidity to pure wind." Orwell had firsthand experience of how the news was routinely rewritten to align with official government fables. Ironically, we have since learned from official MI5 documents released in September 2007 that Orwell was himself the subject of regular surveillance by UK secret services for more than 13 years.

Through the bleak uncertainties of the early 1940s, a small but increasingly literate and well-informed portion of the British population was beginning to question what was appearing in their newspapers and on their radios. Anyone who was fortunate enough to have had any decent formal education (not to be taken for granted at that time) was able to see, by way of basic reasoning and critical analysis, that the news was, at best, prejudiced and inaccurate. Often, it was simply untrue. To combat this, the government enforced news blackouts backed by *gag orders* that legally restricted the publication of certain information. Violators of gag orders could be subject to imprisonment or even execution, should the infringement fall under the classification of a threat to national security—rather a vague categorization in war time.

Independent news blackouts are still commonly used today and were perhaps most plainly visible during the Gulf War in 1990. Often, major TV networks were only able to re-broadcast officially sanctioned U.S. government footage of what was actually occurring in Iraq. According to a poll conducted by the University of Massachusetts/ Amherst researchers, the responses of selected Denver residents indicated that "heavy TV watchers were more likely to support the war." Astonishingly, they were also *less* likely to be well informed about its causes and consequences. Researchers concluded that the more TV people watched, the less they knew. Consider that in the context of the official TV blanket coverage during and after the events of September 11, 2001.

Orwell saw all this coming 60 years ago. His visionary novel, *1984*, essentially projected what Orwell himself had experienced and simply took it to extreme levels. Language was manipulated with the express purpose of limiting the ability of *the proles* (the common man, the proletariat) to talk or think about the events in their world. The ruling totalitarian party had a special PYSOPS department, just like the real Ministry of Information, whose job it was to ensure that terms were suitably redefined, turned inside out, and rendered politically acceptable. The number of words in the dictionary continued to shrink year after year. Serious philosophical, social, or political discussion became unfeasible.

Figures for active vocabularies across different age groups, backgrounds, and countries is notoriously hard to estimate. Frequently quoted figures for America suggest that it's about 10,000 words for the average high school graduate and 20,000 for college seniors, using common wordage. There are also numerous studies showing a general slow decline in vocabularies across America, but the rates and reasons for this decline remain uncertain.

It actually doesn't take as many words as one would think to get a decent operational grasp of the English language. In 1982, W.N. Francis and H. Kucera authored a document called *Frequency Analysis of English Usage.* In it, they found that knowledge of the 1,000 most common English words provides a comprehension of 72 percent of the general English words contained in their sample texts (totalling more than a million words). A vocabulary of 15,581 words is necessary to gain a 97.8 percent understanding of English. Admittedly, this is only part of the equation. In linguistics, *degree of knowledge* is rather different than *depth of knowledge.* Although we can understand the general meaning of a word, before we can claim to have any true depth of knowledge, a rather more stringent set of criteria must be met. Typically, one would have to appreciate the following aspects of a word: *orthography* (written form), *phonology* (spoken form), *reference* (meaning), *semantics* (concept and reference), *register* (appropriateness of use), *collocation* (lexical neighbors), *word associations, syntax* (grammatical function), and *morphology* (word parts). Yes, there's a bit more to it for the budding logophile.

A PSYOP is designed to influence a target audience's emotional and behavioral impulses, so as to establish a desired response in line with the originator's agenda. Depending on the scenario, it will typically seek to create bias, propagate misinformation, or dehumanize, among other things. Simply stated, it places fake images in the mind of the common man.

A solid contemporary example of an evident PSYOP can be found in the invasion of Iraq in 2003. Bush and Blair told America, Britain, and the world that Iraq had weapons of mass destruction (WMD) that could reach us. It was essential that our troops go in and stop the monstrous Saddam Hussein from using them, before it was too late. As it turned out, after further independent investigation, Iraq did not have WMDs. Even the official UN weapons inspector, Hans Blix, went on record stating that the U.S. and British governments were dramatizing the threat of weapons of mass destruction in Iraq, in order to strengthen the case for the 2003 war against the regime of Saddam Hussein. In my view, Bush and Blair (and their allies) *knew* there were no WMDs. They were lying to us.

The governments sought to persuade the people further by publishing a dossier (purportedly collated by the Joint Intelligence Committee) on WMDs. Renowned UK weapons expert Dr. David Kelly was asked to proofread the document. He found serious flaws in it and disputed several claims, particularly the infamous claim that Iraq was capable of deploying biological or chemical weapons within 45 minutes of an order to launch.

Following the ground invasion phase, Kelly was asked to join a UN inspection team tasked with finding evidence of WMDs or WMD programs. Kelly was asked to view and photograph the two alleged "mobile weapons laboratories." He was unhappy with the description of the trailers and later spoke off the record to *The Observer* newspaper, which quoted Kelly (anonymously at first) as having said, "They are not mobile germ warfare laboratories. You could not use them for making biological weapons. They do not even look like them. They are exactly what the Iraqis said they were—facilities for the production of hydrogen gas to fill balloons."

Kelly had a secret meeting with BBC journalist Andrew Gilligan at a hotel in London. They agreed to talk on an *unattributable* basis, which allowed the BBC to report what was said, but not to identify the source. Kelly expressed his grave doubts over the dossier and the inclusion of the inflammatory "45 minute claim," which he attributed to Blair's unsavory director of communications, Alastair Campbell. Gilligan later broadcast his report on BBC Radio 4's *Today Programme*, and it caused a deep political storm. Eventually, the Ministry of Defence purposefully gave sufficient clues to journalists and media savvy pundits that Kelly was Gilligan's source. Kelly was soon asked to appear before two investigative committees in the House of Commons. One of them was publicly televised. He was aggressively and sometimes disrespectfully questioned by members of the committee.

On July 17, 2003, Kelly was working as usual from his home in Oxfordshire. Knowing that he'd been under tremendous pressure, Kelly had received many supportive e-mails from friends. One e-mail he sent that day was to *New York Times* journalist Judith Miller, who had used Kelly as a source in a book on bioterrorism, to whom Kelly mentioned "many dark actors playing games." Later that day, he told his wife that he was going for his daily walk.

He never returned.

Kelly was found dead early the next morning in an area of woodland known as Harrowdown Hill, about a mile from his home. He had allegedly ingested a large amount of painkillers and cut his left wrist.

Perhaps because Kelly had previously worked closely with MI6 (SIS), the UK government thought he would follow the party line. He didn't. Shortly after, he was dead. The disgracefully inadequate investigation that later followed—The Hutton Inquiry—delivered a verdict of suicide. Case closed.

Evidence uncovered in late 2007 cast serious doubt on the verdict of suicide. Liberal Democrat Member of Parliament Norman Baker, who has since written a book on Kelly, revealed (via the Freedom of Information Act) that the penknife Kelly apparently used to slash his wrist did not carry his own fingerprints. Baker said in a number of British newspapers, among them *The Guardian* in 2007: "The angle you pick up a knife to kill yourself means there would be fingerprints. Someone who wanted to kill themselves wouldn't go to the lengths of wiping the knife clean of fingerprints. It is just very suspicious. It is one of the things that makes me think Dr Kelly was murdered. The case should be re-opened."

Independent doctors have said neither the cut to Kelly's wrist nor the drugs found in his body were enough to kill him. They claimed the official cause of death, a severed ulnar artery in the wrist, was extremely unlikely to be fatal. It just didn't add up. Kelly's family and friends insist that he had shown no signs of feeling suicidal. E-mails and the minutes of meetings he attended also showed him behaving perfectly normally, and he was looking forward to his daughter's forthcoming wedding.

Some have a far broader perspective. Former Irish Republican Army (IRA) member Danny Morrison wrote in the *Guardian*:

Although in the Belfast high court (Lord) Hutton occasionally acquitted republicans and dismissed the appeals of soldiers, nationalists generally considered him a hanging judge and the guardian angel of soldiers and police officers. I was amused at the response of sections of the media and British public [to Hutton's exonerating the Blair government]. Do they know anything about how the establishment works?

Dissenting voices, disgusted with the transparent dishonesty of the whole debacle, refused to stay quiet. There was something symbolic about this case. It was an archetypal resonator so negative that it affected everyone, not just Kelly and his family. Consequently, more and more people started to speak out, potentially risking their own neck in the process. In the summer of 2010, former KGB agent Boris Karpichkov raised the flag once more by announcing that he had been told that Kelly was "exterminated" and his death made to look like suicide.

Karpichkov, a KGB exile in Britain, stated that a London intelligence contractor connected with MI5 had told him that Kelly's death was not suicide. He even e-mailed his evidence to Attorney General Dominic Grieve, who went on record stating that he was "concerned" by questions already raised by doctors. Karpichkov, who defected from Latvia to Britain in 1998, said that his source was "agent" Peter Everett, who used to run a private intelligence outfit called Group Global Intelligence Services, contracting former secret service agents to perform detective work for corporations.

Everett told Karpichkov that Kelly had been exterminated for his "reckless behavior." It was not by chance that Special Branch (a British unit responsible for matters of national security) were the first ones on the scene. They moved Kelly's body to another location, rearranged the original position of the corpse, and removed evidence from the scene. It was described as being "washed out," including the removal of all fingerprints. Everett indicated that "the competing firm," meaning MI6, had carried out the operation.

Later that same year, a group of experts, including former coroners and a professor of intensive-care medicine, penned a letter to the British newspaper *The Times* casting serious doubt on Hutton's verdict. Another retired pathologist, Jennifer Dyson, joined in the criticism, stating that a coroner would likely have recorded an "open verdict" in the absence of real proof that suicide was intended. It just didn't make sense. She further criticized Hutton's handling of the inquiry, and joined in the call for a truly comprehensive and impartial investigation into the whole matter. Under increasing pressure, the postmortem that Hutton had requested to be sealed for 70 years was made public. It was to be another simple piece of theater. It confirmed all the findings in the Hutton Report and undermined alternative theories about Kelly's death. Once more, case closed.

People fall for projected images of things, not the things themselves. Projected images do not naturally arise from the people; they are very carefully crafted and designed to elicit a very particular kind of response. The deception is conveyed smoothly between both fictional entertainment and factual historical events. On the one hand, we have the image of glamorous MI6 agent James Bond, handsome defender of the realm and all-round good guy. On the other hand, we have one of the most famous images of modern times, the British bulldog and visionary, Sir Winston Leonard Spencer-Churchill.

During World War II, Winston Churchill was destined to be projected as an iconic prime minister, a patriot, and a man of steel. Despite diverse and consistent criticism, Churchill was stage-managed into a father figure for the largely uneducated rabble. He was the face of victory and English pride on May 8, 1945, as he waved his cigar to massive crowds gathered at Whitehall to celebrate the end of the war. Even in 2002, the BBC polled more than 1.6 million people to find the "Greatest Briton of All Time." Winston Churchill was the man at the top of the pile. Another PSYOPS triumph that has stood the test of time.

Little was made of Churchill's membership of the Freemasons and the Ancient Order of Druids. Involvement in secret orders and occult groups, regardless of their origins, was not part of the marketing plan. Even less was said of his well-known disregard for the common man. Churchill was known to have rejected Hitler's proposal to spare civilian targets. Instead, it seems he goaded Hitler into bombing London by hitting Berlin and other civilian targets first. Hitler was said to be anxious to reach an agreement with Britain that confined military bombardment from aircraft to battle zones only. What followed were equal horrors of British and German bombing campaigns in which tens of thousands of non-military personnel perished. In September 1940, after visiting the first ruined houses and the people standing on piles of bricks, Churchill commented, "They cheered me as if I'd given them victory, instead of getting their houses bombed to bits."

From February 13 to 15, 1945, Allied forces dropped 3,900 tons of high explosives on Dresden, killing up to 40,000 civilians. Though the British claimed Dresden was a legitimate military target, critics have since argued that the city did not have a military garrison, most of the industry was in the outskirts (and not in the targeted city center), and the enormous cultural significance of the city should have precluded the Allies from bombing it. Ultimate responsibility for the British part of the attack lay with Churchill. German historian Jörg Friedrich claims in *The Fire* that, "Winston Churchill's decision to [area] bomb a shattered Germany between January and May 1945 was a war crime." British philosopher A.C. Grayling has described this kind of British area bombardment as an "immoral act" and "moral crime" because "destroying everything contravenes every moral and humanitarian principle debated in connection with the just conduct of war" in his book *Among the Dead Cities*. Günter Grass, a German novelist and 1999 Nobel Prize winner, also called the bombing of Dresden a war crime.

It is unthinkable that a man who could conceivably commit a war crime would later be dubbed "Greatest Briton of All Time." Unless that is, you factor in PSYOPS. Mental conditioning. Churchill just ain't who we thought he was.

Black operations (black ops) are covert missions that usually fall into the "deniability" category, where governments cannot or do not wish to claim responsibility for their actions. This can be seen in connection with secret wars, drug running, assassinations, experimental weapons programs, and so forth. *False flag* operations are another tool in the PSYOPS bag. This is where governments stage and execute their own covert terror operations and blame scapegoat nations or "alleged" terror groups such as al-Qaeda. This also has the agreeable knock-on effect of mustering support for further military operations. Both these tactics are commonly used where international legality and ethical considerations are questionable. Consequently, funding for black ops and false flag events is always "off the books."

There are many modern examples of PSYOPS operations that contain these elements. Though some of these remain controversial, should interested readers care to do some of their own further research, I am confident they will find surprisingly abundant corroborating data.

1. The burning down of the German Parliament (Reichstag) building.

2. Prior knowledge that the Japanese were going to attack Pearl Harbor.

3. The Gulf Of Tonkin incident.

4. Operation Northwoods (a U.S. government plan to stage the assassination of civilians and blame it on Communist Cuba).

5. CIA drug running in Nicaragua.

6. Al-Qaeda as an asset created by the CIA.

7. The bombing of the Israeli embassy in London,

8. A phony al-Qaeda cell (Mossad) in Palestine.

9. 9/11.

Note that not all PSYOPS automatically indicate an inside job. PSYOPS is chiefly concerned with perception management. Sometimes an incident can be "allowed to happen" from ostensibly natural origins, and is then closely steered and manipulated as it develops. Indeed, successful false flag events will usually mandate a convincing "foreign entity" as the instigator.

Black ops also encompass regular covert assassinations of trouble-makers, quite regardless of nationality or political affiliation. Some are more obvious than others. Popular candidates include Gandhi, JFK, Che Guevara, Princess Diana, David Kelly, Robin Cook MP, and Benazir Bhutto. False flag tactics are just as useful with individual assassinations as they are with large-scale military campaigns. Often, a plausible scapegoat/patsy is essential for a successful high-profile assassination. In recent times, apparent suicides, car accidents, and heart attacks are more the modus operandi of black ops teams rather than old-fashioned shootings. And these things go on all the time. Within every major international intelligence agency is a covert team who do this for their day job. What our politicians tell us about national security is irrelevant. Most wars are straight power grabs—illegal invasions for mass resource domination, financial profit, and lowering consciousness—though PSYOPS orchestrators will always tell the people on both sides how to think about these things.

This is most absurdly transparent each time we see PSYOPS name an actual military operation. In modern U.S. warfare for example, I cringe (as do billions of others) each time a new campaign name is unveiled: Operation Valiant Strike, Operation Provide Comfort, Operation Enduring Freedom, Operation Uphold Democracy, and, most insultingly of all, Operation Iraqi Freedom. Sad but true. And should we wonder at the sheer brazenness of these hulking lunges to divert our attention from the truth, let us remember the words of that master of mass hypnosis and archetypal bad guy: Adolf Hitler, "All propaganda has to be popular and has to accommodate itself to the comprehension of the least intelligent of those whom it seeks to reach."

It's quite easy to spot PSYOPS methods on the television nowadays. You can see when someone is being primed, knowingly or unknowingly, to play his or her part in transmitting the *be afraid* meme—helping to rush in new anti-freedom, anti-human laws. Fake reality, fake news.

As the inimitable Bill Hicks once said, "I love talking about the Kennedy assassination. The reason I do is because I'm fascinated by it. I'm fascinated that our government could lie to us so blatantly, so obviously for so long, and we do absolutely nothing about it. I think that's interesting in what is ostensibly a democracy. Sarcasm—come on in."

Disinformation is beginning to falter as a device for confusing the consciousness of the masses. Where it once successfully fooled perhaps 90 percent of the population between 1959 and 2001, I would propose that that figure is now significantly lower, perhaps around the 50-percent mark. This represents a massive elevation in consciousness and a serious problem for group acceptance of the distortion. Consequently, the containment game has shifted gear to focus more and more on behavioral conditioning. The main strategy is now one of having the populace restrain *itself*, rather than requiring subjugation from the top down. To achieve this, the infinite imaginings of human beings must be corralled into one single, homogeneous, commercial endeavor. To put it bluntly, we are petitioned to regard the hustling way of life as the only way of life.

We are to grind out our own dream of material success, or die trying. There are no other modes of operation. This is not about choosing between capitalism/conservatism or socialism/liberalism. This is about the unfoldment of humanity on a journey of divine ascendance. In an existence where there is no value placed on personal development and where only the marketplace has meaning, no time is made available for any sort of private reflection or spiritual contemplation whatsoever. There's no real point in thinking about the world. It's not productive. If somebody absolutely must engage in such obsolete pursuits, then those pursuits must take place within prescribed parameters—official, organized, safe, and handled by approved intermediaries.

Why would any right-thinking person go along with such an unnatural and demeaning way of life? The answer is perhaps a little unexpected: *because he feels he has a responsibility to do so.*

Chapter 14

Cult Indulgences

As we move toward the end of our childhood, we are taught that amassing personal responsibility is a key stage in our social development. We are positively encouraged to welcome it into our lives and shoulder as much of it as we can. It is seen as a mark of maturity: The more we have, the more mature we are. After all, few things appear more grown-up than the stressed-out, task-juggling self-harassment of adulthood.

As a young child, I remember being over at a friend's house one evening when his father returned home from work. We'd been playing upstairs, and so when he walked in through the front door, he didn't know we were watching him from behind the wooden railings of the landing. He carefully placed his leather briefcase on the floor and then flopped down into a chair in the hallway. He sat there motionless for a long time. We silently watched him, not quite sure what he was doing or why. Later that evening, as we all sat around the family dinner table, my friend's father told his wife that he didn't like his job. In fact, he loathed it and had never truly enjoyed his work there for the last 20 years. It wasn't clear who was more dismayed by this announcement, him or her. They talked for a while about the other things that he could do—different kinds of organizations he could work for, potential new career directions, or even starting up his own business. In the end, they agreed that if he could just stick it out for another 10 years with his current employer, he would be eligible for early retirement. Yes, that would be the best thing to do. We continued to eat our dinner. Something felt very wrong at that table. At the time, I didn't quite understand why, but I never forgot it.

The same dynamic continues to play out in countless homes all over the world, each and every day. It is not at all peculiar. Indeed, it is recognized as one of the unspoken but fundamental duties of adulthood—to grin and bear it. However mind-numbingly grinding life can become, we are expected to just keep sucking it up and plodding on. The result is that people are living lives they do not like. They are conducting themselves in a way that is not in accordance with their truth. They are upholding things that they know are dishonorable. Because so many people are caught up in this way of living, it is often genuinely mistaken for being *just the way things are.* The truth is, it is only the way things are if we wish it to be.

Naturally, we cannot always have what we want, all the time. This is quickly learned as children when we realize that not every day can be full of candy, play, and television. If it was, there would be an epidemic of obese, toothless, antisocial, illiterate, brainwashed children stumbling through the streets. Though that might happen from time to time here and there, it's not representative of most young people. Naturally, wise parents teach their children that sometimes you have to do stuff that isn't strictly for your own delight. In theory, helping out around the house, doing homework, visiting relatives, and learning the whys and wherefores of society at large, helps to build a skill set that properly equips the young mind to eventually go their own way in the world.

During the young adulthood years from 21 to 28, the amount of time and energy we get to spend on ourselves is significantly impacted by the decisions we take regarding our domestic and personal affairs. Though we each have absolute freewill to choose precisely what we put our consciousness into, there are enormous social pressures to do certain things in a certain way. Most people simply follow the program and do what they're supposed to do. Even when that program proves to be wholly disingenuous, this is willfully overlooked because rejecting it would mean upsetting too many people and placing oneself in a position of exotic self-determination. When people lack the insight and spirit to design their own lives, or they simply can't be bothered, they tend to go with the unconscious agenda. It doesn't really matter what that is, as long as it's agreeably predetermined and socially acceptable. This is well acknowledged and heavily exploited by those who administer the broader social strategies that shape our culture. It is made all too easy to join the cult of the inauthentic.

The cult has a wide influence and is involved in many aspects of life, but one of its principle initiatives is to encourage all its members to get married, get a career, and get some babies. Though these things can of course happen outside the cult and quite genuinely from truly mindful intent, the cult boasts such a massive multi-billion membership list that, unless an individual consciously decides *not* to join, then he or she becomes a member by default. No actual sign-up is necessary; it is achieved simply by the disavowal of one's own freewill.

Up until fairly recent times, if you really liked someone and wanted to have an exclusive intimate relationship with that person, you got married. The church and/or the state legally joined you together, and you got a house and shared the same surname. If religion played a prominent role in that contract, then you also became bound to your partner for the rest of your life. Even if you came to a point where it wasn't really working anymore and perhaps the shared expression of love and friendship was not all that it could be, you were nevertheless obliged to remain together until death. In some religious traditions, the indenture extends even beyond that.

On a more utilitarian level, if you want to be able to provide yourself with high-quality food, clothing, shelter, transport, healthcare, and leisure activities, there is a clearly defined path to make this all happen: You go to college/university, get a degree, get a good job, and work hard until you are old. Typically, the more responsibility and the longer the hours, the more resources you'll be able to acquire. There isn't really much time for yourself, but that's the price you pay. Work eight hours, recover for eight hours, sleep eight hours. There are those who actually manage to get a job that they like, though of the thousands of people we meet through our lives, they can be counted on one hand. Increasingly, the fierce commercialization of every mode of livelihood serves only to drive the quality and precision of one's craft into the background. The dollar comes first.

The light at the end of the tunnel, if everything goes according to plan, is retirement. If the nest egg has been sufficiently nourished, it is finally possible to stop working and spend time doing the things you'd really like to do. The only snag is that this opportunity to fully embrace the spectacular theater of life is only created in the final act. One might be forgiven for wondering what it was all about. Could it have been done any other way? Was there, at any point, a time of deep contemplation and inner reflection to determine if this was the most truthful and spiritually authentic way of living? Or did things just kind of happen? Perhaps it is just as well that there isn't much time for this kind of introspection. There are too many things to attend to: appointments, errands, projects, paperwork, schedules, chores. Perhaps there is even the patter of tiny feet. That really does change the picture.

The effects, consequences, and energies involved in bringing a child into this world could scarcely be more profound. To seed the incarnation of a new entity—profiled from one's own DNA and endowed with a form and consciousness that are entrusted to the parent for optimal physical, emotional, and mental care—is an awesome undertaking. To have a baby is to owe a lifetime of love, support, and wise counsel to that being. Of the seven billion humans currently living on this planet, how many were conceived from a place of super-conscious, pure, and loving wisdom?

In some cultures, a mother and father will have a dozen children, just so that three or four of them might survive, providing long-term resourcing for the larger group. Reproduction becomes a group survival necessity for those who live in physically demanding environments. For those who live in more privileged circumstances, they can afford to be a little more philosophical about their would-be conceptions. In these situations, starting a family is much more of a lifestyle choice. It's about wanting to become a mom or a dad. Even so, these apparently divergent paths share the same core observance and adherence to their respective traditions. In the West, mainstream society is set up to safeguard the continuance of abundant procreation. Nice young men and women are expected to have babies. It is the way things are.

Many mothers have whispered into my ear that though they unquestionably love their children, if they were given their time again they probably wouldn't have kids. Though none of them would ever wish their progeny out of existence, it is striking how many times mature women have confessed how they massively underestimated the sheer time and effort involved in bringing up a child. They knew there'd be a lot of work involved. That is plain for anyone to see. But quite how much and how all-encompassing it would turn out to be is rarely glimpsed in advance. If it was, perhaps there would be an awful lot less people walking around.

Getting married, having a regular job, and starting a family are all completely neutral activities. To choose to engage in such things is a personal choice and the prerogative of any adult. It starts to go wrong when these life-changing events are stimulated by unconscious cult obligation rather than conscious, free choice. Sounds a little bizarre, but it happens all the time. Particularly with the concept of motherhood, there are certain biological imperatives and hormonal drives that powerfully affect many women. These chemical indicators show that the body is ready for procreation and send potent psychological signals to the brain, exclaiming that "now is the time!" Whether this notice is transformed into flesh and blood is best determined by the existence of a secure, committed, and loving environment—mutually and consciously created by both mother and father. No less one than the other. If this does not exist, then any creation would be little more than neglectful cult indulgence.

Like most cults, the cult of the inauthentic uses isolationist strategies to exercise control over the minds of its devotees. It is vital that previously vibrant individuals are transformed into whitewashed zombies. There are many techniques used to accomplish this, but they can be reduced down into three main areas:

1. *Us vs. Them.* You and all the people like you are doing it right; everybody else is doing it wrong.

2. *Group Think.* Maintaining group consensus is more important than actually getting results and evolving.

3. *Surrendering Individuality.* The group is always more important than the individual.

These three principles keep the cult functioning and operate almost entirely outside the sphere of conscious awareness. If they are brought into the light, the cult immediately begins to lose its dark charisma, and its authority wanes. Like the magician who shows you the secret of the card trick—once the methodology is revealed, the performance is no longer magical and you can't be fooled again. So it is with the cult. You cannot un-see what you have seen. The once-faithful flock begin to abscond in increasing numbers when they begin to act from their own individual spirit.

Persuading people to give all their time away is perhaps the single most important element of cult strategy. This is achieved mainly through coercing people into psychically bonding themselves to a form of work that is often unfulfilling and poorly suited to their natural talents. Over the years, a situation develops where it appears practically impossible to leave that work behind and do something different. They have to just keep doing the same thing. The backdrop may change every now and again, but it's still the same movie looping around and around. There is not much conscious bandwidth left for principles, philosophies, or self-growth. Such things soon drift away and are replaced by pre-packaged simulations, courtesy of the cult. There is only time for work. However the pieces on the chessboard are configured, whatever moves are attempted and anticipated, there can be no positive withdrawal. There is no winning move. It is maddening.

Ideologically speaking, the apparently opposing politics of each side of the game keep people involved by creating a convincing illusion of choice. To the untrained eye, it looks like a fair and open race between the reds and the blues, with the public able to vote for their preferred color. For those who favor even-handed resource distribution and management, there is socialism. For those who prefer the every-man-for-himself model, there is capitalism. If either of these models gets a bit extreme, they may morph into communism or fascism. Taken to the ultimate, the circle closes back on itself and they become the same totalitarian regime. The politics is irrelevant. Until that time, the Republicans and the Democrats duke it out and give the appearance of principled men and women fighting for the betterment of humankind. All the while, their blank maneuverings are endlessly debated by the conservative talk show hosts and the progressive radio pundits. People are hypnotized into believing that this sliver of unreality is all there is. Once again, there can be no ultimate victory. Both sides are but players in a pantomime that is owned, directed, and staged by the same master.

The secret to changing the game is to change one's perception of the game itself. Not how it is played, but *what it is*. When its existence has been fully understood at the inner level, this automatically rewrites the rules of engagement. It becomes possible to stand confidently outside the system and have the might of the universe right behind you. The universe loves insurrectionaries. From a highly zoomed-out perspective, this is a key stage of warrior training and is essential to the unfoldment.

First, it must be acknowledged that the game is not designed to have an outcome. It exists only to draw the player into playing it. There can be no individual conquests. There is only playing the game. The longer the game is played, the further the player is drawn into his or her own inauthenticity and dishonor. By achieving clarity and shifting one's perspective in this way, consciousness is immediately moved away from the erroneous idea that his or her game is the *only* game. The density of its reality is suitably reduced. When the mind rescinds the mental energy that was feeding the game, its gravitation begins to weaken, and the individual is no longer inevitably pulled into playing. Other opportunities become perceptible. It is accepted that real solutions are never televised. Synchronicities align with higher purpose and new paths appear. Intellectual sovereignty and psychological empowerment begin to reveal natural solutions that arise from real people and real communities. Once this principal movement of consciousness has been performed, external circumstances rapidly begin to evolve.

When people stagger around under the weight of their unwanted responsibilities, laboring from one day to the next, dropping things, worrying about dropping things, dreaming about dropping things, life becomes a wretched circus act. Unhappiness stalks them wherever they go. How are you doing? *Much the same, can't complain.* This is a saying in Northern England. It is an idiom often voiced by the defeated proletariat who tend the furnaces of the machine with a grim and peculiar stoicism. They don't believe they can change things, so they cannot change things. They swallow the cult doctrine that freewill is a fanciful luxury, quite separate from the manifestation of the real world and entirely disconnected from the objects of existence.

Though Buddhist and Zen philosophies provide wonderful opportunities for personal growth and spiritual insight, there is a startling disconnect in how their wisdom heritage actually filters down into society as a whole, especially when viewed through the lens of suicide. According to recent figures from the World Health Organization, Japan and South Korea have some of the highest suicide rates in the world, with more than twice the rate of suicide per 100,000 people than America or Britain. Though Buddhism is very popular in these countries, some of its illuminating teachings on unity, honesty, and humbleness are not necessarily reflected in the massive social imperative to *achieve.* From students to businessmen, from youths to seniors, one's standing in the community—especially the outward appearance of it—is hugely significant. The constant pressure of looking like you are "doing well" is a depressing obligation for large sections of the population in these very proud nations. At root, it is an inauthentic way of being.

Until we fully comprehend that the outside conditions are a projection of our internal state, our influence over the train tracks of our lives is negligible. We merely drag ourselves along the standard route, which is not of our design and does not benefit our growth. The good news is that this can all be easily changed. Dissolving the old patterns and claiming the power of freewill are wholly dependent on establishing an intimate acquaintance with the inner self.

For those responsibilities that we have already taken on—ones we suspect we may have originally initiated from a place of unconsciousness—they serve as mirrors of ourselves, so we might consciously track our growth through practicing the patience, empathy, and humility that they require from us. There is no randomness in the unfoldment, however hard we try to make it so. Whatever partners, children, relatives, homes, jobs, mortgages, debts, and duties we have called to ourselves, they deliver the perfect conscious evolution that we asked for. They are pre-ordered, and delivered on time and to our own very exacting specifications. There are few more sacred acts than learning to share consciousness and wisdom for the benefit of others. The unfoldment is always selfless. Sometimes we need some refresher training.

The truth is that we don't really have any responsibilities other than to ourselves. Real accountability starts and stops there. Until we choose to have children, we owe absolutely nothing to anyone—not our parents, friends, husbands, wives, employers, flag, or country. No one. We may, however, choose to give heart and soul to all of these things and more. We may give selflessly, abundantly, and sincerely. But it is not owed. It is given of our own freewill, or it is an empty bestowal. The sovereign spirit cannot be contracted.

What if we were to tear up the contracts of responsibility and remove them from day-to-day living altogether? Without the external answerability in place, would we now suddenly start acting with any less consideration, integrity, or purpose? No, we would not. Would everything slide into chaos and ruin? No. In fact, *more* consciousness becomes available for our deeds because it is no longer being squandered on upholding the fake burden of cult liability. This results in an even higher capacity for noble conduct. All honorable exchanges are performed with total commitment. They are undertaken freely, and they are undertaken gladly.

Central to the illusion of distorted social responsibility is the propagation of continuous adversity. When there is a clear and present danger that threatens the security of the home, the homeland, or even the home planet, people are more liable to band together for the common good.

They do what they're told and suffer conditions that would otherwise be intolerable. The impending menace of war, terrorism, crime, social unrest, economic collapse, and environmental disaster are all fabulous catalysts for establishing and standardizing group responsibilities.

Morning, noon, and night, mainstream television news broadcasts depict strife around every corner. The mirage of public opinion (there can be no single opinion from a multitude of free-thinking men and women)—aghast at the ugliness of life—is manufactured purely to amplify the rallying cry to defend "a way of life," even though it has so plaintively failed to nourish its citizens. One is obliged to ask whether the news fairly represents real life at all. The accuracy of the information, the formulation of its conveyance, and, more importantly, the *context* of it all have to be judiciously scrutinized if we are to truly comprehend the underlying purpose of these official broadcasts of worldly events. Once these things have been properly established, the ability of the news to influence our consciousness is a power that only we ourselves may grant.

Chapter 15

Glad Tidings

When I was a little boy, I used to think that *the news* was a special place on television where grown-ups would go to talk about all the serious things that were happening in the world. Everyone on the screen spoke in very somber tones, and they all wore dull, dark suits, as if someone had just died. This was, perhaps, excusable, as every night the news was replete with images of death and destruction.

In Britain in the 1970s, the BBC (British Broadcasting Corporation) represented the pinnacle of intelligent, responsible, and unbiased news reporting. Most serious-minded men and women watched the BBC broadcasts most nights in their homes. It was, and largely still is, perceived as the best place to find out what's going on in the world. Unlike America, most homes in Britain at that time had only one television set, usually located in a corner of the living room, where it was ideally positioned to become the focal point for many family gatherings and conversations. The BBC was also renowned for quality radio programming, particularly the flagship news station BBC Radio 4, which broadcast two main *heavyweight* news shows, one in the morning and one in the evening. With a TV in the living room, and a radio in the kitchen and the car, it was easy to stay in touch with the BBC's broadcasts throughout the day.

At my innocent and tender age, the news was especially confusing to me because its version of reality was so drastically opposed to the reality we were being taught at primary school. At school, the world was a big, exciting, and wonderful place, full of possibilities and discovery. We learned of the Egyptians, the Romans, the kings and queens of England, dinosaurs, fossils, trains, hovercraft, the beautiful monuments of Europe, and how the Victorians used to live. The words, numbers, and images that were used to articulate all this were always vibrant and colorful. There was a lot of smiling, positivity, and encouragement. Then later, at home in the evenings, this entire buoyant worldview was unceremoniously punctured by watching the news. There was no smiling there, no positive balance, and not even a rumor of encouragement. It was indeed *funereal*.

My chief memories of television news in the 1970s are soaked with pictures of terrorism, acrimonious politicians, and economic woes. There was constant, blanket reporting of the IRA (Irish Republican Army), disturbing video footage of ravaged lands in the Middle East, miserable proclamations from Prime Ministers Edward Heath, Harold Wilson, and James Callaghan, and recurrent industrial strike action by trade unions. One cannot help but wonder at how virtually nothing has changed in the last 30 years.

As has become customary with many Western TV news stations, the patronizing addition of an amusing *and finally* story (such as a duck on a skateboard, or a postcard that was delivered 50 years late) did nothing to mollify the deep sense of foreboding. When the news anchors were obliged to inject some levity into their delivery, their smiles looked more like cracks in granite.

I wondered: At exactly what point on the time line would my positive reality swing into the negative one? I couldn't understand why and how these two worlds could be so fundamentally different. Was everything that we were being taught at school just a silly amusement that would soon be cast aside? Perhaps there was some kind of secret ceremony that all 21-year-olds were subjected to, in which the purity of youth is ritually sacrificed and the dour mantle of adulthood is pinned to heavy hearts.

Fortunately, my parents had the good sense to routinely turn off the television and focus instead on our own family. We talked about our day, told stories, and laughed, all of which helped tremendously in counter-balancing the privations of the news. After dinner, we played board games together, or my father filled the house with music from his guitar and my mother diligently encouraged me to read, write, and draw. I shall be forever thankful to them both. Though my family was as imperfect as any other, we all *tried*. Despite some extremely challenging times early on, we continue to love each other, we are friends, and we go on sharing our stories to this day. I have learned to never stop trying.

Due to this and other reasons, the seeds of doubting consensus reality were sown early with me. I instinctively distrusted the authenticity of those who selected, reported, and delivered the news. Their narrative of world events seemed massively one-sided. Nor did I appreciate the tone of authority with which they proclaimed all this abject misery. No. Something was definitely not right. The news was not only grossly unbalanced and frequently off beam, but it was somehow *anti-human*. Had I known that it would be such a long time in the future before I was to discover why that was, I might have gone round the twist.

The phrase *crossing the Rubicon* is a metaphor for proceeding past a point of no return. It originates from 49 BC when Julius Caesar directed his legions south across the river Rubicon (a traditional barrier between the Roman province of Cisalpine Gaul and Italy proper) toward ancient Rome, in defiance of the Roman Senate. Upon crossing the river, Caesar is reported to have shouted "Alea iacta est!" ("The die is cast!").

In terms of the awakening process, crossing the Rubicon is a key revelatory stage when you realize, beyond any doubt, that reality is not at all how you thought it was. The stark recognition that you have been living in a false paradigm created by someone else begins to sink in. It is here, at this bleak philosophical crossroads, where most people experience such a disturbing degree of cognitive dissonance that they instinctively turn back. Too much to process and the implications are huge. So, even knowing that there is a greater truth on the horizon, they choose instead to return to the distortion, with all its comfortable certainties.

In 2008, award-winning journalist Nick Davies caused quite a stir in UK media circles. The title of his article for the *Independent* newspaper summed things up nicely: "How the Spooks Took Over the News." In his articles and his book *Flat Earth News* (2008), Davies illustrates how "shadowy intelligence agencies are pumping out black propaganda to manipulate public opinion—and the media simply swallow it whole-sale." It is refreshing to observe how this information can land slap-bang in the middle of the mainstream outlets. Without doubt, it certainly reaches a lot of people and helps to consolidate awareness of how easily the news is skewed toward a pre-determined message. Even more inter-estingly, Davies also suggests who the perpetrators are and why they're doing it. This is rarely discussed in any serious way in the mainstream.

In the *Guardian* newspaper, Davies described how our media have become mass producers of distortion, and he evidences this with clear, unambiguous examples. He convincingly delivers the message that "the mass media generally are no longer a reliable source of information"—that is, for those who need any more convincing. Regardless, he stands out as pretty much a lone voice taking an admirable and revolutionary stance, amid hordes of supercilious hacks in a mainstream vortex of dishonor.

Davies is careful to characterize the problem as a structural thing; it's not really about attacking individual journalists. He points to the mo-mentous change of press ownership as the pivotal event responsible for mutating quality news into fake news, switching from the historic pa-triarchal proprietors to the mega corporations, like News International owned by Rupert Murdoch's News Corp. We know that the raison d'être of the corporations is to turn a profit. Quality and truth are quite irrelevant. So over a short period, Davies believes that the instinctive logic of commercialism gradually replaced the objective logic of jour-nalism. The consequences were devastating for the integrity of impar-tial news reporting. The corporate ownership of news has now all but destroyed the principle of truth-telling by grossly politicizing the news agenda and severely reducing the actual time available for journalists to do their jobs. This tends to propagate *churnalism* (bad journalism; journalists that churn out rewrites of press releases) and hence bias. And we're not talking about the gutter press here. We're talking about the so-called quality newspapers.

Davies has unearthed some incredibly damning information. In his February 2008 article for the *Guardian*, he wrote:

I commissioned research from specialists at Cardiff University, who surveyed more than 2,000 UK news stories from the four quality dailies (*Times, Telegraph, Guardian, Independent*) and the Daily Mail. They found two striking things. First, when they tried to trace the origins of their "facts," they discovered that only 12% of the stories were wholly composed of material researched by reporters. With 8% of the stories, they just couldn't be sure. The remaining 80%, they found, were wholly, mainly or partially constructed from second-hand material, provided by news agencies and by the public relations industry. Second, when they looked for evidence that these "facts" had been thoroughly checked, they found this was happening in only 12% of the stories. The implication of those two findings is truly alarming. Where once journalists were active gatherers of news, now they have generally become mere passive processors of unchecked, second-hand material, much of it contrived by PR to serve some political or commercial interest. Not journalists, but churnalists. An industry whose primary task is to filter out falsehood has become so vulnerable to manipulation that it is now involved in the mass production of falsehood, distortion and propaganda.

The news is nonsense. This can no longer be construed as some crazy kind of unconventional or activist opinion anymore; it is plain, well-evidenced, undeniable fact. We must seriously discipline ourselves to stop being suckered by what we see on television and what we read in the newspapers. A far better alternative is to seek out one's own news. Believe nothing unless you have done your own research. Use the Internet. Practice being a prudent and discerning researcher. Employ equal measures of intuition and critical judgment at every turn.

It is sobering to contemplate that the Internet was not even widely available before 1994. Before that time, there were no other, easily accessible alternative news sources. You got your news from the TV and the newspaper, or you got nothing. You could haul yourself down to a decent public library and spend a few days trawling through archive newspapers and microfilm. But who has the time? Very few. So while the Internet is here, let us use it.

Nick Davies has figured out that the media is a propaganda machine and perhaps there never was a golden age of independent, equitable journalism. However, Davies appears unaware (as most people are) of the sheer penetration of the control system. For example, he states that (after 9/11), "For the first time in human history, there is a concerted strategy to manipulate global perception." For students of the esoteric and the transcendent, it is an elementary teaching that control system containment techniques have been in place from the very beginning. Thousands of years of deception and suppression—though admittedly, that is a rather mind-bending stretch for those without a basic grounding in the hidden history of mankind. You have to digest the works of a few dozen alternate historians and arcane researchers (employing proper practices of due diligence and discernment, naturally) to begin to understand that the real strands of history are revealed through esoteric symbolism and the traditions of ancient mystery schools that gave birth to the Abrahamic religions of today. The official history books and encyclopedias give only very limited, surface-level data. You have to dig deeper.

Though Davies is eloquently and accurately unveiling media collusion in a government/spook-sponsored program of mass deception, the public sort of *don't care*. And that is the genius of the control system—its ability to channel apathy. It is not enough to demonstrate that the corporations and governments have become corrupted. Most people already know that. Sometimes Joe Public might initially be shocked at the squalid details of exactly how crooked they can get, but it's still not going to shift the train tracks from the habitual circular layout.

I foresee a time when it will be proven beyond reasonable doubt that the actual events of 9/11 bear very little resemblance to the official government account. It will be further proven that various international intelligence agencies conspired with senior political and media figures to cover up what really happened. The events will be shown to have little or nothing to do with Arab terrorists. And guess what? *No one will care.* A few politicians and military personnel will go to jail. Enough time passes, and people don't care. They forget. They're watching talent shows and gritty police dramas on television. Everyone knows something is fishy about 9/11, but what to do about it? Who gives a damn that there were never any real reasons to be in Afghanistan or Iraq, killing more than a million people? Whatever. Let's watch reality TV.

The decline of quality news reporting is, of course, not limited to traditional print media. In 2011, Conan O'Brien lampooned the heavily scripted nature of U.S. television news by showing 18 separate news stations delivering a news item in identically scripted dialogue. It was quite an alarming spectacle. The veneer of intelligent reporting and impartial interpretation rapidly melts away. You can be sure that 95 percent of viewers have no idea that their news is so tightly prescribed. The smiling old guy with white hair or the attractive young woman with the pearly-white teeth is all that is necessary to establish credibility.

Ever since the days of Nixon and Kissinger, anyone who has kept an eye on politics has been aware that conspiracy and corruption are standard government practices. Assassinations and espionage are the staple diet of operational agencies like MI6 (Britain) and CIA (America). Any ridiculous claims to the contrary do not stand up for long. Amid the wearisome Princess Diana courtroom charade of 2008, Ian Burnett QC, for the coroner, asked former head of MI6, Sir Richard Dearlove, the following question: "During the whole of your time in SIS (MI6), from 1966 to 2004, were you ever aware of the service assassinating anyone?" Dearlove replied: "No, I was not."

You've got to laugh.

Michael Moore's 2004 film, *Fahrenheit 9/11*, is a classic example of the limited utility of pursuing documentary based exposés. He turns the spotlight on the military and U.S. administration's apparent ineptness and secrecy in handling 9/11, but fails to explore the idea that the real circumstances of 9/11 were much more mysterious and profound than anyone could imagine. That would be crossing the Rubicon into unknown territory. He won't do that. Moore does succeed, however, in highlighting corporate corruption, illegal invasions, and political favoritism. But again, even the casual viewer already knows that. Although Moore's analysis of government responses and dodgy deals resonates well throughout the film, the effect does not last. The viewer leaves the theater and still votes Democrat or Republican, still thinks football is important, and still believes that the mainstream news is real.

The predicament of many maverick journalists and film-makers—treading the fine line between exposing high-level deception and maintaining mainstream credibility—is quite explicable to me. However, without a spiritual solution, there is *no* solution. Just describing the problems is not sufficient anymore. Somebody has to do that, and thank goodness they do, but notions of lobbying Congress, demonstrating in the streets, leafleting, boycotting stuff, even taking up arms—all are utterly pointless. If we play the game with their rules on their chessboard, they will always win.

Jump off the moving train. Take the spiritual path.

If human consciousness allows itself to be manipulated through the fear-based and trauma-based systems that are entrenched in our news broadcasts and entertainment, then the control system can implant a reality of its own that severely constricts the natural evolution of human consciousness. It keeps people self-limiting and passive. They become mere cabling for the unreality network.

Breaking the fake news trance and going through the subsequent mental unraveling is hard, but it's worth it. Once through the other side, the profound insight and enhanced awareness are deeply liberating and sources of immense internal power. It is also a highly honorable act, moving oneself closer to the truth. All the tortuous, gloomy sociopolitical problems like employment, crime, immigration, health, housing, war, the economy, education—they all begin to make sense. They aren't a mess because our representatives in the government are inept; they are a mess by design. All that matters is that the wheels keep turning and the workers keep working. Keep them busy. A life's work to own a house. A decent payout at 65 if you're lucky. Lunacy. Inhumanity.

Once you have the distortion *coordinates*—the cipher that makes sense of all the surface weirdness—everything begins to slot into place. The mist of confusion disperses. You can *see*. And those coordinates are horribly uncomplicated: Most of the human population on the planet lives in a consumer plantation designed to provide physical and spiritual slave labor to an elite few. Reality and truth are concealed in order to maintain and protect the powerbase. None of this has anything to do with politics or ideologies.

The news is like a movie: quite unreal and removed from the living world. The contrived reality that is presented, though justifiably claiming a high degree of consensus, bears no resemblance to the physical, emotional, and spiritual human reality that we actually live in. The news-makers just dish out the approved agenda, designed solely to encourage the proletariat to think less, behave, and enjoy the shiny distractions of consumerism. So we end up with a thousand channels of soul-destroying shows on cooking, cars, and house renovation, presented by some of the most unfortunate examples of humankind ever gathered in one place—the sort of people who badly need some hard time scrubbing public toilets with a toothbrush for a chance of ever salvaging their deluded egos. Intelligence and integrity are indeed rare on TV. They occur spontaneously and by magic once every blue moon. The rest of the time, the airwaves are filled with undead corporate hustlers, ready to swallow the demonic distortion on command.

The mainstream media reporting of terrorism is an object lesson in how official information is hopelessly compromised. This is nicely illustrated by examining what *terrorism* is generally understood to indicate, and what the word *terrorism* actually means.

To understand the true nature of the "war on terror," it is essential to look into the origins of perhaps the most infamous of terrorist organizations: al-Qaeda.

Al-Qaeda was created and funded by the CIA in 1979 and has been controlled by them ever since. A group of Arab Muslim fighters called Maktab al-Khadamat (MAK for short) was originally formed to augment the Afghan Mujahideen who were fighting the Russian occupation of Afghanistan in 1979. MAK was funded, directed, and trained by the United States, working through Pakistani and Saudi secret services. A certain Osama bin Laden (Saudi-born) was a founding member of MAK, along with Palestinian militant Abdullah Yusuf Azzam. After a costly nine-year war, the Soviet Union finally withdrew from Afghanistan in 1989. The CIA operation was a success. They'd ousted the Russians from this strategically important region and replaced them with a bunch of low-tech Arabs who could easily be ejected at any time, and without the diplomatic dilemmas inherent in engaging with a major player such as the Soviet Union. Al-Qaeda, like many CIA assets, was expendable from their very inception.

Eventually, in the late 1990s, the CIA decided that it was time to officially demonize Osama bin Laden and Ayman al-Zawahiri, and had them issue a *fatwa* (a binding religious edict) that calls for Muslims to kill the enemies of Islam and their allies, wherever they may be. This was to be the start of some major social engineering on the part of the control-system controlled CIA. And they did a brilliant job.

The CIA took some disgruntled rebel Arabs and mutated them into the international poster boys of terrorism. Al-Qaeda is a phantom menace, a boogeyman that can never be caught, because it does not exist in any kind of comprehensible or coherent form. Therefore stories of its victories, defeats, destruction, or rebirth can be summoned at any time. A superb documentary, *The Power of Nightmares* (ironically screened on the BBC), claims that al-Qaeda is so weakly linked together that it is hard to say it exists in any sense apart from Osama bin Laden (now officially deceased) and a small clique of close associates. The lack of any significant numbers of convicted al-Qaeda members, despite a large number of arrests on terrorism charges, is cited as a reason to doubt whether a widespread entity that meets the description of al-Qaeda exists at all.

Now let's take a closer look at the word *terrorism*. According to the *Cambridge Dictionary*, terrorism is simply defined as "(threat of) violent action for political purposes." Wow. Isn't that something that could be applied to any country in the world? Especially the UK and America?

Yes, it is. In fact, do not all major countries use terrorism? If they didn't, they would be absorbed by other countries that had no qualms about violent action for political purposes. So terrorism can justifiably be described as an *instrument of statecraft* and a fundamental aspect of the survival of any nation. Within this more precise definition, the idea of our governments endeavoring to stamp out terrorism and trying to safeguard people against terrorist outrages is exposed as utter drivel.

In itself, the word *terrorist* does not tell us very much. Was Nelson Mandela a terrorist? Depends on your definition. Technically, yes, he was. But the terminology chosen to describe various political upheavals, struggles, and disputes is entirely subjective and open to widely conflicting interpretations. Where violence is involved, there is no difference between a revolutionary, a freedom fighter, and a terrorist. They are the same thing. In the end, it is the writers of the history books and the perspective of the reader that determine the wording and its implications.

And so it becomes apparent that the modern phenomenon of terrorism is a device used to mislead the public into believing they are under threat by strange evil-doers. In reality, governments themselves use terrorism as a covert device to strengthen and forcibly expand their own empires. They always have done and they will always seek to do so. The myth of the good guys versus the bad guys perpetuates itself.

Problem-reaction-solution, sometimes referred to as the *Hegelian dialectic*, is a classic technique used by the control system to steer events in their favor by manipulating public opinion. To see just how dramatic the effects can be, consider these famous examples of this tried and tested methodology.

◊ *February 303 AD.* The Roman Emperor Diocletian needed a crisis to accelerate the suppression and eradication of the Christians. This was accomplished when he had his guards set fire to his own palace in Nicomedia on two different occasions. A crushing set of edicts then followed, as the Christians were blamed for the blaze.

◊ *February 1898.* The Spanish-American War was a turning point in the history of the United States, signaling their emergence as a world power. The destruction of the battle-ship USS *Maine* in Havana harbor was a critical event on the road to that war. The U.S. Navy Department immediately formed a board of inquiry to determine the reason for the *Maine's* destruction. When the Navy's verdict was announced, the American public reacted with predictable outrage. The destruction of the *Maine* acted as a catalyst to accelerate the approach to a diplomatic impasse between the United States and Spain. There are many doubts as to what really happened.

◊ *February 1933.* A Berlin fire station received an alarm that the Reichstag building—the assembly location of the German Parliament—was ablaze. The fire seemed to have been started in several places (indicating foul play), and by the time the police and firemen arrived, a huge explosion had set the main Chamber of Deputies in flames. The police found Marinus van der Lubbe, shirtless, inside the building. Van der Lubbe was a Dutch insurrectionary council communist and unemployed bricklayer who had recently arrived in Germany. Hitler and Göring arrived soon after, immediately stating that the fire was set by the Communists, and promptly had the party leaders arrested. Hitler declared a state of emergency and encouraged aging president Paul von Hindenburg to sign the Reichstag Fire Decree, suspending the basic rights provisions of the Weimar constitution. We know what happened next.

◊ *Operation Northwoods.* Operation Northwoods was a 1962 plan to generate U.S. public support for military action against the Cuban government of Fidel Castro as part of the U.S. government's Operation Mongoose anti-Castro initiative. The plan, which was not implemented, called for various false flag actions, including simulated or real state-sponsored terrorism (such as hijacked planes) on U.S. and Cuban soil. The plan was proposed by senior U.S. Department of

Defense leaders, including the highest-ranking member of the U.S. military, the chairman of the Joint Chiefs of Staff, Lyman Louis Lemnitzer.

Many major terrorist events that unfold around the world are staged for effect. Whether on home soil or in foreign lands, not all the bombings, hijackings, viruses, assassinations, and atrocities are quite as spontaneous as they seem. Why? Because terrorism is an instrument of statecraft. Though terrorism is currently a crucial piece on the control system game board, it may soon be superseded by even more outrageous strategies. Technologies and realities that many people believe are still pure science fiction have been in operation for decades: weather manipulation, artificial tectonic plate stimulation, airborne chemical manipulation of organic matter, incoming objects in the solar system, and even simulated alien invasion. Bigger and juicier than any false flag terrorist stunt could ever hope to be. Such drama. Terrifying, pathetic, fascinating, and hilarious, depending on your perspective. If the character of local and world events is always negative, then something is wrong. Equally, if it is relentlessly upbeat, there is an imbalance. Both are reflections of the same dystopian construct. Both are untrue.

We plot a unique course through the polarities of life, steered by the quality of our consciousness, our spirit, and our knowing. Along the way, we cannot expect to have a precise and delicate preparation of useful information delivered to us from mainstream broadcasts. We have to gather knowledge for ourselves, from multiple sources, using the most appropriate tools and techniques, both ordinary and non-ordinary.

Real news is only ever *our* news. It is the news that we determine for ourselves—balanced, reasoned, and true to our own heart and spirit. The focus of that news may be solely on our immediate community, or it may embrace parallel narratives and images from overseas and outlying territories. Is what is spoken in the local post office any less significant than what is declared on the White House lawn? Are the energies in our home as powerful as the energies generated at the CERN particle accelerators in Geneva? How close do we have to be to the murder of another human being to understand the truth and impact of his or her life? It is not about proximity either way; it is about resonance.

It would be unwise to underestimate our ability to remotely intuit the energetic substance of an event, or indeed to be afraid to gauge the integrity of its chronicling. We may not be cognizant of the logistical details, but we can discern the root emanation. We can *feel* the essence of it. When we learn to filter out the associated egos (including our own), the cultural paraphernalia, and the anchored belief systems, we may arrive at the core of any happening. And every happening is essentially the same: energy transforming from one state into another. We gather as much information as is appropriate to accurately and equitably track an event. We must then personally interpret its meaning within the broader spiritual ecology. No one can do this for us. The clearer our vessel of consciousness, the deeper and more multi-dimensional our natural comprehension will be.

Only we can know what energetic input is appropriate at any particular stage of our unfoldment. We learn to vigilantly and intuitively distinguish what information, narratives, people, and experiences are best aligned with our unique expression of consciousness. Sometimes we seem to have a lot of influence over that, and sometimes we don't. The lower self cannot always see the deeper teachings of our immediate circumstances. However, if we always move with integrity and freewill, we will not go far wrong. As a rule of thumb, the amount of natural creativity in any particular thing—whether it is physical or non-physical—is always a respectable gauge of its authenticity. Creativity, in this sense, is not just about art; it is about getting to the truth of a thing. This process of discernment often begins with a very personal encounter. Perhaps even a playful one.

Chapter 16

Input, Output

Deep in the human experience of consciousness is a powerful impulse to *create*. It is through our creations that we grow, share, and steer a graceful path of ascendance. To create is to give. To learn is to teach. In the process of creating we attain discipline, think laterally, focus our will, and magnetize happiness.

Some people believe that they are not creative because that can't draw too well, or they can't think as inventively as Leonardo da Vinci. This misapprehension arises from our childhood, where we are all too often conditioned to harbor rather constrained ideas about what constitutes *good* creativity. These ideas usually revolve around how realistic our creative representations are and the level of technical ability we are able to demonstrate. Yet, when a child produces a crayon drawing of a dinosaur, is its creational value less than a portrait by Albrecht Durer? No. Its realism and technical prowess will naturally be entirely different, yet these are not the only appropriate measures of value.

It is easy to confuse art with creativity, but they are very different things. Art can be esoterically divided into two classes: synthetic/unreal art, which is concerned with control, and organic/real art, which is concerned with freedom. You can easily tell the difference. The synthetic stuff doesn't really resonate much heart, passion, sincerity, or spontaneity. It is largely self-referential and seldom aims above the mundane, whereas the true organic manifestation of art is always full of the good stuff; it is effortlessly universal and invariably contains transcendental elements. Creativity frequently produces organic art, but sometimes it does not produce anything that we would ordinarily recognize as art at all. Our creations can come simply in the form of thoughts, dreams, conversations, humor, memories, hopes, or realizations. Often, there is no resulting tangible form, yet the creative *outcome* can change our whole lives.

I went to art college when I left high school. It was an enlightening experience on many levels. From an academic standpoint, I relished the opportunity to explore different genres and modalities of art, such as abstract expressionism, surrealism, and conceptual art, which had hitherto appeared to me to be just some sort of intellectual joke. I was keen to get to the bottom of that particular enigma, or at least understand what the back story was.

The epitome of the confusing abstract expressionist was Mark Rothko (1903–1970). Rothko was a Russian-born American painter who used simple, broad bands of color to explore his chosen subject matters. He is one of those painters whose works can all too easily elicit the uninformed yet perfectly legitimate response: "My two year old daughter could've painted that. How is that art?" When one understands what Rothko was aiming for, the question begins to answer itself. Firstly, he was deconstructing form. That is plain to see, though most people lose the thread right there and then. A bit like wondering what the hell Mondrian was doing with his little red, blue, and yellow squares, plopped in a grid on a white background. Quite mystifying out of context. Rothko was using art to explore the inner landscape at a vital level, necessitating an intimacy that must transcend form. One intent was to re-spiritualize the Western relationship with art by destroying outward appearance, and elevating the purity and primacy of direct experience. He attempted to achieve this with the subtle interplay of carefully chosen colors, the largeness of the shapes, and canvas placement and dimensions that encouraged the viewer to become absorbed in the work.

For Rothko, the journey of the creation is the juice. In the act of creating, something stirs deep inside the psyche and what was a previously silent communication is slowly brought to life. There is a correlation between the profundity of that exposure and the disintegration of structure. Rothko went very deep and it shows—so deep in fact that, at times, his work is decidedly uncomfortable to take in. A similar principle can be observed in Jackson Pollock's splatter paintings. Though I personally don't like the end result quite so much, Pollock was making a significant statement about liberating oneself from the conventions of politics, aesthetics, and morality. His paintings represented the act of this emancipation and a radical disentanglement from tradition.

The creational value of art by da Vinci, Durer, Rothko, and Pollock, and the crayon drawing of a dinosaur are *equal*. Considered as synthetic products, they are assessed and priced drastically differently. Considered as organic human art, they each tell us something potentially remarkable about the human condition.

At root, the creative impulse is a willingness to transmute energy from one form into another. We shift its density, we recalibrate it to expresses something unique, we take hold of the raw material and sculpt it into a configuration that conveys our growth and ascendance, and then we openly share that with others who are on the same wavelength.

Knowing that every creation is valid, the barriers to manifestation fall away. Taking oneself seriously enough to imagine that even a subtle creation can be striking and profound, is a delicate but vital mind shift toward recognizing the fidelity of one's own creative endowment. Doodles *are* fine art. Scribbles *are* novels. Tickling the ivories *is* a piano sonata. One becomes the other by way of confidence, not ability.

There is one other little matter to consider before the full flow of one's own creative engagement can make its presence felt: the ever-present inducement to *consume*.

Moving through the modern mediaplex of screens, pages, feeds, portals, and broadcasts, one would think that consumption is a 24/7 imperative for all human beings, a strange obligation to gorge oneself with endless input. For example, to have an addiction to news is considered quite acceptable and even secretly commendable. Morning, noon, and night, quick fixes or unhurried binges are available everywhere: at home, in the car, on the subway, in the street, at the office, on the shop floor, or even in the restrooms of certain American airports. Like the chain smoker who reaches for a pack of cigarettes upon regaining consciousness each morning, the news junkie reaches for his or her smartphone, tablet, computer, or TV remote to see what lurid tribulations are slithering out of the informational cauldron today.

War, money, and slime. Not exactly the most inspirational subject matters in the world. Nevertheless, these are the things that are habitually obsessed over by the media controllers, constituting most of the available broadcast bandwidth that is pumped out every day. Admittedly, slime is rather a broad category, though it does seem to reasonably suit most of the additional political, corporate, celebrity, and entertainment segments of the news broadcasts.

I recall once being stranded by a particularly impressive snowstorm in Burlington, Vermont. The landing gear of the aircraft that was supposed to take me home to New York had completely frozen solid. The plane wasn't going anywhere. As I walked out of the warm airport lounge and into the freezing street, my eyes watered from the sub-zero blast of the wind, and the tears turned to ice on my cheeks. American East Coast winds are noted for their peculiarly bone-chilling powers. Thankfully, I found a hotel with vacancies just a short distance away. I had 24 unexpected hours to myself. I got my provisions and buried myself in the welcome coziness of the hotel room. Bags thrown to one side, clothes stripped off, into bed, and asleep in 30 seconds. I awoke a few hours later. My mind was awake, but my body hadn't caught up yet. Foolishly, I reached for the remote and flicked on the TV. I watched the news. More and more and more of it. I willingly submerged myself in an uninterrupted gush of reports, bulletins, dispatches, and statements. It was curiously hypnotizing. The sugared unreality infected my psyche, and I was drawn into the whole thing with embarrassing ease. I was experiencing the temptation of these deadly broadcasts. It'd been quite a while since I'd subjected myself to such a barrage of news. It wasn't pretty.

I sat through 10 continuous hours of it, from all the major stations. There were absolutely no inspiring or honorable communications from or about the real world. Of course, nothing at all was remotely connected to the majestic human journey of ascendance amid all the hundreds of news bites and commentaries. Just the same tripe repeated over and over: war, money, and slime. Even so, I could not help but notice how habit-forming all this morbidity was. Then the sledgehammer of knowingness cracked open my perceptive stupor. I realized that it was not news at all—not in any way that makes any reasonable sense. It was something entirely different. It was *doom porn*.

Filling oneself with input temporarily quells the emptiness that arises from a deficit of self-expression—of *output*. Whether that input is focused on doom, cooking, sex, soap operas, talent shows, sport, or high culture, the desired outcome is the same: tranquilization. It just so happens that at the end of the 20th century and the beginning of the 21st century, one of the most socially acceptable input habits is mainstream news.

There is a maxim that has been voiced by a number of wise thinkers and visionaries over the past two decades: *Consume less, create more.* Embedded in these simple words is an equation that is abhorrent to the consumer way of life that has been foisted upon much of America, Britain, and Europe over the last half-century. It is a worrying thing for those who idolize control when the very lifeblood of capitalism—consumption—ceases to be a pleasurable or automatic pursuit for large sections of society. Yet this is precisely what is happening. People are starting to disbelieve the line they have been fed that consumption is a hallmark of a healthy civilization. *It is not.* Personal, organic, human creativity requires very little large-scale corporatized consumption. People just feel so much better when they create something. No matter how large or small, creations bring a natural sense of accomplishment that is hard to beat. The more time we spend creating and the more we resonate that feeling of imaginative achievement, the less and less appealing the old ways of consumption become. The habit is kicked.

Not all portals deliver the mainstream unreality broadcast. Over the last 10 years, inexpensive and free, open source technology has enabled a growing number of creative individuals to produce authentic, high-impact independent media, in written, audio, and video formats. Bloggers, podcasters, writers, and artists have created a whole new stratum of output that is more alive with meaning and legitimacy than anything we have previously known in the last few thousand years. It is now viable to completely replace the old conventional media with something that is actually relevant to human life. Healthy output = healthy input.

Such is the penetration and efficacy of this new and unfettered media, that what used to pass for high-brow political, cultural, and philosophical programming in mainstream broadcasting is suddenly starting to look a bit lame. Where people might've once contentedly tuned into well-respected and publically funded radio programs for some plausible discussion on matters of substance, their output now comes across as increasingly meek, bourgeois, and somehow feigned.

From around 2006 onward, the quality, professionalism, and overall production values of the more committed independent media producers started to rival and even exceed that of the old kingpins of primetime broadcasting. Certainly the all-important *content* was leagues ahead of anything that could be found on regular television and radio. Despite the establishment scramble to co-opt, sequester, and generally get in on the act, their attempts to replicate this new media were hopelessly bland. They lacked the heart.

For me personally, there was a huge sense of satisfaction when I stopped paying the ludicrous (and mandatory) British television license, because I no longer watched live broadcast television. It was easier than I thought to give it up. Shortly after, I gave away the television, too. I have not had one for years now and can't imagine a scenario where that will change. Even my old friend the radio has precious little to offer nowadays. But things have changed for the better. There is such a wealth of fascinating podcasts, blogs, audio books, and videos out there (most of them free) that I could easily spend the rest of my life imbibing quality media about real life, made by real people. But once more, even that would be a little too much input.

Balance is central to the art of living as a naturally ascendant human being. Balancing input and output is the same as with any other play of polarity. Sometimes input is exactly what is needed, though it should be a conscious choice as to what that input is and what it is for. How relevant is it? What is its truth? The output of one's creative expression represents a spiritually uplifting and gracious movement of consciousness. It enlivens, teaches, heals, and encourages others to embrace their own creative endeavors. If we can move with the natural flux of the universe's own creative momentum, we can draw upon its infinite beauty and inventiveness for our own inspired creations. This is something that cannot be thought about—only felt. Allowing an open creative exchange between ourselves and our world means that whatever we bring into being is infused with that singular divine spark. All of our creations become living symbols of truth.

Before we can fully embody a truer resonance in our communications, we have to first bring it into the felt experience of our day-to-day being. This means that it is sometimes appropriate to be exposed to situations where there is an absence of truth. By observing the dynamics of unconsciousness—by living through the wrongness of a particular scenario—we come to appreciate the incredible transformative power of truth. This teaching is most consistently demonstrated in our dealings with other people. Although it is certainly instructive (and admittedly easier) to learn from those fine fellows who have attained a degree of enlightenment and self-awareness in their being, there is frequently even more to be gained by being temporarily marooned with those who have definitely not enjoyed such realizations.

Chapter 17

Ogres Bearing Gifts

Life often places us in proximity with difficult or unpleasant people. Many otherwise perfectly agreeable situations can be reduced to rubble by the presence of an individual who chooses to conduct himself in an inconsiderate manner. As noted in Ecclesiastes 10:1, "dead flies cause the ointment of the apothecary to send forth a stinking savor."

On the surface, it certainly seems like plain-old bad luck when we get lumbered with an annoying character. Indeed, wherever there is a certain diversity and volume of human activity, there is invariably a ripple of some unwarranted nuisance. Insensitivity, bad timing, misplaced profanities, and general egotism appear to be the stock-in-trade of the professional bungler. The behavioral characteristics of these provocative individuals vary in scale from the mildly tedious to the downright obnoxious.

My own path into properly comprehending this phenomenon was a textbook example of being compelled to wise up for the sake of my own sanity. I was obliged to deal directly with a number of challenging people, with each presenting classical modalities of antisocial behavior. Only through being plunged into the thick of it could I attain the deep realizations regarding unconsciousness and disavowal that have since become so pivotal to my understanding of human spiritual dynamics.

It began with a man named Cooper. He was the first truly contemptible adult I'd seen up close and personal, from the perspective of being a young adult myself. Of course, everyone has their moments, but what was unusual about this guy was the staggering consistency of his vileness. Day after day, year after year, he was just nasty to everyone. He especially enjoyed making various middle-aged secretaries cry, once he'd vented his spleen at them for any minor errors in transcribing his audio dictations. He sent grown men out of his room to properly adjust their tie before they could re-enter his office. His offensiveness and ferocity were legendary. It was rumored that at some point during their careers, he had made all of his colleagues cry, both female and male, young and old. To this day, I still don't understand why someone didn't just knock his block off. Clients complained and colleagues despaired, yet he held his senior position for more than 30 years as a partner in the business, before finally moving abroad to enjoy his retirement. Goodness knows what he's doing now.

In my first year of knowing Cooper, I'd only ever encountered him in the office. One glorious summer afternoon, however, I happened to see him shuffling down the street with his head bent low and a demeanor that just resonated defeat. It was as if an ogre had temporarily ventured out from under his gloomy bridge and had gotten lost in the world of humans. Without any emotional attachment whatsoever, I began to intuitively understand what was occurring with him. I *saw* him. Outside of his little fortress of solicitation, he was essentially powerless. No one knew him, women looked through him, men disregarded him, and even nature herself seemed to have given up on supporting his growth. His drooping eyes and grimacing lips tasted no wonderment in the exquisiteness that shone all around him. Spontaneously, I observed him with total lucidity and understood what was wrong with him: He treated people so roughly because it temporarily relieved the agony of his own inner pain.

There are no bad guys, just disturbed guys.

Cooper knew he was messed up and chose to live an overtly hostile life almost as a piece of radical, nihilistic theater. He felt it was too late to go in and do any healing or rewiring of his fractured mind, so he just played up the bad guy and to hell with it all. I got the strong impression that someone had treated him like this when he was at his most vulnerable. It had broken something inside him. Although the outward symptoms are very pronounced (which present undeniable challenges) with men like Cooper, the root of the suffering is correspondingly easier to identify. In total, I had perhaps 10 dealings with him over an 18-month period. A month after contemplating the cause and purpose behind his grown-up tantrums, I never saw him again.

The second fly in the ointment was George. I encountered him about two years after Cooper. George was the uncle of my boss at the time, occasionally coming into the office for a few days to help with the administration. As my forte was software and I spent most of my time on client sites, I rarely saw him. Each time I did, however, I was in awe of his pomposity and conceit. He could barely bring himself to look at me, let alone talk to me. When he did grace me with his attention, his communications were always tinged with discourtesy. As I was singularly polite and well mannered, I found this baffling. I couldn't figure out what I'd done to upset the man.

Though the office dress code was fairly casual, George always dressed in exceedingly formal attire, and marched around as if it were 1943 and we were organizing an Allied attack on Berlin. The most trifling and commonplace of office interactions were treated with the utmost solemnity—so much so in fact, that I noted his histrionics actually got in the way of doing the work itself. He would often stare into the distance and regale us with accounts of his previous triumphs in the business world and how he had frequently embarrassed or wrong-footed other people. His stories usually concluded with him having the final say in some long forgotten saga, the memories of which would have him quietly chortling to himself.

One evening, a friend of mine picked me up from work to take me to my karate class. We changed into our white karate gis in the bathroom and were about to leave when I heard George snorting behind me, apparently at our appearance. I said, "Oh, this is just the traditional Japanese dress for this form of martial arts." He replied, "You should try a proper man's sport like boxing. None of this foreign nonsense." We left without a word.

It was a small company, and there were only seven of us in the office at any one time. We used to take turns walking down to the sandwich shop each day and bringing back lunch for everyone else. George had been around for more than a week and had had sandwiches brought to him every day. On that Friday, I ventured to suggest that maybe it was his turn to go and get lunch. I had not meant this to be a provocative proposal in any way. He glared at me, and his face turned purple with fury. "How dare you!" he scowled. "Do you think *I* should go and bring sandwiches for *you*?" Everyone else in the office fell silent. George returned to his paperwork and ignored me for the rest of the day. I went to the shop and got everyone's lunch. I placed George's sandwich carefully on the side of his desk, having already resisted the temptation to somehow sabotage his food.

I returned to my chair and stared hatefully at the back of his head while I ate my lunch. Had I possessed the telekinetic power to set his head on fire, I would've done just that. Thankfully, I did not have that ability. Something far more incredible did occur in that moment however: I caught myself feeling indignant, upset, and unappreciated. I felt myself at a very deep level, yet with a peculiar objectivity. It dawned on me that my own worth was in no way connected to this sad man and his distorted psyche. I could be who I was, keep doing my own personal best, and not worry at all about what came out of his mouth. My feelings of resentment immediately began to evaporate. By removing the emotional sting and perceiving as truthfully as I could, I was able to get past the personal filters of my own pride and see what was really there.

George had very low self-esteem. He had spent a lifetime defining himself by his actions in the workplace. This is always a very foolish thing to do. Although his outward behavior was arguably less caustic than Cooper's, his ignorance of his own mental state was far deeper. His survivalist ego was running the show almost exclusively and only occasionally handed the reins over to his true self. On the one occasion that I did perceive a more balanced man inside, it was a rather gentle entity, almost feminine. As with so many people, I understood that something had happened to this true self many moons ago, and the associated trauma had permanently wounded him—so much so that his ego insisted on controlling everything from then on. Unlike Cooper, George's main defensive strategy was not attack; it was self-importance.

George's capacity for empathy, growth, healing, and authenticity was virtually zero. To observe him from an energy portal perspective, he was channeling his consciousness only through his throat and his root. Information and preservation—that is all. These facets, stripped of insight, knowing, heart, and honorable will, resulted in a profound inner barrenness.

There are no bad guys, just disturbed guys.

By far the most fascinating figure of spiritual infelicity was Clark. Unlike Cooper and George, Clark came across as a really nice guy. Most people who met him liked him. Strange, then, that though he was such a well-intended chap, it was so unbelievably energy-draining for me to be in his presence. He sucked the life-force out of me like Nosferatu the Vampire.

Clark was very much the antithesis of what I was trying to do with my life at the time. I was trying to grow, be more fluid, integrate spirit, be reflective rather than reflexive, and cultivate philosophical independence. He was habitual, stubborn, materialistic, and knee-jerk reactive, and all his opinions were crude rehashes from the mainstream media. He powerfully symbolized everything that I was trying to move away from. The clue was already right there in front of me, had I had the wisdom to see it.

Irritation may seem like a minor obstacle to overcome with a person, especially compared to rudeness or aggression, yet it can stealthily erode the sanity of those who are exposed to it for prolonged periods. Clark's inherently irritating behavior arose from his obsession with trying to be funny. Some people are just naturally funny, and some people are not. The same joke told with identical wording can be recited by two different people and elicit either spontaneous hilarity or embarrassed silence, based solely on the way the joke is told. Clark tried very hard, but he just wasn't funny. One or two of the kindest people in the office would indulge him by laughing at his imitation wackiness, but for everyone else his Spider-Man socks and amusing walks were just stupid.

Now to give the other side of the picture, at another level, Clark was also very generous, full of life, moral, and hardworking. The business customers liked him very much, and he was an extremely loyal ambassador for the company. He was a good man.

Over the two years that I worked with Clark, we often shared the same physical office space. He seemed to follow me around quite a bit, sometimes of his own volition and sometimes via apparently fateful synchronicities. I recall once we had a major office re-organization, where whole departments were shuffled around in an effort to achieve optimal efficiency, and he ended up sitting at the desk right next to me—for a year. I was mortified. He would hum the French national anthem as I worked on spreadsheets and would pretend to do the backstroke as he reversed himself across the room to the Xerox machine. Believe me: The veneer of amusement wore rather thin after a few hundred repeat performances.

Just as I felt I was either going to strangle him or suffer some kind of schizoid embolism, Clark and I were asked to represent the company at a conference in Brussels, Belgium. So off we went. I remember sitting next to him, right at the back of the plane. We both ordered coffee and croissants. Though I was rather nervous about flying at the time, we sat chatting together in an uncommonly cordial and easy manner. He started telling me about his mother and how she'd never spent much time with him when he was a kid. He found it difficult to talk to her even now. I listened attentively. He told me he had a brother, whom he had never previously mentioned, who suffered from severe mental and physical disabilities.

At 34,000 feet above the English Channel, Clark told me that his brother had always been a source of deep embarrassment to him and it was only recently that he'd taken a more compassionate and true-hearted perspective, allowing a real friendship to blossom between them. Perhaps for the first time, they had gotten closer and started to really enjoy each other's company. I could tell Clark was getting emotional. I put my hand on his shoulder. He momentarily froze. We had never touched each other before. I smiled into his eyes with all my heart and said, "That's the best thing I've heard for a long time. Doing what you've done takes guts." He nodded. He knew that I meant it.

A little later, I walked over to the little bathroom on the airplane, went inside, and locked the door. As I looked at myself in the mirror, tears streamed down my face as I tried to muffle my sobbing. I felt thoroughly ashamed of myself and appalled at the times I had presumably made Clark feel uncomfortable, unappreciated, or diminished in some way. I had been so wrapped up in my own apparently sacred journey that I had disregarded the equally sacred journey of someone who was right there next to me. How could I miss what was so obvious for such a long time? What precious teachings had I entirely overlooked from this generous, soulful, and thoroughly honorable man? I pulled myself together, cleaned up as best I could, and returned to my seat.

Clark, ever the diligent worker, was tapping away on his laptop in preparation for his presentation later that afternoon. I reached over and closed the lid, nearly trapping his fingers in the process. He looked at me with bewilderment. I said, "Clark, I just want to say sorry if I've ever treated you poorly or said anything stupid. I didn't mean to. You're just so different to me, and I haven't been able to deal with that in the way I would've liked. I'm sorry." He reached over and shook my hand. "That's okay," he said, "I appreciate that. Water under the bridge, mate. Water under the bridge."

We went to the conference, did some good work, and had a few laughs. Without any further substantial conversation about ourselves or our personal lives, the enmity that had existed between us for so long had drifted away. Our communications subtly changed. I behaved a little more warmly and accepting, and he calmed down a bit. We were friends.

After the conference, back in the UK, I remember sitting at home and reflecting on Clark, our history, our recent conversations, and what might come next. Completely unexpectedly, a deep recognition hit me like a bolt of lightning. I perceived the teaching that Clark was bringing to me. *Clark was me.* He was the shadow me. He was an inversion of my spirit. What I was good at, he was bad at. What he succeeded in, I failed in. We were there to learn from each other, and both light and shadow were absolutely necessary and equal. We were helping to balance each other. As soon as I internalized this, the wisdom that had been for so long encoded into these seemingly mundane and exasperating interactions suddenly began to unlock itself. I could appreciate its perfection and artistry.

I finally grasped that in the process of developing my own intimate spiritual awareness, I had wandered unthinkingly into the conceit of discounting those who were not practicing the same thing. True enough, Clark was actively upholding the self-diminishing diktats of an inauthentic life and ultimately behaving in a destructive way, both toward himself and those around him. Yet if Clark was me, then the growth and healing that I was bringing into my consciousness was also emanating from him. He was part of my unfoldment, just as I was part of his. He was helping me, and I should've been helping him. Perhaps I did in some way, but it could've been much more conscious and graceful.

I *saw* Clark for the first time on that airplane. An infinitely richer narrative began to emerge, and I accepted that my rejection of him had been terribly egoic and narrow-minded on my part. I owned my mistake. I resolved that such things were no longer appropriate for my journey and that my dealings with everyone at every level would be full of integrity and honor. I judged that it was unacceptable for me to treat anyone poorly. It would never happen again.

Not long afterward, I returned to the office after a little vacation, only to find Clark's desk empty. No papers, no laptop, no plastic flower monsters, no novelty banana pens, no Clark. A colleague came in and told me he'd gone. His sudden departure was quite unrelated to his work, to me, or to anything one might ordinarily expect. I felt a mixture of disappointment, release, and completion. I was glad for his journey and knew that wherever his growth took him next, he would be a happier man. It was as if the universe, once we had completed our energetic exchange, then promptly ushered us on to new terrains. Our paths diverged. I had identified the root wisdom and the life code was rewritten.

There are no bad guys, just disturbed guys.

My interactions with Clark were some of the most valuable of my life. During the two years that I had spent wrangling with his odd behavior, the more I tried to disown the situation, the harder it manifested. Though it was indisputably taxing at the time, the gifts of growth and honesty were massive. Ignoring negative energy patterns only ensures that they will return again and again in different guises and with sharper teeth. This recurs until we finally make the choice to face the shadow, step into the middle of it, and begin to consider it as part of ourselves.

It is instructive to note that there is an inverse correlation between the decreasing density of the three difficult characters and the increasing value of their embedded wisdom, Cooper being outwardly the hardest, then George, then Clark. Though Cooper's physical behavior was more overtly antagonistic than anyone else's, the teaching that he imparted was basic and relatively simple to get to. With George, I felt I had to go through a little suffering to get to the knowledge. So suffer I did. With Clark, it took a great deal of confusion and pain before I could understand what was occurring at the higher level. When I did, however, the wisdom was colossal.

We do not need to suffer to get to the wisdom. We can do it effortlessly if we only allow ourselves to flow without like or dislike. This is a hard lesson. There is a huge difference between a conceptual understanding of this and a realized attainment. It has to be lived sincerely and with heart before it can be understood. No torment is necessary if one channels consciousness through the mind and the heart in equal measure. It is only when there is imbalance that there is pain.

Difficult people often play the roles of *agents provocateurs* in our lives—stirring things up, pressing buttons, and obliging us to look at powerful triggers and emotions that lie deep inside us. Though sometimes our initial reaction is to just wish these people would go away, the impeccable timing of their arrival is a dead giveaway that the universe is placing their hidden counsel within our grasp for a reason. We might have to get over ourselves to see it, but when we do, the growth potential is remarkable. It is very much a mutual energy exchange; both parties benefit when consciousness is brought into every interaction, regardless of when they become conscious of it. It may often fall upon oneself to create a reciprocal space for mindful communication, especially when there is a clear disparity in consciousness. This is a further teaching in humility. It is a gift of compassionate recognition. Opponents cease to be opponents when we understand their higher teaching.

The unfoldment compels us to explore every part of our being and encourages us to consider every conceivable element of life as an instrument for growth. Ultimately, this brings us to a realization that positive and negative experiences resonate from the same single core, particularly when we stop considering one of them as good and the other bad. In the end, it appears that good and evil, right and wrong, are human conceptions and nothing more. So what is positive and negative? They are pulsations of being and non-being. Light and shadow. Sometimes there needs to be a fresh construction in our life, and sometimes it is essential to undergo a thorough deconstruction. They ebb and flow, as does consciousness itself. The tone of any energetic exchange is always perfectly tuned to present maximum evolutionary potential.

When a good amount of inner work has been done, the flow of non-ordinary incoming vectors usually intensifies. In other words, the weird and the wonderful make their enigmatic entrance. Until a point of internal equilibrium has been reached, such events risk going unprocessed, unheeded, or even entirely undetected—that is, if we are too caught up in the distortion of consensus reality. In addition to our emotional and psychological preparedness, we have to open ourselves up to meet the extraordinary. We have to personally allow for normal proceedings to be adjourned. Stand at the center and be still. When we stop upholding the old model of normality, we clear the way for a personal encounter with the unbridled magic of life.

Chapter 18

Paradox

The unfoldment welcomes paradox into our lives. All manner of anomalies and phenomena, once kept at a respectable distance, may be called forth to pierce the film of daily routine and raise an eyebrow. The kind of reality-wobbling experiences that would ordinarily be encountered perhaps once or twice in an average lifetime, appear unaccountably bountiful in the experiential realm of the ascendant spirit. The more they happen, the more the perimeter of the familiar is obliged to draw back. Ever deeper layers of the universe open themselves up, divulging vast passages of iridescent majesty. Eventually, there comes a point when one has to concede that the whole idea of normality is as flaccid as a soggy noodle.

Every time we come upon something new, we extend our boundaries. Because the universe is ceaselessly generating novelty, these opportunities for conscious growth lie around every corner. Without even stepping out of the front door, something poignant may be found in the pages of an old book, or on the radio, or in a casual observance in the kitchen—something previously unspecified that is now perfectly timed to transform one's whole outlook on life. People often have profound realizations while taking a bath or shower. While they bask in the hot water and soothe their weary limbs, the mind loosens and reflections of the day drift by; ambitions and dreams fuse together into new realities. Before they know it, they've resolved to sell the house, learn the clarinet, and move to Papua New Guinea.

Though many of our conscious evolutionary jumps are relatively commonplace, they are no less special when they happen to *us*: our first day at school, our first trip on an airplane, the first time we make love,

173

the first time we swim in the ocean, the first time someone we know passes away. We find ourselves contemplating the mystery of mortality for the first time. As Hamlet pondered, "To die to sleep, To sleep, perchance to Dream; Ay, there's the rub, For in that sleep of death, what dreams may come, When we have shuffled off this mortal coil." All these happenings irrevocably change us. Life *is* change. Consciousness refines itself throughout our unfoldment, developing more balance, discernment, and insight as we continue to grow.

When we encounter a paradox—something that is contrary to received opinion, or directly conflicts with our reality model—it brings an altogether different class of potential personal upgrade. Paradoxes are by their very nature confusing. That's what they do. They interrupt the habitual, discursive thinking of the brain and throw down a wildcard. They serve as boundary markers for a consciousness that is moving toward the optimal elasticity of an old concept. It is therefore highly instructive to note when and where a paradox is encountered on the chart of one's conscious growth. They always seem to show up at just the right time. Even so, they often arrive with a jolt. For a split second, consciousness blinks. The brain tries to process the paradox, but there is no corresponding entry in the database. Everything stands still while the brain performs a system-wide search for an analog—a similar reference point that, unlike the paradox, happily conforms to the commonly accepted conditions of the human world. If none can be found, then the phenomenon that produced the paradox is either ignored, discarded, or ridiculed.

Traditional Zen teachers would employ a kind of riddle known as a *koan* in their teaching practice. The koan is a mental device designed to interrupt the accustomed flow of reasoned thinking in students by creating a logic-confounding problem. By being asked to contemplate questions that have no rational answer, the student is forced to formulate alternative methods for resolution and insight.

Perhaps the most famous example is when a Zen Master posed the following to his student: "Two hands clap and there is a sound. What is the sound of one hand clapping?" There is no commonsense answer of course. More poetically, an aspiring Zen monk asked Master Kegon, "How does an enlightened one return to the ordinary world?" Kegon replied, "A broken mirror never reflects again; fallen flowers never go back to the old branches." Or, my personal favorite, on being asked by a student, "What is Buddha?" Zen Master Wenyan replied, "Dried dung."

Often with koans, the teacher asks the student a seemingly simple question, such as "What is Buddha?" and the student naturally tries to answer in a philosophical and respectful manner, proposing answers such as "Buddha is within us" or "the enlightened heart of all humans" or "I am Buddha" and so forth. The teacher would invariably then bash the student over head with his bamboo stick. Crack! All thought-out answers are wrong. A few bruises later, and the student finally gets it. Crack! The wise teacher can tell when the penny has dropped and the answers are from heart-centered intelligence, where there is often a deeper pool of wisdom than in the superficial conceptions of the brain.

The point of paradox is to encourage the student to transcend dualistic thinking—to short-circuit the cerebral impulse to jump either to this or that, right or wrong, up or down. Because the desired state of unitary wholeness is a difficult thing for the normal mind to grasp, the conflict that paradox creates is skillfully leveraged to temporarily suspend customary modes of thinking. How does it do this?

Milton H. Erickson (1901–1980) was an American psychiatrist who specialized in family therapy and medical hypnosis. His unconventional use of hypnotic technique, coupled with his radical theories on the subconscious, serve to neatly illustrate the intriguing range of practical tools available to the sincere teacher. One of Erickson's trademark procedures was the confusion technique (or, as my friend likes to call it, the Jedi mind trick). When a person is confused, his conscious mind is busy and occupied, and is very much inclined to draw upon previous unconscious patterning (or instructions) to make sense of things. A confused person is in a kind of trance of her own making and therefore goes readily into that trance without resistance. In this state, she is vastly more susceptible to suggestion. Confusion can be created by ambiguous words, complex or endless sentences, pattern interruption, or myriad other techniques—all aimed at initiating what is known as *trans-derivational searching*.

A trans-derivational search (TDS) is a psychological and cybernetics term, meaning when a search is being conducted for a fuzzy match across a broad field. It is a fundamental, automatic, and unconscious part of human language and cognitive processing. Arguably, every word or utterance a person hears, and everything he sees or feels and takes note of, results in a very brief trance while TDS is carried out to establish a contextual meaning for it. You can often see it in people's faces (particularly when that search takes a little longer than usual). The skilled teacher can utilize this process to "get into" the mind and speak to the spirit, or heart, rather than the brain.

Verbal techniques such as the use of open-ended statements and focused ambiguity can help to induce a longer TDS. The teacher may prefix a sentence with "You know those emotional things you were thinking about yesterday...." The average mind cannot process hearing this phrase without at some level searching internally for emotional thoughts from yesterday. The brain wants to do this, as it always desires to fill in the blanks and have the equation balance out properly.

Similarly, a statement can be opened with a phrase such as "the many colors that fruit can be." This starts the mind considering, even if briefly, various different fruits sorted by color. Ambiguity is perhaps an even more potent TDS instigator. Dialogue is commenced with a purposefully ambiguous question or statement such as "Do you remember the blue horse from your childhood?" Without sufficient context, vagueness in a statement may trigger TDS in order to seek resolution of the question. The student wonders, "Did I have a blue horse as a child? Was it a children's TV show? Was it a popular toy? Is it a euphemism for something else that I don't know about? Should I ask for clarification or keep searching?" All the while, the TDS chugs away in the background. Mixing clichés and stock phrases can also trigger TDS, as the mind tries to reconcile the discrepancies between expected and actual utterances in sequence. "Rome wasn't built so too many cooks can make light work of it."

Erickson also utilized a technique called hypnotic handshake induction, whereby the automatic routine of a handshake (which is a chunk of learned body memory behavior) is unexpectedly interrupted with subtle gestures that leave the subject in a state of mild catalepsy. He or she goes into an extended TDS in search of meaning to a deliberately ambiguous use of touch. With the normal behavior diverted midway, the subject is stopped in the middle of unconsciously executing a behavior without a corresponding pattern. The mind crashes, defaulting to a trance state until either something happens to give a new direction, or it reboots itself. A skilled hypnotist like Erickson can use that momentary suspension of normal protocol to deepen the trance. Though this can be used for both medical and entertainment purposes (as in stage hypnotism), the same mechanism is also used by spiritual teachers to break through ingrained mental conditioning.

Paradox teaches us that logic and language aren't necessarily the best tools for attaining real gnosis about ourselves and the world. As these are the two primary tools that most humans use to navigate their way around, this leaves the investigator in an ontologically sticky situation. How can one acquire knowledge about something if the customary methods of acquiring knowledge are useless? Perhaps, then, it is not about the knowledge at all—not as we ordinarily perceive it.

It was back in the early 1990s in Britain, that I first came across a very enigmatic set of anomalous manifestations known as crop circles. A friend showed me an article in the newspaper, containing half a dozen stunning photographs of these huge, otherworldly glyphs imprinted in wheat fields. I found them spellbinding. They exhibited an amazing degree of originality and elegant geometry, the likes of which I'd never seen anything remotely like. Though they intrigued me, I had gotten swept up in the narrative of my own life and just hadn't given myself sufficient time to look into them with any real focus. I'd thumbed through some books, looked at photographs, and read various research papers, but that was about it. All the while, I could not help but absorb myself in the primitive enquiry of wondering who makes them and how. Understandable, really. It took quite some time before I would move beyond this initiatory red herring.

Some of the first known reports of strange crop formations appeared in Lyon, France, around AD 815. An early illustration appeared in an English pamphlet from 1678 called "The Mowing-Devil Or Strange News From Hartfod-shire." During the 1970s and 1980s, as home photography and travel became more accessible to more people, there was a resurgence of interest in firsthand accounts and sightings of crop circles. Mainstream media coverage really peaked in the late 1980s and early 1990s. British rock group Led Zeppelin released their *Remasters* album in 1990, featuring a prominent crop circle image on the cover. This was probably the first time an international audience had seen such images. Then, in 1991, two old geezers—Doug Bower and Dave Chorley—revealed themselves to be the men who hoaxed the world, by creating hundreds of crop circles with planks of wood and lengths of rope. The whole phenomenon then quickly vanished from public view. Nevertheless, year after year, increasingly extraordinary circles continued to quietly appear in large numbers.

For those who care to trace the sequence of events and filter out the historical sediment, Doug and Dave were part of an absurdly obvious PSYOP, yet another in a long line of intelligence community–sponsored, "nothing to see here" propaganda jobs. Like all the best stooges, they were most likely unaware of their complicity in successfully steering consensus focus away from anything metaphysically heretical. The objective of the crop circle blackout was of course to neutralize any mass engagement with this wholly unexpected phenomenon, partially because it really did have the potential to compromise the boundaries of the approved syllabus.

This diversion was achieved, quite simply, by binding the word *hoax* to the term *crop circle*. Twenty years later, and the hoax association is now solidly established as part of the unthinking hive response. Today in England, if you were to ask the average person in the street, "What do you think about crop circles?" they would most likely respond, "Hmm. They're all hoaxed, aren't they?" Frequently, this does not in any way represent people's own considered view; they are simply parroting the message they've heard in the mainstream media. As a wise old man once told me, "Never ever be afraid to say 'I don't know.'"

Concepts are all well and good, but it is not until paradox is brought into the substantiality of direct personal experience that it gains real value. I felt it was high time that I actually got my hands dirty (or, as it turned out, my feet). From 2001 to 2009, I made many pilgrimages to the hallowed and ancient landscapes of Wiltshire, the county in South West England where the vast majority of global crop circles appear. I learned much. Some of my most epic experiences and moving revelations have emanated from the fields, woods, hilltops, and villages of Wiltshire. Not to mention the pubs. Indeed there have been many fine ales quaffed along the way, but even more nourishing were the fascinating conversations and personal narratives that took place there. I had the privilege of sharing in many incredible exchanges, courtesy of authentic human souls who had evidently opened themselves to their own unfoldment.

I have walked in dozens of the largest and most intricate crop circles on record. I have slept in them, meditated in them, held night vigils in them, had lunch in them, and done some other things that are best not talked about here. I have analyzed their geometry, have measured ratios and circumferences, and have taken innumerable photographs. I have learned to distinguish the authentic from the inauthentic, the terrestrial from the ultra-terrestrial. I have observed how the crop itself is elaborately woven together in organic, river-like patterns, with the plant stems delicately bent over without being snapped. I have sat with the amateurs and the experts, the faithful and the scientific, absorbing all their theories and interpretations. There has been lunacy and there has been brilliance. I have been baked under the summer sun and half-drowned in the monsoon rains of 2007. I have seen orbs of blue light zipping across the fields and watched glowing orange spheres hovering in the twilight sky. I have been buzzed by military helicopters, met with ex–secret service agents, been photographed by zoom lenses poking through bushes, and had my hotel room gone over by clandestine figures. Quite an adventure.

Though every single day gifted me some new knowledge or inspiration, one of my greatest experiences occurred when I was walking alone, barefoot, through a formation near Alton Barnes. It was quiet. There were only two other people in the circle, and they were respectfully going about their own studies. As my feet pressed into the warm soil and my eyes lingered upon the exquisite basket-weave of the crop, I felt a distinct warmth in my heart. It was a pleasant sensation, as if a loving hand was gently massaging my chest. I sat down, lay back, and looked up into the cloudless blue sky. The warmth spread through my whole body. A deep sense of bliss permeated my being, and I just felt inexplicably happy. Not only that, but somehow I felt *loved*. Though I have had the great fortune to have been loved by some amazing women, this was different. It was more profoundly encompassing and absolute. I almost felt overwhelmed by it, as if any further increase might cause me to spontaneously combust. But it felt so good. I whispered to myself that it felt divine. *Divine.*

Nothing existed except that moment. I could feel something downloading itself into me, through me, from me. It was like a soothing current of emotional gnosis—a glimpse into a near future where this state would become an important part of my life. I lay there for a long time. The other people had left and no one else came by. I eventually propped myself up on my elbows and looked around. The formation was on a gentle hillside slope, so I could easily look down on the landscape spread out before me. It was stunning—a perfect day in a perfect place. There was nowhere else on the planet I would rather have been. Tears filled my eyes, and I perceived the entire natural panorama with an unprecedented level of clarity. No filters. No thinking. I could feel the supremely coherent aliveness around me as my consciousness stretched out. I just lay there and allowed myself to become part of it. Perhaps for the first time in my life, I absolutely wanted to be here. There was no pain, heaviness, discord, or effort. It was an honor to be part of this magnificent sacred creation.

The tone and method of my engagement with crop circles changed from that day on. It was a change for the better. I realized that high-resolution cameras, laser tripwires, light-amplifying goggles, and thermal-imaging equipment only ever find epiphenomenal traces of phenomena—logical glitches and nuts and bolts reflections. Intriguing for sure, but not effective channels of discovery for truly understanding the teaching of crop circles. Though there is indeed often captivating information embedded within the physical geometry of the glyphs, this is potentially a very surface level of data, or even a cosmic joke—designed to engage a certain mindset that is as yet unprepared for the real juice.

The more circles I have experienced, the more I have come to know that only when all linear systems of thought are taken off-line and consciousness can flow freely through an untainted channel, does the primary teaching begin to unveil itself. Open-heartedness is more valuable in this respect than the intellect. There is little to be gleaned by the mind that is fizzing with mental noise and egoic spasms. The psychic tides must be allowed to naturally rise up and reform the inner landscape, submerging old reductionist concepts and sculpting new densities of graceful being.

There is one further anomalous experience that warrants telling, as it has some exceptionally singular qualities. The events I am about to describe also had a highly personal connection and, as I would later discover, were to have a profound influence in shaping my immediate life path.

James was quite a rare thing in England in the 21st century: a successful farmer. He had a wonderful family, a large house in an idyllic English valley, and a strong business. Aside from farming wheat and cattle, James and his wife, Deborah, also ran an upscale bed and breakfast out of their own home. That's how I met them.

In the summer of 2009, my friend Jay and I decided to spend a couple of weeks in Marlborough, Wiltshire, from where we could happily explore the sacred megalithic sites of Avebury, Silbury Hill, West Kennet Longbarrow, and some of the lesser-known sites, as well as take in a good number of fresh crop circles. We were also not too far from the ancient town of Glastonbury, where friends of ours were staying. Naturally, we also factored in the profusion of marvelous pubs so as to guarantee the proper refreshment of stomach and mind. I booked us into a bed and breakfast that I knew little about, other than noting some great online reviews and a lovely rural location, only a stone's throw from Marlborough town center.

The day we arrived, Jay and I sat around the kitchen table with our gracious hosts, enjoying their hospitality and politely answering their questions about our somewhat esoteric research into mysterious sites and the enduring enigma of crop circles. We had assumed that, being farmers, they would have a naturally skeptical and dismissive attitude of such things, so we played our cards close to our chest, while at the same time being as sincere and thoughtful as we could. We didn't want to freak them out; we'd only just met them. A little later, we ventured out to reconnoiter the land, walk round the town, and get some stuff for our explorations the following day. We ate out, discussed our plans, and relaxed. When we returned to the B&B a few hours later, we were totally bushed and immediately retired to our rooms.

As so often happens when one has been taking in the country air, sleep was long and deep that first night. I went out like a light and could've slept 12 hours straight. So it was, the next morning I was awoken by the sound of Jay knocking on my door. "Are you getting up or what? I've been up for ages. It's quarter past nine!" he informed me through the door. "Give me 10 minutes," I said. For everyone else in the house, 9:15 a.m. was late. However, the magnificence of Deborah's cooking was enough to rouse even the most dedicated dreamer from velvet oblivion. When I got downstairs, Deborah, her daughter, and Jay, were all gathered around the table. We ate, talked, and shared stories. We could not have chosen a better place with lovelier people if we'd tried. As I sipped my coffee, I looked out of the window. It was a beautiful morning, and I could see James in the distance on his tractor. Deborah said he'd been out since 5:00 a.m. My eyes widened, and I felt like an idle bohemian in a room full of movers and shakers.

Just as we were about to go out for the day, I heard a faint humming sound overhead. No one else noticed it at first, but it persisted, slowly growing louder. Then Jay noticed it. I could see him tuning into it as his body became perfectly still. We promptly excused ourselves and went outside. Two helicopters were doing surveillance sweeps over one of James's fields, and a small single-prop plane was circling high in the blue sky. We all went to investigate.

We walked to a distant field on the estate to get a better view of the aircraft, trying to figure out what they were doing. The plane was still circling above, making occasional, straight fly-bys. The choppers were there, too, hovering surprisingly low. We walked to the intersection of their flight patterns. I caught Jay smiling to himself as we walked along side by side. He had figured it out before I had. After a long, circuitous route through the surrounding grass fields, we came upon a truly striking spectacle: A massive crop circle had appeared in one of the fields—one of James's fields. To me, it resembled a huge ethereal sea-creature, composed of circles, spikes, and crescents. It was a large and charismatic design, with bold geometry and pregnant with mystery. It took another whole hour before I realized the broader significance of this event: The crop circle had appeared on the farm where we were staying on the very night we arrived. It was inescapably *personal*.

We walked into it. The field buzzed. The hairs on my arms and neck stood on end, as if a sizeable static electric charge was passing through my body. No one said a word. Even James and Deborah's young daughter just silently walked around the beautiful geometric shapes that had been fluidly laid down in the wheat. Ironically, it wasn't until a little later when we saw the aerial photographs that we got a proper sense of the overall design, so massive was the formation to navigate on foot.

Deborah called James on his cell phone. He made the 10-minute drive from the other side of the estate, and I greeted him at the top of the crop circle field. His face was expressionless. We walked down into it together. The formation itself was set into waist-high crop, and, as the field was on a slight hill, James couldn't see it until we were right on top of it.

The sheer size of the thing was overwhelming. Initially, James was speechless. I couldn't tell whether he was angry, bewildered, or in shock. I gave him a minute to collect his thoughts. Even as we stood there, other people started to arrive. We could see them in the distance, down the hill, vaulting the steel gate, and making their way up to the crop circle. Thankfully, most of them were walking along the tram lines (the tracks the tractor leaves in the field) to avoid trampling any of the precious crop. Deborah sprinted to an adjacent field, swiftly closing the gate to prevent the resident bull from causing an unthinkably bizarre scene.

Within a couple hours, news of the formation spread across the crop circle Websites and forums, and more visitors started to arrive. Buses pulled up on the main road and unloaded their eager passengers. Visitors from around the planet—who had specifically come to England for the crop circle season—made a beeline for this field so they could experience the phenomenon firsthand. (A fresh crop circle is always hot property.) James remained surprisingly unflappable, considering the circumstances. Images of the crop circle were already being published, scrutinized, blogged about, and debated over the Internet. The field was world-famous before the day was out. It would now forever be known as the site of the 2009 Ogbourne St. Andrew formation.

Jay and I assumed the roles of temporary park rangers, making sure everything was cool and the visitors were conducting themselves appropriately. We felt especially responsible for the well-being of this particular piece of land. Fortunately, there were no problems. Everyone was super-considerate. James attached a donations bucket to the entrance gate (as is customary with many crop circle sites), the proceeds of which would go to two local charities that he and Deborah supported. My friends from Glastonbury arrived, and we met them inside the crop circle. It was actually the first time I'd physically met them, as our previous communications had been conducted remotely over the Internet. One of them lived in France and the other in America. It was quite an occasion. (Little did I know at the time, but one of those friends would later become my wife. But that is another story.)

With all the commotion, the significance of a number of key elements did not fully impact me until later that afternoon. Specifically, (a) the circle appeared the night we arrived, (b) James might've wondered whether Jay and I somehow made it in the night, (c) James might've made it to promote his bed and breakfast, and (d) what were his feelings and conclusions about this paranormal event, now he'd had a few hours to reflect on it?

In discussing this with James, we satisfied ourselves that neither of us had either the inclination or the know-how to make such a thing for ourselves. Furthermore, I pointed out to James that this formation fulfilled all the criteria of being a genuine circle, as opposed to a man-made one.

At Jay's suggestion, in order to put the whole affair into some sort of context, we decided to record an interview with James. With his consent, it was then published on a number of U.S. and UK radio shows, Websites, and media portals. It was widely listened to throughout 2009, and was a thoroughly engaging story for all paranormal investigators, talk show hosts, and lovers of mystery.

Later that evening, we talked much more candidly with James and Deborah. They did the same with us. The wine and coffee flowed freely. We all acknowledged that we had borne witness to something that, by anyone's standards, could be rightfully described as remarkable. With more than 1,300 square miles of land in Wiltshire, with countless farms and fields, the creators of the formation had chosen this farm and this field. Directly or indirectly, they had also therefore chosen James, Deborah, Jay, and me.

Our hosts demonstrated a degree of open-mindedness, warmth, and authenticity that I found extremely humbling. We weren't the only ones who had been playing their cards close to their chest. They shared many stories, mysteries, and secrets of the land with us. As long-time stewards of this sacred ground, they had evidently been privy to all kinds of happenings and extraordinary events throughout the decades. As James put it so perfectly, "When you have such a close relationship with the environment—the animals, the earth, the weather, and all the powerful forces of nature—you get used to seeing miracles." Perhaps the crop circles were just another order of nature that we have yet to comprehend.

Two months later, I addressed an audience at the Beyond Knowledge Conference in Liverpool, host to prestigious speakers from across

America and Europe, including speakers who'd worked with NASA and Britain's Ministry of Defence, plus various other experts and specialists in esoteric science and history. Alongside my other work, I presented my photographs from Wiltshire and told the whole story. The audience loved it. Aside from the beautiful crop circle itself, and the perennial questions of how it was created and by whom, I told them that these glyphs are physical teachings in paradox. They invite us to extend our conscious boundaries and explore new levels of awareness. They transport us into the ancient landscape of the English countryside and place us right in the heart of nature.

Though I was ordinarily more interested in discussing the spiritual and philosophical aspects of my work, rather than simply dwelling on phenomena, I knew in my heart that the circles were significant at that point in time. They were teaching us something profound about ourselves and how we perceive reality. I explained that there were a basic set of characteristics that distinguish genuine circles from man-made ones: the degree of precision, the fact that the plant stems are not broken but curved over, the incredibly short time frame of creation (as little as seven seconds), the buzzing static electricity feeling at fresh sites, the presence of particles from high in the atmosphere and space, as well as continued British military surveillance of the formations. My aim was to persuade a good percentage of the audience, who might've previously been dismissive of such things, to contemplate them a little more evenhandedly. I think I succeeded.

Six months after standing inside the Ogbourne St. Andrew circle, I left England and moved 4,600 miles west. Something had shifted inside me, and my unfoldment determined that it was time to go deeper. All my conscious patterns, domestic routines, and familiar terrains were transforming. I followed the movement of energy that flowed through me and trusted the universe. I wrapped up my affairs in England and got on a plane to Reykjavik. From there, I flew to Seattle. Aside from a large suitcase, a backpack, and my laptop, all my other worldly possessions were in boxes in my grandfather's garage. I felt as though a huge psychic weight had lifted from me. Everything was different. It felt good.

In contrasting the fundamental transformation of my inner life with the many external non-ordinary phenomena that I have seen, I cannot say which is more valuable: an inward personal miracle, or an outward physical miracle. At root, I know that they are not at all separate from one another, and so perhaps the question does not have a ready answer. Yet to understand the principle of miraculous happenings, it can be helpful to approach the problem by working backward, from the outside in. By consciously focusing our gaze on the manifest marvels of the world, we begin to appreciate how we are directly connected to them. It is in grasping the relationship between the two that we arrive at a truer apprehension of ourselves.

Though I'd had my interest in the outward mysteries stimulated from a very early age—by the likes of Lyall Watson, Arthur C. Clarke, and Erich von Däniken—I somehow knew that my personal path was not about throwing myself into the role of researcher or alternative historian. At some point, I just *accepted* that the world was inherently mysterious. That view has remained largely unchanged over the last 30 years (and if anything, has only deepened). I was more interested in *why* physics-bending phenomena are generated, rather than trying to prove their authenticity. Even so, the conspicuously recurrent presence of miracles in both ancient and contemporary narratives provides us with a golden opportunity to once more examine how it is that we decide upon what is real.

Chapter 19

Something From Nothing

The "feeding of the 5,000" is the single living miracle to appear in all four canonical gospels of the Bible. It gives a striking account of human compassion, divine intent, and extraordinary manifestation. As if that weren't enough, it is immediately followed by an even more rousing and oft-quoted deed. Both incidents serve to demonstrate how thoughts can be given form in consensus reality, under certain special conditions.

After learning that John the Baptist had been beheaded, Jesus left for a remote spot over the Sea of Galilee for some much-needed solitary contemplation. However, a large crowd had followed him on foot from the nearby cities and gathered near him. Jesus saw their number and felt moved to go among them, healing their sick. When evening came, Jesus' closest disciples suggested that he should ask everyone to go home and have their evening meal, as there was not enough to eat in this desolate place. Jesus told them that wouldn't be necessary. He got the crowd to sit on the grass and he took the only food that was available—five loaves and two fish—"and looking up to heaven, he blessed, and brake, and gave the loaves to [his] disciples, and the disciples to the multitude. And they did all eat, and were filled." By an act of divine will, the empowered spirit of one man brought about what was most apposite in that moment. His thoughts became forms—real-world physical objects that nourished thousands of people.

Following this, Jesus immediately asked his disciples to board a ship and sail out from the shore, into the midst of the sea. He then sent the multitudes back to their homes and made his way to an isolated mountain to finally be alone. After a while, he returned to shore, from where he could see the ship being tossed about in the waves, as a high wind had arisen. Jesus walked toward them, across the surface of the water. When his disciplines observed what he was doing, they thought he was a ghost and were petrified. Jesus saw their fear and said to them, "Be of good cheer; it is I; be not afraid." Peter suggested that if it were Jesus, he could give Peter the power to walk on the water, too. Jesus beckoned him forward, and Peter proceeded to walk on the water toward Jesus. As Peter felt the cold whip of the wind around him, he suddenly became afraid, and immediately began to sink and shouted, "Lord, save me." Jesus grabbed him and said, "O thou of little faith, wherefore didst thou doubt?" When they all got back onto the ship, the wind immediately ceased and the disciples recognized the truth of their teacher.

As any good Bible scholar will tell you, these incredible back-to-back miracles (quoted here from the King James version of the Bible, translated and edited from 1604 to 1611) represent the most vigorous teachings in faith in the divine. Few things could be more immediate to a human being than eating food and surviving an unruly ocean. Jesus was clearly testing his spiritual initiates. When he saw their doubt over the shortage of food and the impending danger of the sea, he demonstrated what was possible when doubt is removed and faith is absolute. Note, in the first account, that Jesus looks up to heaven before his remarkable feat, and in the second, he goes alone to a mountain to pray. He sets his *self* apart, connects to the divine and respectfully harnesses its ineffable power to bring about physical changes. The rules of reality are suspended because in his teaching, his intent is true, honorable, and specifically configured to create a spiritual opening in his students.

The Tibetan term for a manifested thoughtform is *tulpa*. A tulpa can be either a physical object, a force, or an actual life form. It is a mental emanation created using a specialized form of focused will. Tulpas are discussed in various spiritual traditions (though with differing terminology) including Mahayana Buddhism, Hermeticism, alchemy, and various European occult schools, as well as Mesoamerican, Russian, Chinese, and Mongolian shamanism. Though the notion of the tulpa is ancient, the concept was most recently re-introduced to contemporary

Western mysticism in the 19th century by Alexandra David-Néel, a Belgian-French spiritual adventurer. She gave many intriguing firsthand accounts of her experiences with tulpas and the men who create them, including one episode where a *bonpo* (a practitioner of the Bon spiritual tradition in Tibet) produced a tulpa using sound waves.

David-Néel purported to have manifested a tulpa herself, in the image of a monk. It lived in her apartment as a kind of guest, where its form grew gradually more fixed and life-like. When she later left the apartment to go traveling, the tulpa included himself in the tour party and behaved much like any other traveler: walking around, taking breaks, surveying the landscape. It was also witnessed in her tent by a herdsman who assumed it was a real, live person. David-Néel remarked that, over time, the tulpa started to lose its original chubby monk features and became leaner and developed "a vaguely mocking, sly malignant look." As it became increasingly troublesome and bold, she decided to dissolve it, an exercise that took more than six months to complete. As she observed in *Magic and Mystery in Tibet*, "my mind-creature was tenacious of life."

The idea of the tulpa is not quite so provocative when we consider that within Buddhist and Hermetic philosophy in particular, the manifest world is held as purely *mind* or *mental*, with every physical thing being merely the outward expression of non-physical thoughtforms. So, a tulpa is simply a localized thoughtform within the grand thoughtform. A dream within a dream.

Certainly, Tibetan Buddhism represents one of the most enigmatic sources of esoteric wisdom that we currently have available to us. Its origins are *old*. Consider, too, that some of the adherents that we think of as Buddhist are not really Buddhist at all—not in the way that it is commonly understood. As with other major world religions, when Buddhism came to town in the seventh century, it suppressed existing indigenous Bon beliefs and practices as part of its holy mission to convert, enlighten, and save. Consequently, the smart Tibetan esoteric mystic (in the same vein as his European cousins) has a long tradition of wearing the robes of the presiding religion when appropriate, thereby maintaining a low profile and helping to preserve the sacred knowledge. Such concealment does not even necessarily compromise the integrity of the practitioner, as he understands the roots of the domineering religion far better than anyone else. He can therefore authentically uphold the virtuous tenets of its philosophy, ignore the political fabrications, and still give heartfelt expression to its exoteric moral shell.

All the same, with so many wonderfully abstruse ideas arising from this very specific Asian province, one cannot help but wonder at just why that is. What's so special about that particular part of the world? Why the uncommonly well-observed code of secrecy that shrouds much of esoteric Bon practice? Understandably, most systems like to keep their stuff under wraps, but the Tibetans go to extreme lengths, with whole communities going into social, political, and physical exile to protect their knowledge. If their crazy, mystical notions about the universe are so deeply antithetical to Western modes of thought anyway, why bother concealing them?

One does not have to dig too deeply into arcane history before the controversial subject of a certain continent that "was lost to the sea" presents itself. We have come to mythologize this place as Atlantis. The very word *Atlantis* automatically triggers a similar set of responses that one might expect when using terms like *fairies, vampires,* or *UFOs.* It's not real, right? It is a delicate business, extricating oneself from the memeplex of associated fictions that have grown up around the whole concept of Atlantis. To sort the real from the unreal, conscientious readers are encouraged to undertake their own independent research into this fascinating subject. For now, let us suppose that a large island existed many eons ago that was home to a highly advanced civilization. That island was destroyed by earthquakes and reclaimed by the sea. Those who had foreknowledge of the cataclysm left for carefully chosen locations in the East and West (among other places) in order to preserve their spiritual roots and the unique cultural and technological understanding that they had accrued over thousands of years. One such sanctuary in the East was what we now call the Himalayan region, the colossal mountain range that straddles the border of India and Tibet.

There is a legend that tells of the great Chinese mystical philosopher and Taoist sage Lao Tzu, who, once he felt he had completed sharing his philosophical teachings, rode an ox to these mysterious lands, crossed the border, and never returned.

The Atlanteans had found a place that was not only agreeably high above sea level, but that was also home to groups of highly spiritually attuned, remarkably humble, and naturally kind-hearted humans—a rare combination. If information from the ancient world was shared with these folks, perhaps the geographically isolated nature of the terrain itself also helped to preserve the purity of this knowledge over thousands of years. The ability to create tulpas was one of the metaphysical tools or reality-hacks that they were gifted.

The actual function of the tulpa is often rather more prosaic than one might assume. Far from simply being a bizarre feat of conjuration from an overzealous sorcerer, the tulpa was often brought into being to assist with domestic chores around the home, workplace, and temple. Particularly in harsh environments, the ability to enlist an extra pair of eyes and hands could be a positive blessing. Even more valuable than having a tulpa help with fetching and carrying, a tulpa could also be asked to locate crucial resources for the community and even cure illnesses. Outside the protection of modern healthcare, this was a most cherished skill.

At Runswick Bay, in Yorkshire, England, folklore tells of a *hob* (a diminutive mythological being) that lived in a cave called a *hobhole*. This particular hob was known to be able to cure children of whooping cough (a condition that can be fatal to small children without proper treatment). Loving mothers would carry their sick child to the beach and walk to the mouth of the hobhole. There, they would cry, "Hob hole hob, my bairn's gotten t'kink cough, tak it off, tak it off."

Jewish mystic and Talmudic scholar Judah Loew ben Bezalel was a highly influential rabbi in Prague in the late 16th and early 17th centuries. He was known as the Maharal (teacher) of Prague and was renowned for his creation of a *golem*, a living being he produced using the same esoteric principles that God used to create Adam. Though it is said that the golem was created using clay from the riverside, this is mystical symbolism for the primordial or principle substance—the stuff that all life is created from.

The golem was brought to life for the specific purpose of helping to defend the Jewish population in Prague against *pogroms* (organized attacks on particular religious or ethnic groups). The mighty golem undertook its task with great ferocity, slaughtering non-Jews (gentiles) and spreading tremendous fear. Although some versions of the story have the golem attacking both gentiles and Jews, and even its own creator, the standard account sees Loew submitting to the emperor's wishes to have the creature destroyed. Loew achieved this by erasing the first letter of the word *emet* ("truth or reality") from the inscription on the golem's head, leaving the word *met* ("dead"). The inanimate body was then stored in an attic in the synagogue, locked away until a time when it might be needed again.

This incredible story has even been confirmed by several high-ranking orthodox Jews, such as Menachem Mendel Schneerson, a prominent Hasidic rabbi who led the Chabad-Lubavitch movement in Brooklyn, New York, up until his death in 1994. Schneerson wrote that his father-in-law had witnessed the body of the golem firsthand in the attic of Alt-Neu Shul. A number of other notable rabbis have also confirmed the existence of the golem.

Perhaps then, there is an order of beings walking among us who are not quite what they seem—a kind of humanoid subspecies that is officially un-documented. When Hebrew, Christian, and Islamic texts talk about strict classifications of mankind, it can sound awfully divisive or even dangerously elitist. However, if we go to the early sources of some of these religious systems—before the foundational texts were condensed and standardized—we may detect that not all gradations of humanity are necessarily for the purposes of decrying non-believers.

Certain pre-Christian Gnostic sects classified mankind into three types:

1. Those of ascending spirit nature (*pneumatics/pneumatikos*).

2. Those with the freewill to determine their own destiny through spiritual endeavor (*psychics/psychikos*).

3. Those of descending flesh nature (*hylics/choikos*).

The hylics are wholly of the *demiurge* (the lower God who created the world according to the appearance of the divine template, yet lacking in harmony). They did not derive directly from the imperishable light. They are thoughtforms without spirit. Sounds familiar. Their essence will perish when it is time for matter to perish.

The final paragraph of the Gnostic tractate *On the Origin of the World* (part of the Nag Hammadi library), states: "For everyone must go to the place from which he has come. Indeed, by his acts and his acquaintance each person will make his nature known." *Acquaintance* is a special term for sacred knowledge or divine lineage. So, the tulpas will be dissolved, along with the demiurge, who, once he's killed his own "gods of chaos," will then proceed to "turn against himself and destroy himself until he ceases to exist." All the realms of the demiurge will also crumble as "their heavens fall one upon the next and their forces will be consumed by fire."

When one reads the Gnostic tractates in this light, there are abundant references to "the men of unrighteousness," "those who dwell in error," and "those who hope in the flesh and in the prison that will perish!" Are these references to a different kind of human—humans without the gift of eternal life or a pathway back to the divine creator? As proclaimed in the *Apocalypse of Peter*, "not every soul is of the truth, nor of immortality."

Traditionally, individuals with magical knowledge created tulpas to *help out*. They were given a little piece of consciousness to consider as their own, then sent off to complete specific tasks, or to generally assist around the workplace or home. British and European folklore is replete with tales of sentient supernatural entities that are either bound to their original creators or to the land itself. They are the *tomte* of Sweden, the *nisse* of Norway and Denmark, the *haltija* and *tonttu* of Finland, and the *wights* and *hobs* of England.

Tomtes often looked after a farmer's home, children, animals, and crops, particularly at night when everyone else was asleep. Many stories tell of their magical abilities, such as shapeshifting, invisibility, and feats of enormous strength. They were also quite independent minded, did not suffer fools or mistreatment gladly, and were quite capable of making their own way in the world, should circumstances necessitate it.

When Christianity came to the Scandinavian lands, all talk of such supernatural entities was considered a threat to the unity of the church. It was heathen enchantment—the work of the devil—and had to be stamped out forthwith. Millions of European farmers risked accusations of witchcraft and execution if they were judged to have created, worshipped, sheltered, or conspired with *false gods* or *demons*. So the whole thing went underground almost overnight. The pagan peoples (from the Latin *paganus*, meaning "rural, villager, civilian") learned to keep their mouths shut. Any continuing practices or talk of the non-ordinary would henceforth have to be conducted in total secrecy.

In the 12th century, the Roman Catholic Church formalized the destruction of indigenous spiritual knowledge and practices in the shape of The Inquiry on Heretical Perversity (Inquisitio Haereticae Pravitatis), better known as The Inquisition. In order to erase the old ways and install their new ways, even more crucial than executing spiritual practitioners was to impound the wisdom of the people, the lore of the folk—the *folklore*. One policy was to collapse complex knowledge down into crude umbrella terms. It can be likened to reducing the *Oxford English Dictionary's* current 600,000 English words down to 600. Change the language and you change the way people think, communicate, and remember. Consequently, today, the entire paradigm of those supernatural entities has now been abridged into something we think of as *pixies*. Children's storybook material. Unreal. That is precisely what the religion of the empire wanted. Expunge and discredit.

In light of this, one could say that tulpas have been absent from European thinking since approximately AD 1300. That's sufficient time for most people to forget. It only takes a couple of generations to have witnessed the empire's brutal punishment of *ungodly* practices, before thousands of years of history vanish like white breath on the winter air. It would not be until the 20th century, during a spontaneous revival of mysticism in the early part of the century, and then a resurgence of interest in shamanism in the latter part, that the idea of tulpas would once more arise in the collective consciousness.

University of California anthropology student Carlos Castaneda served an unexpected and wholly enigmatic apprenticeship with an old Mexican sorcerer named Don Juan Matus, the details of which he started sharing with the world in 1968. Over a series of extraordinary and controversial books, Castaneda recounted dozens of paradigm-cracking feats of magical attainment and reality manipulation. One such episode involved Castaneda himself being taught to manifest a live squirrel—a tulpa—into Don Juan's hand.

For newcomers, it should be noted that Castaneda's material is still rather troublesome, because it is essentially semi-fictional. Nonetheless, for me and many of my most esteemed colleagues in the field of spiritual philosophy and mystical study, the excellence of Castaneda's work is indisputable. Whatever he was doing and wherever the information was coming from, the knowledge in those books (particularly his second, third, and fourth books) is absolutely first-class. Quite where he got it from is anybody's guess, but there's nothing quite like it. To this day, his books are standard course material for all students of ancestral metaphysics, de-conditioning, and magical tutelage.

A little later in the 1980s, the burgeoning field of UFO research introduced the somewhat-bizarre idea of the *men in black (MIB)*—peculiar, shadowy men wearing 1950s-style black suits who would often show up at prominent UFO or paranormal related events, and even during significant natural and manmade disasters. Witness reports often cite them as typically operating in groups of two or three, being vaguely androgynous in appearance, and being rigid in physical mannerisms and speech patterns. A number of channeled sources state that these 1950s time-traveling shadows, which seem to be able to appear and disappear at will, are in fact tulpas. They are tulpas created to collect specific sets of data from realms where their creators cannot easily go.

A tulpa's ability to disappear is a very commonly observed behavioral characteristic. In some parts of Sweden, folklore tells that one would very rarely, if ever, see a tomte. You would only see the effects of its labor. Tomtes liked to stay out of normal human sight. Only a few wise men and women (seers/shamans) could observe them directly on a daily basis. Because of this, if a tulpa was ever to wander off and go on its own private adventure, finding the tulpa would be nigh on impossible.

The idea that tulpas can quite easily liberate themselves from their creator and go AWOL is fascinating. David-Néel, in her 1929 book, *Mystiques et Magiciens du Tibet*, recounts the thoughts of a Tibetan *gomchen* (spiritual adept) named Kushog Wanchen, with whom she was discussing the subject. He said:

> Visualizing mental formations, either voluntarily or not, is a most mysterious process. What becomes of these creations? May it not be that like children born of our flesh, these children of our mind separate their lives from ours, escape our control, and play parts of their own? Must we not also consider that we are not the only ones capable of creating such formations? And if such entities exist in the world, are we not liable to come into touch with them, either by the will of their maker or from some other cause?

He went on to caution David-Néel about the processes and realities of conjuring tulpas: "It is only prudent to beware of opening channels without due consideration. Few, indeed, suspect what the great storehouse of the world which they tap unconsciously, contains. One must know how to protect oneself against the tigers to which one has given birth, as well as against those that have been begotten by others."

It is estimated that in the 99-year span from 1900 to 1999, the world population ballooned from 1.6 billion to 6.1 billion. Today, the number is estimated at 7 billion. The rate is slowing down, though there are still an awful lot of people here. In Times Square, in New York, around 500,000 people a day move through its colorful streets, restaurants, theaters, stores, and hangouts. Every creed and persuasion of individual is represented there, every day, 365 days a year. Place yourself in the middle of that mega-torrent of human traffic. Might some of these people be tulpas? How many? What would the overall percentage look like? If an individual's clarity of consciousness was a reasonable measure of his or her spiritual connectivity—indicating direct emanation from source—then that percentage could be very high. We must be very honest with ourselves in considering how many truly conscious people we have met in our life—not at specific conferences or gatherings of conscious people, but just in the street, at the grocery store, in the workplace, within our own social circles. You can usually count them on one hand.

An unconscious person is not a negative or bad person; he is simply someone who is choosing to be asleep, to remain separated from his spirit. This is generally a defensive tactic that comes about quite reflexively. It is an innate protective impulse to prevent a weakened psychic-emotional complex from being exposed to uncertainty. For a tulpa, however, who is ostensibly without a spirit, unconsciousness is not a choice; it is the default setting.

The intriguing question is: Would knowing that many of our fellow men and women are tulpas make any significant practical difference to our life and how we regard those people? Certainly, this incendiary slice of knowledge shifts the foundations of the whole game, but what is the actual effect in terms of felt experience? Should the *unspirited* be treated with any less sincerity, politeness, or compassion, just because they don't have the same lineage as organic human beings? Sentience is sentience, regardless of origin. If an entity conducts itself with integrity, honesty, and grace, then perhaps it can rewrite its own basic programming and become more than the clay from which it was formed.

Perhaps the wisest of tulpas can create a soul vehicle for themselves and begin the sacred journey of unfoldment just like anyone else. Is it conceivable that they can attain spirit through personal endeavor, in a similar manner to the Gnostic psychics? Hermetically speaking, we are all thoughtforms anyway. We are all emanations within the mental universe—all thoughtforms of the divine. Considered from the Tibetan perspective, traditional tulpas are just one step removed from that.

Without doubt, they might anticipate a rather more circuitous path back home, though it is no less sacred in its ultimate realization.

In the Hermetic book *The Kybalion*, there is a passage that should bring some comfort to the tulpa who aspires to the infinite:

> There are many planes of Being—many sub-planes of Life—many degrees of existence in the Universe. And all depend upon the advancement of beings in the scale, of which scale the lowest point is the grossest matter, the highest being separated only by the thinnest division from the SPIRIT of THE ALL. And, upward and onward along this Scale of Life, everything is moving. All are on the Path, whose end is THE ALL. All progress is a Returning Home. All is Upward and Onward, in spite of all seemingly contradictory appearances. Such is the Message of the Illumined.

Anything that *is*, is quite naturally part of what Hermetic philosophers call *the indrawing*. This is an evolutionary impulse that all sentient forms participate in, whether they know it or not, whether they like it or not. In this respect, the question of spirit—that is, having one or not having one—reveals itself to be a question of *identity*. If the whole divine emanation is seeking to gather itself back into unity and nothing can be left out of this process (despite apparent polarizations and endings), then the only difference between a spiritual entity and a non-spiritual entity is a *knowingness* of one's path and a sense of the eventual indrawing. Even though a non-spiritual entity might dissolve and appear to lose its identity altogether, it is merely reverting back to the original energetic density and state from where it came. There is no fear or loss in that realm. The identity was always illusory. Nothing is lost. The Gnostic demiurge and his super-being minions will dissolve as identities, because they never were independent identities at all. That was their naïve conceit.

The *only* identity is the original emanation of divine truth. Everything else is a temporary construct. Any fear related to any loss is to fear something that never existed in the first place. The material beings do not know this in their hearts and so there is disturbance. The spiritual beings know this in their hearts and so there is harmony.

Regardless of the level of awareness, the power to manifest thought-forms is a potent and natural component of consciousness. Spending time in the 3D temporal zone of cause and effect—the clockwork of our ordinary world—helps us to comprehend the effects of our mind on the things around us by slowing down the process of manifestation. We get to see exactly what occurs when we think, feel, and act in a certain way. If we were to create a thoughtform from a place of imbalance, whether we were materializing a piece of fruit or a sentient being, we would inevitably pass on our mental deficiency, and our creation would soon embody the same unstable energy signature that created it. We need to achieve a precise balance for our creations to endure. That balance stems from our ability to acknowledge, process, and express our will from a place of centeredness. It is the whole purpose of the inner work. In this regard, nothing is more significant than developing an impeccable knowledge of our emotional self.

Chapter 20

Sublime Flux

Emotions have a profound influence in shaping our life path. They have greater power and deeper penetration than the abstractions of the intellect and have an uncanny ability to discern the real essence of a thing. For these reasons, emotional awareness is a foundation for conscious growth and one of the most important elements of the unfoldment.

Emotions are intrinsically multi-dimensional in nature, in that they operate on a number of different levels simultaneously: the physical, the non-physical, and the higher realm of the spirit. They have the power to reach out and touch things in a way that nothing else can. They can elevate or disintegrate, heal or wound, purify or diminish. Sometimes we can control them, and sometimes they get the better of us. To enhance our understanding of what emotions are and how they support the unfoldment, we must first explore their enigmatic presence in our day-to-day lives, both from a commonsense standpoint and a more esoterically attuned perspective. To achieve this, it is useful to go to the felt experience of their most prominent manifestation, which in our strange times is most conspicuous in their negative aspect.

Many people encounter the same problems over and over again in their lives—recurring experiences of unfulfilling relationships, dissatisfaction with daily routines, uncertainty over direction, domestic strife, or a general sense of purposelessness at the throbbing monotony of the rat race. We hear these stories all the time. Though they all have their own particular nuances and characteristics, the underlying principles remain constant. Indeed, it is commonly accepted that such things are to be expected in life. There is a tacit agreement that people are expected to quietly "get over it" and "get on with it."

It is not the way of the unfoldment to just ignore what feels wrong. If a negative emotional response arises within us, it is trying to tell us something. We have all felt it—that energetic constriction that ranges in intensity from mild disquiet to gut-wrenching dread. Indeed, it is one of the unifying aspects of the human condition. As surely as we must all draw breath, so we must all encounter the same irresistible phenomenon: emotional turbulence.

This spontaneous dissonance occurs when challenging new experiences trigger incompatible old wiring. The new experience resonates a *note* that, when superimposed over the old wiring, falls either sharp or flat—in other words, it is discordant. The knee-jerk response is to discard that which does not fit into the music of the old wiring. Emotions work in the same way. The only difference is that we are shifting up a gear, to higher frequencies and greater energetic fidelity.

The secret is that emotional turbulence is not meant to be suppressed. It is a teaching mechanism. It signals a perfectly organic state of psychic flux into which an immediate potential for growth is encoded. Indeed, it is at this very point that the individual must make a choice: accept the emotional upwelling, leading to integration and growth, or deny the emotional upwelling, leading to disavowal and inertia. When we grasp exactly what our emotions are doing, making the right choice becomes much easier.

Traditionally, submarines use sonar to detect other vessels in the ocean. Active sonar works by putting out a pulse of sound, called a *ping*, and then listening for echoes of that ping, which reflect back from other objects. From the echo, various attributes of the object can be determined, such as its size, speed, heading, and so forth. In a similar manner, consciousness is constantly pinging our circle of awareness. When an experience of potential growth is encountered, the returning echo is often *felt* as an emotion. The sooner we acknowledge it, the more latitude we have in exactly how we choose to deal with it. The later we acknowledge it, the fewer options we have and the more turbulence its impact can have on us.

By constantly ignoring ping echoes and refusing to engage with the inner work of the unfoldment, a certain type of spiritual emptiness is created, which I have termed *the void*. At a low level, it is one of the worst enemies of the intelligent human. It can be compared to the "black dog" that English writer Samuel Johnson (1709–1784) used as a metaphor for the haunting presence of his own debilitating depression. At a higher level, the void actively demonstrates that the circle of awareness, and sincere engagement with one's unfoldment, cannot be ignored indefinitely. Only when they are embraced can the void be made whole and a state of true equilibrium reached.

By delineating the techniques that have been devised to elude the void, we provide opportunities for identifying and resolving any emerging or latent avoidances in our own lives. It also helps to shed light on some of the baffling behavior of those around us. If we can heal ourselves, we directly contribute to a wider healing by preventing the transfer of our own negative patterns to our friends, families, and children. For those who directly seek our help, we empower ourselves to share something of universal substance.

There are three primary techniques of avoidance: displacement, delay, and dysfunction. They are used both independently and in combination.

Anything that demands sufficient mental energy (intellectual or sensory) can effectively relegate the specter of the void back into mere background noise, at least for another day. There is a rich repository of socially acceptable displacement activities to draw from. These can be broken down into three categories:

1. *Quick fixes*: food, shopping, movies, games, intoxicants.
2. *Leaving the scene of the crime*: walking out on a difficult situation without resolving it.
3. *Long-term strategies*: excessively absorbing professional careers, devoting oneself to others, religious zeal, cultural immersion.

In themselves, these activities are entirely neutral; they are what they are. It is only when they become artificially amplified to the point that they represent the totality of one's chosen energetic focus that they become distorted. Of course, there are socially unacceptable displacement routines, too—mental and physical acts that subvert energy into the direct abuse of oneself and others.

For those who cannot restrain their woes by their own hand, the current conventional medical wisdom is to proffer a range of pharmaceutical products to suppress any offending emotional upwelling, temporarily rendering it mute. As long as there's a steady supply of pills, the chemical counterbalance is worth it. People can get out of bed in the morning and go about their business. This does nothing to address the root of the problem in any meaningful way. Depression is at higher levels than ever before. From the underclass to the super-privileged, this devastating malaise seems to move unhindered through the populace. It is not just a chemical malfunction of the mind; it is a symptom of the void and, ultimately, represents a perennial invitation to realign with the truth of one's higher purpose.

Delaying fundamental inner work until another time is a common practice. It can be tempting to falsely supplant doing the inner work (particularly dealing with emotional patterning), with the arrival of a particular event or achievement. When I get that new job. When we move to France. When I lose 30 lbs. When the kids leave home. When I find the perfect partner. "Then I'll be ready!" If and when these events do occur, another event is summoned up to once more project the time for self-examination into the future. When I've retired. When I've read the complete works of Shakespeare. When I've got $250,000 in the bank. When I've learned to play the glockenspiel. And so the years roll on. This is untruthful. The time for the inner work is always now.

Continued deferment of the organic unfoldment of one's spirit eventually results in a significant diminishment of self-esteem. The void sucks it out of people. Buried deep within the subterranean caverns of the psyche, a little voice repeats, "You are not following your true path." This is the most terrifying murmur conceivable. To drown out these fateful tones, a persistent and sizeable over-riding pain is required. And this is exactly what people create, albeit subconsciously, by maintaining a highly dysfunctional element in their lives. It usually takes the form of a relationship, but it can take other forms, too, such as a particular environment, ongoing manipulated dramas, magnetized ill-fortune, or a psycho-somatically induced disorder.

With the dysfunction in place, all the resentment, anger, and pain that have accumulated from years of spiritual renouncement can be channeled into the object of dysfunction—the bitch, the bastard, the chaos, the pointlessness, the sickness, the soulless job, the evil empire. This distorted logic gives license for heedless self-indulgence.

This is perhaps the most insidious avoidance technique, and it can have ruinous consequences. As Nietzsche observed, "He who despises himself nevertheless esteems himself as self-despiser." This gives a further insight into the mechanics of this ritual self-harming.

Continually ignoring negative energy patterns ensures they will return again and again. Each time they do, they gain density, becoming harder and harder to reject, gradually creeping toward crisis. A single, ignored negative emotional impulse can move from apathy to discontent, from dysfunction to despair. We cannot just let things go unresolved, try as we might. Negative energy patterns cannot simply be abandoned. The immutable flow from mind to matter, from consciousness to creation, does not allow us to disregard a given challenge on our path of ascendancy. Each challenge must be faced, met, and understood in order for the negative patterning to dissolve.

Even if the individual makes it to the finish line—death—without consciously engaging with her unfoldment, she simply gets rebooted back into another parallel life experience, re-incarnating with exactly the same issues, predilections, and circumstances. Same challenges, different scenery. It is inescapable. So guess what? We might as well deal with things right now.

We can only ever be our own teacher. Though we may encounter wise men and women who share their wisdom with us, it is only the *inner* teacher that can translate and crystallize incoming information into our own solid knowing. We must be open to growth—open to change. An open person freely receives and transmits energy and is undaunted by how it will change him, as he is not so easily dislodged from the center of his own being. He has innate balance in everything he does.

A closed person imagines that she is the self. She believes that she is her personality; her likes and dislikes; her attitudes, history, and knowledge. If this were true, then even the slightest breeze of new energy could potentially change what she is, in ways that are impossible to predict. So she shuts down the portals of conscious discovery, and attempts to deal only in fixed and narrow certainties. She makes an enemy of change. As a consequence, she is obliged to stave off the unfoldment because it doesn't work without openness.

Let us be quite clear: Self is an expression of spirit. It is not what we are; it is an illustration of our journey. It has an essential role to play in the purification of our mind and the deepening of our consciousness. When all is well, it can be rightfully considered as a constant and faithful ally on our singular human adventure. It is always there with us and knows us better than anyone else. Self holds a space for our evolving character. It allows us to track our behavioral development and acts as a pivot point for all our linear conscious experiences. We need the self just as we need the ego. Without both, we cannot fully welcome our ascendance or appreciate the unique teachings of what it means to live as a spiritual animal.

The Tibetan Buddhist tradition of the *sand mandala* is an excellent metaphor for the self. Groups of monks spend weeks meticulously crafting large, ornate, multicolored discs of sand on the ground. These highly elaborate designs are lovingly articulated with powerful sacred iconography, and demonstrate breathtaking levels of skill and patience. Once completed, the mandala is then ritually swept away. The fabulous geometry is once more reduced to piles of sand, which are carefully gathered into a jar, wrapped in ceremonial silk, and taken to a nearby river. Here, the sand is returned to its natural source. This unique art form serves to draw attention to the transitory nature of material existence and focuses consciousness on the process rather than the product.

When we grasp that we are not anchored to self in the way we once thought, our emotions take on an agreeably lighter aspect. We can see their truth more clearly. We can better understand what they're showing us about ourselves and our world. We realize that we do not need to take them personally; we need not hide from them, defend them, or cling to them. Our emotions guide us to what is true, beyond the logical grasp of the intellect. They help to bridge the gap between mind and spirit.

The universe is designed to support the energetic movement from the dense to the less dense, from the gross to the subtle, from the void to radiance, from benightedness to knowing. If we regard our emotions as conduits for this gnosis, we see their true worth. Inch by inch, we shift our consciousness out to the perimeter of the known self and closer to the felt experience of the spirit. The fear that we may fall off the map as we approach this mysterious frontier is perhaps understandable, yet quite unnecessary. There is nothing to fear. As we approach the line, it moves ever forward from our range of perception, reaching further into the distance to reveal a new event horizon. It is not the line that moves; it is us.

Emotions are interpretations of the energy flow between spirit, mind, and self. In the same way that the eye detects different frequencies of radiation and interprets them as color, so the subtle energy portals in the body detect and interpret the conscious exchange between spirit and self. The resultant interference and defraction are translated into what we call an emotional response. The principle is similar to how holograms work. In essence, emotions demonstrate how our higher purpose is manifesting into our life. When we feel an incoming growth ping, spirit is attempting to rewire the old conditioning. When we feel a surge of knowing—as we do in moments of profound personal revelation—spirit is harmoniously integrating with mind and the self witnesses it. Everyone is happy.

There are many systems of spiritual philosophy and practice that show us ways of repositioning the self for more direct encounters with spirit. Particularly in Buddhism and Taoism, we find frequent references to concepts such as detachment, non-action, mindfulness, rigorous self-examination, and meditation. They are methods for recalibrating the mind for purer, more authentic perception. They reduce the static of brain chatter so the signal of consciousness can be more clearly conducted. For the contemporary Western mind, these techniques are so often necessary because our culture has persistently encouraged the survivalist ego to assume the overall authority of the self. Under its captaincy, self can all too easily become radicalized and reflexive. All incoming encounters get crudely categorized into things that provide material advantage and things that do not. This is an immensely disobliging program to run with.

There is a natural ebb and flow of spirit as we go about our daily business. Sometimes we feel very physical and anchored to the root of the earth. Everything is alive, vibrant, and sumptuously carnal. At other times, we are inexplicably ethereal in our being and can feel the slenderness of the illusory reality around us—as if it might melt away at any moment and allow us awesome contact with the truth. As spirit moves into mind, self fades. As spirit recedes from mind, self consolidates. The art of living as a human is to find the point of perfect equilibrium where there is no longer any distinction between the two.

Emotions, like everything else, are vibrations—specific configurations of moving energy. Each type of feeling has a distinct composition, with its own unique, energetic characteristics, which may be thought of as analogous to charge, gravitation, and velocity. This goes for both negative emotions (contractions), like fear, hatred, and despair, and positive emotions (expansions), like joy, love, and compassion. They are all emanations from source, formations in the field, no less substantial or insubstantial than anything else that manifests. A voice, a stone, color, heat. Strictly speaking, positively and negatively charged emotions do not signify good and bad. A negative ion is not bad, as the negative pole of a battery is not bad. It is just the reverse polarity of the positive.

Polarity is the fundamental dynamic of the third density, constantly compelling movement and refinement.

The old narratives of good versus evil, light versus shadow, are seeking re-integration and completion in their age-old game of conflict. The current accumulation of negative manifestations in the world is the collective projection of billions of personal disavowals in the hearts of humankind. The macro reflects the micro. As above, so below. Our internal shadows are propelled through the void to play the role of the external *other*—the enemy that would be so easy to pin it all on. But this is not the truth of it.

To hasten the re-integration of opposites, we must manifest wholeness into our own lives through our own emotional intelligence. To heal our world, we must heal ourselves. When we shift our perceptions from self to spirit, the polarities of positive and negative collapse into themselves. There is no further division between self and non-self. There are no more advantages and disadvantages. The unity of consciousness flows through our thoughts and deeds, and its supreme equanimity guides our actions. Nothing is gained and nothing is lost. There is only the graceful movement of the primary emanation.

Chapter 21

Undoing Woundedness

Some men and women go about in a state of mental woundedness for their whole lives. Though the wounds themselves usually go unseen, their influence over day-to-day affairs could scarcely be more profound. They shape a person's likes and dislikes, their fears and prejudices, their self-esteem, where they go, what they do, and who they choose to share a bed with.

Wounds are energetic blockages that are brought about by emotional trauma. Woundedness is a state whereby the individual overcompensates for these blockages by distorting his or her natural expansive behavior to become restrictive and defensive.

It is rare for a person to directly reference a wound under normal circumstances. As is so often the case, if everything seems to be going according to plan in the outside world, why look inside? And so things remain as they are. Then, one day, something happens. Something breaks. Something goes wrong. Depending on the individual, there is either an explosion or implosion of mental energy. These energetic movements can be interpreted as various forms of anxiety and depression. Indeed, it is not until the natural procession of life is tangibly impeded that the mysteries of inner conflict are given any serious thought. Before then, woundedness is considered to be just another common affliction of modern society—a collective symptom of an unhappy world.

The presence of wounds can be felt as an unaccountable sensation of *old pain*, a pain so distressing that the mind will construct all manner of barriers to avoid it. These barriers habitually result in some form of energetic contraction—something that millions of people have been led to believe is part and parcel of everyday life. There are many drugs that

213

attempt to bury the symptoms, but the knowledge of how to deal with the actual causes is rare.

Being anxious or depressed is the mind's way of subconsciously running *static*, whereby the inner landscape is obscured by a haze of overwhelming negative energy. Though this negativity is highly immobilizing to the flow of consciousness, it is exactly the desired outcome, because it successfully masks the old pain. With or without professional help, many people do not feel that they have sufficient strength, courage, or knowledge to go to the source of their discord. They like to think that it's just something they can put behind them, as they stoically march onward. The truth is that woundedness cannot be left behind, because it follows us around wherever we go. It is inside us.

The majority of wounds are created in the first 14 years of life, usually emanating from traumas experienced in the familiar environments of home, family, friends, and school. Being exposed to physical, mental, or emotional shock when the mind is at such an impressionable age results in the formation of what we might call *crisis response wiring*. This is an involuntary defense mechanism that the mind formulates in order to evade potential wounding that parallels the initial traumatic event. It is a seemingly rational tactic based on prevention. The problem is that years and even decades later, the old response wiring remains firmly in place. It is still fully operational and can be inadvertently triggered at any time. It can be activated by any number of things: a powerful emotion, a sequence of words, a particular smell, a piece of music, or even an entirely imagined scenario.

When consciousness flows through the old wiring, the old pain is experienced (whether there is a conscious memory of the initial wounding or not) and the energy system of the body profoundly contracts. Reflexively, some form of attack, escape, or shut-down is initiated to counteract the suffering. It depends on the individual as to what form that response will take. It may mean a surge of anger, or walking away, or getting inebriated, or becoming emotionally frozen. Even subtle ploys like making everything into a joke can be discerned as methods for offsetting woundedness.

The nature of the response wiring and the resulting behavioral symptoms will vary in relation to the character of the initial event. If someone was humiliated in the schoolyard, this can present agoraphobic impulses and incomplete self-expression. If someone was abandoned by her mother, she may live with constant separation anxiety and have problems with low self-worth. If a child is beaten by an adult male, his response wiring will likely extend into adulthood and lead to an underlying distrust of men that will negatively affect him for the rest of his life. The wiring that is set up for each wound requires a certain amount of conscious energy to sustain it. The deeper the wounding, the more conscious drain there is on the individual. It is an exhausting business maintaining one's woundedness. For those on the spiritual path, this consciousness has to be reclaimed.

People develop all kinds of elaborate strategies to protect themselves from activating old wounds. Some of them can look relatively harmless at first glance, and even fun, but they are always damaging to growth. I knew one man, John, who spent 40 years sleeping around with hundreds of different women as a way of disavowing a deep, emotional wound that he carried. He loved to talk about his sexual exploits, reporting back all the graphic details from his liaisons in hotels, supply closets, dentists' restrooms, vineyards, coat check rooms, widowers' bedrooms, backyard hammocks, and Polish brothels. Yet it was clear that he was utterly incapable of having any sort of meaningful or intimate relationship with a woman.

By his own admission, John had certainly never been in love. I later learned that his wound was inflicted quite unexpectedly, one day at the family dinner table, when his mother casually let slip that he had been conceived by accident. As John cut his roast beef into neat chunks (understandably, he remembered this particular meal in vivid detail), he realized that his magical entrance into the world had been totally unintentional. Sure enough, his brother and sister were 15 and 20 years old than he, and to John, his parents had always seemed quite elderly compared with those of his schoolmates. John interpreted this as "not being wanted" and felt a deep sense of rejection.

Because his mother did not communicate this news in a very thoughtful or considerate manner (due to her own woundedness), every time John recollected those times when his mother had told him "no" or whenever she had seemed to turn away from him, John then saw it as evidence of his fundamental unimportance. He did not feel loved and had very low self-esteem. As a means of indirectly punishing his mother, John spent his whole life punishing other women by devaluing their sexuality (as well as his own) and further propagating woundedness into the lives of others.

In terms of the dynamics of woundedness, in John's case, the wound was rejection, the crisis response wiring formulated a strategy of detached revenge, and the negative emotional patterning presented itself as destructive sexual expression. Not only do we see a clear example of how woundedness has seriously harmful effects on an individual's life, we can also observe how it invariably spreads to other people, too.

Woundedness, crisis response wiring, and the subsequent negative emotional patterning can all be undone. There is no need to carry the pain and weight of these things any longer than one wishes to. There are a number of fundamental elements to consider. When each is fully realized and charged with personal experience, they enable a truer self to emerge, free from distorted behavior.

First, we must acknowledge that negative emotional patterning is not only terribly limiting to one's multi-dimensional expression as a human being, but it is also wholly optional. To behave in a physically or emotionally destructive manner, however seemingly justifiable or moderate, and regardless of whether or not it affects anyone else, is always a choice. Therefore, the act of healing oneself begins with an act of empowered will: *to choose to transform*. Without the fundamental and authentic decision to modify one's own inner core, no amount of distraction, therapy, pharmaceuticals, or philosophy will ever make any real difference.

Because we are not given the knowledge or tools to work on ourselves, there is no common framework to use as a reference point for addressing woundedness. Many people feel that the only practical alternative, therefore, is to displace wounds by some other overriding sensation. Crude, but effective. If this appears to have done the trick for a good few years, it will most likely become an ingrained and recurring behavioral pattern. Unfortunately, displacement tactics always have some sort of injurious byproduct, with the level of disturbance being directly proportionate to the intensity of the original wound that they're trying to mask. (Entrenched low-level poor behavior stems from light wounding; chronic high-level sociopathic behavior derives from severe wounding.) Either way, change begins with the will to reshape oneself.

Strange as it sounds, it can be hard for some people to let go of the old pain. Becoming a martyr to one's own private anguish is common. The woundedness and all the strategies that have been assembled to offset it become enmeshed into a person's sense of identity. Objectionable behavior can easily be mistaken for just some weird aspect of someone's natural disposition, far too obscure and thorny to worry about quite how it got there or how it might be extracted. People will say, "I'm just antisocial," or "I'm just an angry person," or "I just don't do trust," or some other pretext for dubious conduct. They have permitted the old pain to become part of who they are.

For those who uphold woundedness for extended periods of time, there is a belief that letting go of the pain somehow equates to no longer caring about the event that caused the initial woundedness, however distant or invisible that may be. Particularly when this relates to close family or intimate relationships, it can resonate powerful feelings of guilt and rejection. This is erroneous thinking. To endure self-imposed suffering does not show strength of character or moral fortitude. It impresses only those who suffer the same ill. It is escapism.

Basic gnosis 101. We are not our body. We are not our brain. We are not our personality. To define ourselves by any of these is naïve. Therefore, to worry that we may lose some part of ourselves if we rewrite the old lines of identity code is totally unwarranted. Changing the identity by removing pain does not change who we are; it changes how we choose to depict ourselves and how truthfully we allow consciousness to move through us. We must never be afraid to transform and evolve the identity.

Wounds are always passed on. We get them from other wounded people. Wounds transfer themselves from one person to another and will continue to do so for as long as consciousness is diverted away from them. Generations upon generations may transmit physical and mental damage to their own kin, continuing to bestow emotional frailty and spiritual decay upon each other, until someone, somewhere vows to stop passing it on. There can be few higher authentic expressions of compassion than to *go into* one's own original wound and heal it. When it is healed, not only does it immediately free the individual from the pain and weight of carrying this sorrow, but it will *never* again be passed on. A long cycle of diminishment is brought to an end.

The wounds we receive, though they have unique features associated with our circumstances and environment, all emanate from the same source, and all contain the same root suffering. Even in the space of one brief century, a grandfather may easily pass his wounds onto his son, and he to his son. Imagine extending this dynamic out a few hundred more times. How many millennia might that cover? One wound can do untold damage across a time line that reaches far beyond the event that produced it. What was the *first* wound? Was it the original wound of mankind itself? Was it contact with the tree of gnosis that showed both truth and untruth in the heart of man and the imbalance at the root of the world? Is this the pain that was lain bare when man was finally unchained from his unknowing trance? Nothing has been lost.

Healing is a commitment to positive transformation. Whether we have a single wound or a dozen, the underlying process is the same with each. To choose not to conceal and ignore wounds anymore is to be prepared to restructure oneself—to live without the wound and to affirm its termination within oneself. All these things are required to positively charge the healing process.

The crisis response wiring itself needs to be deeply and honestly considered. This is challenging, because it means recollecting and even reliving the original emotional shock that brought it into being. In other words, one must go into the resonance of the original wound. This requires courage and focus. To help approach this, it is vital to understand that, no matter whether the initial trauma derived from an intentional or unintentional act, whether from a person, an accident, a misunderstanding, or pure malice, *it wasn't personal to you*. It emanated from a place of unawareness. It was a wound being passed on. As we have seen, if one were to trace back the inception of the primary wound, its origins may lie thousands of years ago.

Certainly, it can be useful to identify the event that caused a particular wound. Was it a remark at the dinner table? A fist in the face? A glimpse of something disturbing? A humiliation, a rejection, or a loss? In some cases, hypnotic regression can help the subject to draw back the veil of the subconscious mind and access the historical hard drive of the brain. Everything *is* in there, even though the ability to recall specific data about an incident may be obstructed. The brain may deliberately attract forgetfulness to a particular trauma, so we can get up and go on living immediately afterward. Later on, however, a point may be reached where the appropriate tools are at hand and the wound can be safely illuminated.

Even without any remembrance whatsoever, it is possible to perform a kind of *trace back*. A strong negative knee-jerk reaction to something or someone, who is perhaps totally blameless, is always a clue to the presence of old response wiring. It can be followed back into one's inner self—in the moment it happens—and the trigger can be isolated and mapped. For example, talking to a portly businessman with blond hair and a lisp makes you uncomfortable because…run trace back…it reminds you of your old physics teacher who once humiliated you in front of the class. Sudden emotional eruptions are opportunities for psychic upgrades.

As well as strong emotional reactions, the presence of prejudices is a dead giveaway for the triggering of old wounds. Generalized negative judgment, against a type of person, or race, or style, or manner, or anything, is more often than not the result of old, inappropriate wiring.

Not all wounds are old. They can be picked up at any time in life, though the frequency and depth are noticeably reduced as one's understanding of the mechanics increases. The more consciousness flows through the mind, the more that potential incoming wounds are harmlessly deflected. Challenging events still occur; they just don't harm us anymore. Like the martial artist who has been trained in high-level, defensive body movements, their ability to smoothly and efficiently repel would-be attacks becomes second nature. There is a graceful motion of body, consciousness, and spirit, moving intuitively in concert to neutralize the incoming negative energy strike.

The mind is not always in the state of poised readiness that we would like it to be. Sometimes things can just catch us unawares. Especially when the mind is diverted or fatigued, we can succumb to a new wound. Though in times of great adversity and war, these wounds can of course be significant, in regular, non-violent domestic life, the wounds are most often light and shallow in nature. Even so, the effect of the response wiring and behavioral distortion can be just as dramatic as heavy, trauma-induced incidents.

In my early 20s, I had an extremely negative camping experience that affected me for years afterward, even though, at the time, I considered myself to be an intelligent, perceptive, and tolerant young man. I had naïvely supposed that any outlandish misfortunes that might befall me would be promptly identified and processed. Not so. It all seems rather farcical now, but at the time, it was a most grave and spiteful business.

My girlfriend and I had spent a wonderful day hiking around a particularly beautiful corner of the South West English countryside. It was all hills, valleys, woodland, streams, laughter, romantic picnics, and tales of mystery—a truly memorable day.

It was getting late and the sun was beginning to set. We were dog-tired from the many miles we'd walked, so we pitched our tent on a little camp site, made some tea, and lay back to reflect on our exploits. Within 15 minutes, we were so exhausted that we feel into a deep, velvety sleep. Shortly afterward, a group of excitable German tourists arrived and pitched their tent right next to ours. They were loud, obnoxious, and hugely thoughtless for what seemed like an eternity. Though we tried to block it out with earplugs and bury our heads in our sleeping bags, it was no use. I yelled at them to shut up, which they did for a little while, but they soon resumed their (what I now recognize was a) drug-fueled hyper-conversation. What made it worse was that I understood a little German and could make out some of their absurd blabber. They were discussing the various merits of French and German cheese, and trying to determine which was superior. It was grotesquely surreal.

Though I was a peaceful man, I contemplated beating them up. As there were three of them, I tried to calculate their body mass and age by the tone and nuances of their voices. After a few minutes of attempting this feat, I realized that even Sherlock Holmes would struggle with that one, so I gave up and came to my senses. We dressed, went outside, pulled our tent down (though it should've been theirs), trudged several miles down the road in total blackness, found an empty field, pitched the tent for a second time, and collapsed inside it.

We awoke the next day in sweltering heat. It felt like we were in the Mojave Desert. My girlfriend reached over to see how I was doing and jumped back with a start when she saw me. I was covered from head to toe in mosquito bites. Not a square inch of my body was free from their havoc. My face alone bore maybe 20 or 30 bites. I looked dreadful, and they itched like hell. They must've gotten to me while I was pitching the tent and I'd carried them back into the sleeping bag, too. Thankfully, she had gotten off lightly with only a few bites. Outside, in the blistering midday sun, we could see that we'd managed to pitch the tent right next to a stagnant old pond, surrounded by cow dung and alive with all manner of insects. Black clouds of them swarmed around the thick, fetid waters. I covered myself in insect bite cream and wore sunglasses and a big hat for the rest of the week.

About two years later, I was sat on a train traveling from Manchester to London, quietly reading a book and sipping coffee. Two well-dressed gentlemen came into the carriage, looked around, and took the two empty seats opposite me. Then they started talking to each other—in

German. I glared at them from over the top of my newspaper. My hands became fists and I could not stop myself from crumpling the newspaper into a ball. The two Germans looked at me quizzically. The same wrath bubbled up inside me once more and, for a brief but worrying moment, I could've killed the pair of them with my bare hands. The crisis response wiring was still fully operational and my consciousness fired it up in milliseconds.

This amusing but instructive example taught me that our customary tools of civility, patience, and intellect have very little to do with woundedness. Self-awareness is not the same as intelligence. To see clearly into oneself, one has to create stillness. Without that, we only get fleeting glimpses of misshapen reflections.

I recognized that the mental shock derived from a number of factors combining together to penetrate my psyche. Firstly, the idyllic serenity of that day in the countryside, where I wanted everything to be perfect, was rudely shattered by the arrival of something unforeseen. The inconsiderate nature of the drugged foreign tourists, not to mention their peculiar conversation, simply served to exacerbate matters. Most importantly however, I was *exhausted*. My cerebral and spiritual faculties were at a low ebb. Mindfulness and vigilance were switched off. Season this with a hint of misfortune, some foreign accents, and a few thousand mosquitoes, and you have a recipe for a minor wounding to take place.

Wounds usually cause the brain to lay down some pretty rudimentary wiring. As we have seen, the brain invariably devises some form of fight or flight strategy to avoid anything remotely similar to the initial trauma. The further in time we move away from the initial event, the less appropriate that wiring may become. To help accelerate the process of undoing woundedness, it is useful to re-pattern oneself with more appropriate internal pathways and external responses. If we know that the old response wiring has created behavior that is harmful to ourselves or others, we can change it. To make those adaptations, we have to first demystify the wiring, thereby making it less scary and the response more understandable.

Deconstruction involves breaking something down into its individual constituent parts. By dismantling the overall structure, we can better comprehend its efficacy and composition by analyzing its components. If we deconstruct a common piece of behavioral wiring—fear of the dark—it proves to be a far less ominous phenomena.

Why are we afraid of the dark? Without light, our field of visual perception is massively reduced, and awareness of our environment is equally diminished. The ancient part of our brain knows that certain predators can see very well without light: wolves, crocodiles, snakes, big cats, and so forth. Simply stated, they can spot us before we can spot them. Being unsighted in proximity to such creatures would, of course, place us at a distinct and potentially fatal disadvantage. Thus, in our not-too-distant past, nighttime was a period of insecurity, where our tribal ancestors would be obliged to gather around the fire, secrete themselves in caves, and diligently watch over each other. In some parts of the world, this is still the case. To wander through the jungles of Guatemala or the plains of Botswana at night is probably inadvisable for all but the wisest of bushmen.

The ancestral *body memory* of fearing the dark is about physically avoiding specific predators. Contemporary Western insecurity over the nocturnal hours is more closely related to a collective social anxiety relating to the unknown, rather than specific threats. The sinister fables, images, and movies that we have all inevitably been exposed to usually involve something malevolent prowling around at night. Yet, for people who do not live in a wilderness area, the statistical probability of being killed by a predator is practically zero. You are more likely to be flattened by an incoming meteorite. Most fatalities are liable to happen in broad daylight, as people go about their normal business of crossing the road, driving cars, and eating junk food. So if we are technically safer in the shadow of the night than in the day time, our only real enemy is our own mind.

In Frank Herbert's 1965 novel, *Dune*, there is a litany against fear that could be mentally recited in times of real or unreal peril: "I must not fear. Fear is the mind-killer. Fear is the little-death that brings total obliteration. I will face my fear. I will permit it to pass over me and through me. And when it has gone past I will turn the inner eye to see its path. Where the fear has gone there will be nothing. Only I will remain."

This mantra nicely illustrates the hidden secret of fear: Fear is a mind construct and can be undone in the mind. Though we can heed the bodily signal of potential danger, we do not need to let fear commandeer the imagination and submerge us in dread. There is no physical or mental benefit to that whatsoever. The stronger, purer, and more honorable our mind and deeds, the less we have to fear.

Deconstructing fear allows us to design a better, multi-dimensional response. If we stand alone in the pitch black of our backyard at night and feel a shiver of trepidation, that electro-chemical signal of potential danger can now be more accurately gauged and interpreted. We can separate the real from the unreal. If something is amiss, we pay attention to the danger signal and take appropriate measures. If everything is fine, we can begin to countermand the danger reflex. It is wise to leave it equipped, as it is merely trying to keep us safe, but we can assuredly modify the dominance of its signal and unplug it from the imagination.

This conscious re-patterning can be applied to any old wiring and subsequent negative responses. The more luminous, elegant, and effective the new behavioral patterning, the further back it will reach to the original wound, infusing it with consciousness and removing its resonance of pain.

Self is a conduit for the unfoldment of spirit. The clearer it is, the more truthful our expression and the more fulfilling our experiences. When we consciously acknowledge the existence of our woundedness, the healing process begins. When we choose to transform ourselves, recognize the transmittable nature of wounds, understand that it's not personal, and actively re-pattern our responses, we undo the entire cycle of woundedness. Our self-imposed restrictions fall away and the mind flows freely. It all begins with an act of will.

In ages past, the sacred knowledge and hands-on techniques necessary for creating emotional well-being were studied and practiced within the numerous mystery schools that were prevalent in Europe, the Middle East, and Asia. It was well acknowledged that emotional and psychological composure were essential foundations for conscious transcendence; the initiate had to have his house in good order before he could have any hope of rising above its material constraints.

The interconnected disciplines of mysticism, alchemy, science, healing, and philosophy—which many mystical groups fused together—have since become somewhat obscured by the dominant monotheistic religions of the last 2,000 years, eager as they were to normalize their texts for consumption by the common man. Yet the roots of wisdom have not been totally erased. With a little scrutiny, it becomes clear that the penetrating power and truth of mystical practice are never far from the surface of the modern landscape.

Chapter 22

Mystical Utterances

Many of the world's foremost religious and spiritual traditions have become disconnected from the truth of their original meaning. Where once there was an abundance of vibrant teachings in transcendence and spiritual philosophy, we now find only coarse fragments of dogma and moral allegory. This is not to say that many of the foundational texts are totally devoid of their ancestral wisdom; there is still a great deal of meaningful discovery to be had. However, in order to get to it, one has to have specialized instruction in decoding the texts, as well as generous slices of time and inspiration. This is where the significance of mysticism comes into play.

Mysticism is normally defined as the study and practice of making contact with ultimate reality through direct experience and insight. The word comes from the ancient Greek word *mystikos*, which indicates "one who has been initiated," either into the so-called ancient mysteries or, more generally, into that which is hidden from normal human comprehension. As to what is meant by ultimate reality, this differs from one tradition to the next, but it usually focuses on notions of divinity or higher realms of being.

Mysticism differs from commonly understood ideas of spiritual philosophy in that it puts a particular emphasis on experiential practice. In order to fully grasp the path of transcendence, you have to thrust yourself into it. It is acknowledged that the attainment of the vicarious spiritual student—relying chiefly on other people's ideas and accounts of spiritual enlightenment—is decidedly limited and unlikely to produce tangible or lasting results. There is also the temptation for such second-hand knowledge to be employed as a long-term substitute for one's own personal gnosis. The importance of self transformation is summed up nicely in *The Matrix* (1999), when the character Morpheus tells Neo, "Sooner or later you're going to realize just as I did that there's a difference between knowing the path and walking the path."

Hermeticism is a particular school of mysticism that is said to have arisen from the mysterious figure Hermes Trismegistus. Modern scholars suppose that he is a symbolic character, possibly a syncretic combination of the Egyptian god Thoth and the Greek god Hermes. But that is debatable. Hermeticism values experiential knowledge—gnosis—in a most profound way. It draws attention to the idea that the micro world of man's mind and the macro world of the universe are reflections of the same thing. The spiritual axiom "as above, so below" derives from the legendary Emerald Tablet, which is said to have been the work of Hermes Trismegistus.

The concept of the individual having a natural faculty for transcendence, rather than requiring the exclusive license of an outside agency, was a major headache for the church. To be able to attain spiritual salvation without an officially sanctioned savior or redeemer figure undermined state authority. It was a dynamite notion—all the more so, as many mystical traditions were very unambiguous on this point. Evolution beyond the constraints of the material human form was viewed as a biological imperative—something we are simply designed to do from the start. There is no requirement for intervention or external identification. Not that enlightened masters or divine avatars don't show up from time to time. They do. But we don't *need* them to move forward. They return to offer wisdom and guidance, when appropriate. But really, they want us to do it for ourselves.

It is not surprising to me that mysticism is still eyed with a degree of suspicion and incredulity in the modern epoch. In the collective mainstream imagination, it conjures images of solitary, roving wizards, hokey séances, and strange happenings in incense-filled chambers. It all seems so incompatible with the age of industrialization, mega-corporations, and secularism. The incongruity stems from a powerful, conditioned belief that tells us that, if something cannot be readily measured, categorized, or quantified, then its real world relevance is questionable. To put it bluntly, it has no place in machine culture.

In ages past, the ruling religious authorities were equally skeptical about the various extraordinary methods of the independent mystic and the fantastic sacred knowledge that they wielded. They didn't like the accentuation of direct personal spiritual revelation, as this potentially short-circuited conventional church doctrine and hierarchy altogether. So the church controllers set up their own mystery schools tasked with reinterpreting, destroying, or, better yet, *sequestering* any pre-existing, empowering mystical traditions. This included the knowledge, the practices, and the practitioners themselves. Anyone who opposed this assimilation was sidelined or executed.

Only very recently was the dominance of the church separated out from the ostensibly democratic governments of Britain, and Europe. In many Asian and Middle Eastern countries, religion continues to remain firmly entrenched within the apparatus of the state, the formal education system, and wider society as a whole. It is difficult for the Western mind to grasp the fact that, in these places, religion is not merely a system of elective spiritual practice; it represents the very heart of the culture itself. When so closely bound to the social order in this way, the rule of the religious authorities is total.

Antidisestablishmentarianism—the longest natural word in the English language—derives from this very issue. In 19th-century Britain, the *disestablishmentarians* sought to separate the church from the state. The *antidisestablishmentarians* sought to preserve the bond. Hence the term. To a degree, the argument is still ongoing to this day, with questions arising over Britain's queen's current position as "Supreme Governor" of the "Church."

The independent mystic of old needed to be a very special sort of person. For one, he had to be able to read and write. For thousands of years, this ability, which we now tend to take for granted in the West, was an extremely rare and powerful skill. Before the start of the Industrial Revolution in Britain in the late 18th century, very few regular people were literate. The art of the written word was the sole province of the ruling elites and their administrators—the privileged upper classes and religious clerics—with whom they shared certain entitlements. It is ironic that with the dubious march of industrialization, from Britain to Europe, and then to America and the rest of the world, literacy was finally brought to the masses. Pre-18th-century literate mystics therefore had to be either completely self-taught, wealthy enough to pay for a private education, or born into titled families.

As well as cleverly safeguarding the treasure of their sacred knowledge, the mystic also had to be constantly mindful of their own physical safety—not a thing to be disregarded when practicing spiritual independence in previous centuries. Gladly, many mystics successfully identified and outsmarted the church's assimilation process by clothing their esoteric wisdom in the robes of the presiding mainstream religion. Names, symbols, philosophies, and rites were frequently coded into officially approved doctrine and became all but invisible to the uninitiated. Yet the knowledge was there. It was lying low, ready to be decoded and unpacked by other initiates, or even in the distant future by more enlightened scholars and civilizations.

This did not stop Christianity, Judaism, and Islam from producing their own powerful and insightful mystics, although they were operating from a totally different paradigm. It is therefore crucial to recognize that every major world religion has come to have both an exoteric outer shell and an esoteric inner core. It is the exoteric shell, with its panoply of scriptures, commandments, and behavioral requirements, that determines the lives of most religious worshippers—whereas, the inner core always remains unknown, intentionally concealed and watchfully guarded. Only those initiated into the inner mysteries are permitted access to the original sacred gnosis, which, even after millennia of obfuscation, still contains revelations that are shockingly divergent from the beliefs authorized for public consumption.

There is a striking consistency in the central knowledge base gathered by so many apparently diverse and even opposing mystical traditions. This is not altogether unanticipated when one considers that the major monotheistic faiths of Christianity, Judaism, and Islam also have remarkably similar spiritual roots, despite their history of warring. Millennia of fierce ideological conflict and countless millions of lost human lives make it deceptively easy to forget that the pivotal messenger of God and the holy prophet to the people—Abraham—is common to both Christian, Jewish, and Muslim sacred lore.

The central figure of Jesus is considered by both Christians and Muslims to be a descendant of Abraham. Muslims, too, regard their holy prophet Muhammad as a direct descendant, through Ishmael (Abraham's child). The Jews identify Abraham as the forefather of many important tribes, including the Israelites, Midianites, and Edomites. He was also the grandfather of their third patriarch, Jacob (also later known as Israel), a crucial figure from whose descendants Judaism defines itself. In modern encyclopedias, each religion is still formally classified as Abrahamic. Though each has its own brand of spiritual philosophy and exhibits differing forms of symbolism and ritual, they all share this same single historical ancestry. If that is so, then the committed mystic, who had laid his hands upon the deeply esoteric knowledge that emanated directly from the original prophet (whom we might reasonably assume was himself a mystic), was placed in a rather precarious position.

If it could be shown that the original creed and the ideological roots of these global giants were identical, it would expose the treachery of the men who had sequestered these traditions for the purposes of lowly political control. Perhaps this is obvious now, with our contemporary access to the Internet and innumerable data sources, but, a few hundred years ago, this knowledge would have represented a game-changing piece of intelligence. Conflict between the different faiths was critical for long-term globalist policies. Perceptions needed to be tightly controlled. And they were—right up until the 17th century. Not long ago at all on the historical time line.

Whether or not an initiated mystic was operating from within the church, was pretending to, or was totally independent, the knowledge he had was beyond measure. Not only did mystics hold the real genesis of the authorities origins in their hands (stretching eons before Abraham), but the substance of the knowledge itself revealed a massive disconnect in the way the churches were representing personal spiritual ascendancy and the actual truth of it. And so the mystics were obliged to become hidden sages, and have largely remained so ever since.

Though not quite the same matter of life and death, the modern heralds of scientific reason have been equally obliged to handle mysticism with kid gloves. Particularly with the current trend for science to proclaim itself as the sole arbiter of reality, any suggestions of mystical influence must be hurriedly played down. Yet the path of unfoldment never fails to stir things up. Ironies are as common as epiphanies.

Though many eminent philosophers have contemplated the metaphysical underpinnings of one's being in the universe, few have done so with the penetration and open-mindedness of certain physicists. One might imagine that it would be the other way round. Yet despite the initial academic habituation of pioneers like Niels Bohr, Werner Heisenberg, Erwin Schrodinger, and David Bohm, through the felt experience of their own intimate experimentation and inquiry, they succeeded in consciously deconstructing their own scientific paradigms in order to afford a glimpse of the underlying architecture of the universe. Of course, much of the metaphysical contribution from these fellows derives from their work in the field of quantum physics—though it is hard not to observe a higher spiritual consciousness in the overarching themes of their respective works, whether explicit as in the case of Bohm, or implicit as with Bohr.

Even with Socrates, who can justifiably be regarded as a major contributor to the modern scientific dialectical method, we can detect an element of undoubted mysticism to his work. Socrates and his Greek peers observed a "daemonic sign" in his philosophical technique. That is to say, Socrates regularly heard an "inner voice" that dissuaded him from taking certain negative paths. Socrates himself considered this to be a gift of "divine madness" from the gods—one that helped steer his actions and thoughts toward the most rewarding outcomes. That same gift, he tells us, brings us mysticism, poetry, art, and even philosophy itself. Socrates' interpretation of the "sign" as daemonic suggests he considered it not just simply an intuitive subconscious faculty, but something of divine origin, quite independent of his own thoughts.

It is broadly acknowledged that many prominent philosophers, including Baader, Schelling, Hegel, Schopenhauer, and Heidegger, were significantly influenced by the bold assertions of various mystics. I feel that they inspired some of the most meticulously crafted philosophical texts of the last few centuries. Even so, it can be seen that the philosophers were often compelled, both by their intellectual apparatus and their academic paradigms, to conceptualize much of their spiritual insight into scholarly linguistic schemas of abstraction and "bottom-up" materialism. This can be most clearly tracked in the movement of ideas from Jakob Bohme, to Georg Hegel, to Karl Marx. An instructive, if curious, relationship.

All academic institutions have the potential to restrain their mainstream adherents to the received wisdom of the day, whether scientific, philosophical, or religious. However, it seems that the mystics were demonstrably more willing to take risks. Even in the face of the overtly authoritarian religious dogmas of their day, mystics such as Meister Eckhart, Jakob Bohme, William Blake, Helena Blavatsky, G.I. Gurdjieff, and Teilhard De Chardin launched themselves into the deepest realms of experiential metaphysics to a degree that was unthinkable to all but the most intrepid of philosophical scholars. We are forever beholden to them for their profound, transcendent, and ever-so-slightly crazy spiritual fortitude.

Chapter 23

Within and Without

The greatest achievements from the greatest men and women are often feats of the imagination. Acts of ingeniousness always arise from the subtle but miraculous crucible of the inner realm. Throw in a healthy dose of tenacity and application, and that quiet spark of potential transmutes into a spectacular blaze of materialization.

Imagination is the beginning of reality. It is the holographic engine for creating certain energy configurations that we call *form*. With the proper concentration of will, intent, spirit, and discipline, those forms can achieve a level of consistency that may convey them from the inside to the outside, should we so wish. The dream of consciousness shifts its density and becomes an actual concrete thing, a thing we can witness and experience. The more coherent and solid it is, the stronger its manifestation in consensus reality and the more people can share in it.

A clue to the mechanism of the imagination lies in those situations when we find ourselves hitting a brick wall of logic or facing some kind of tricky dilemma. At these times, we often hear people say "use your imagination!" This is very prudent advice indeed, though it has to be said that it is typically shared without full knowledge of quite what it means. Even so, it is commonly supposed that the imagination is somehow capable of a kind of lateral thinking that the linear mind often struggles with. This mysterious dynamic that appears to defy the usual circuitry of cause and effect is why the imagination is so esteemed by wise.

Many prominent works of art, music, science, and literature have been claimed by their creators to have just "come to them." Sometimes the inspiration comes from the dreamscape of their nocturnal unconsciousness; at other times there are waking flashes of illumination that bring revelations in broad daylight. It seems that closer proximity to the vigor of the imagination is achieved when the ordinary workings of the mind are diverted or even taken off-line altogether. Dreaming represents an especially potent nexus for encounters with the imaginal.

Schumann believed that many of his musical compositions were channeled to him by his deceased colleagues and other musical luminaries (including Beethoven). Beethoven himself, when struggling with the fourth part of his masterpiece, *Symphony No. 9 in D Minor*, was said to have dashed into the room exclaiming, "I got it. I just got it!" From this gift he then refined and reworked the idea until it became the final choral finale. Many romantic English poets credited their visions as direct sources for some of their most renowned works, including Wordsworth and Coleridge. The same can be said of Charlotte Brontë with her classic novel *Jane Eyre*, Mary Shelley with *Frankenstein*, Robert Louis Stevenson with *Dr. Jekyll and Mr. Hyde*, and even modern-day works like *Misery* by Stephen King. American inventor Thomas Edison, whose developments led to the phonograph and the long-lasting light bulb, attributed many of his strokes of genius to his habit of taking frequent catnaps at his desk. German-born physiologist Otto Loewi won the 1936 Nobel Prize for medicine for his work on the chemical transmission of nerve impulses, the genesis of which came to him through a dream. Elias Howe invented the sewing machine from a dream. Abraham Lincoln saw his assassination in a dream. Einstein, Wagner, Handel, Descartes, Jung—all have identified their visions and dreams as responsible for some of their most significant works. The list goes on.

Whether they saw it in a dream, heard it in a moment of repose, or just simply copied down the details from an otherworldly source, it is as if it already existed somehow. The thing coming down the pipe of creation was *already there*. But how could it be? There is a hushed but eerie sensation that at some level, the core inspiration for our finest creations is not really *ours* at all. We unearth it, we channel it, we articulate it—but it's not ours. Though we can legitimately lay claim to a splendid discovery, the actual origins are quite another matter.

The first stage in unlocking the potential of the imagination is to actively recalibrate the erroneous perspective we have on it. We really don't understand what it is, what it's for, or how it works. I cannot remember a single occasion in my primary, secondary, or higher education when the nature of the imagination was discussed at all. One would think that it would've been at least mentioned in several years of visual arts training, but it wasn't. I had to find out for myself.

The mainstream view of the imagination is simplistic and reductionist. For example, it is commonly believed that some people have big, vivid imaginations, and some people do not. This is not accurate. It is more useful to say that some people *value* their imagination as a source of inspiration, and some people do not. Even in everyday life, it is this basic perspective shift that distinguishes the exceptional from the ordinary.

The official position is that the imagination is a lighthearted plaything used by kids and artists. More often than not, as we go from school into college, from the workplace into family life, and from maturity into our senior years, we find that our stunningly resourceful imagination has been largely surplus to requirement. Nobody mentioned anything in particular about it, and we didn't go looking.

Despite paying lip service to the brilliance of the human imagination, the mega-corporations and think tanks of unhappy gangster capitalism can't afford to have too many imaginations running around the place. It upsets the applecart and starts making things go a bit wobbly. So they simply downgrade it. They pretend it's not there, and even if it is, it is of no real consequence. Hence, the imagination is perceived as largely immaterial to normal, grown-up proceedings. It is at best a privileged toy, at worst a distraction from serious productivity. The abiding resonance is that adults do not need imaginations to be happy and successful; they just need to work hard. Even for those who are employed in ostensibly creative industries, raw innovation and uncontaminated flair are often inhibited by the pressure to adhere to popular trends and market expectations. Doing it by the numbers has replaced many free-form frontiers of creative impact.

An increasingly corporatized cultural environment—which people are willingly consenting to—places less and less value on individuality and natural expression. *Machine culture* disguises the crushing uniformity under a veneer of surface customization that makes people believe that they can still do things their own way. The result is that large chunks of the global population purchase identical third-rate machines from two or three multi-billion-dollar organizations. *There is no choice.* I have witnessed this many times on the subways of New York: all manner of humanity transformed into cardboard cut-outs by their little gadgets of audio-visual nourishment. Is this so hugely different from the good old days of communal train travel? Not really. The newspapers have just become electronic.

The imagination is a highly resilient force. It is like a stargate or portal that opens up in the mind, affording access to other realms—other densities. It wants to open up and refuses to stay closed indefinitely. Moreover, it has a mischievous habit of making its presence felt at the most inopportune moments, often swinging the whole context of a situation into its opposite. It defuses the melodrama and sparks apathy into engagement. That is why it is safe for children and artists, but not for proper grown-ups. That is also why it has to be switched off as soon as possible through social conditioning. Persuading people to buy into uniformity, submission and mass symmetry is a very clever way of obtaining financial, emotional, and psychic permission to harvest their imagination.

The television screen has a particular capability for altering consciousness. Primetime viewing during one of the biggest public holidays in the UK a few years ago was in the shape of the Tony Mitchell disaster film *Flood*. The tagline for the film is "It's coming straight for us." What actually arrived was an enormous slice of negative imaginal programming.

Flood is a bit like an English version of *The Day After Tomorrow*. It showcases impressive CGI visuals of major population centers being consumed by water, with all the inevitable ensuing pandemonium, ill-equipped authorities, and selected personal dramas. Leveraging the contemporary enthusiasm for doom porn, *Flood* enjoyed heavy mainstream media attention and was watched by millions of British families. The very next day, BBC news carried the headline "Flood Risk Fear over Key UK Sites." The similarities in the fictional *Flood* imagery and actual aerial pictures of London were astonishing. These striking images were seeded into the public imagination within 24 hours of each other. For the esoteric researcher, the subconscious resonance is absolutely intentional—the news augmenting the prior fictional narrative with a bleak consensus reality and an identical transmission of fear, panic, and vulnerability.

As we have said, the imagination is constantly wanting to open itself up to our own sovereign spiritual self. It doesn't really like being hijacked by anyone else. Even when it is overwhelmed by some traumatic event, it just goes into a sort of temporary stasis. It cannot be destroyed.

I remember when my imagination took its first serious dent. I was 7 years old. I was playing with a friend in a small, wooded area of his parents' backyard. There were only about 10 trees, but to us it was a vast and mysterious forest, full of adventure and fierce dragons. We had a handful of little, yellow plastic discs from a board game that we had imagined into gold pieces. We'd previously buried them in the soil, so we could later go back and pretend to discover them as treasure. We were armed with mighty, dragon-slaying swords to defend ourselves against the evil monsters who were guarding the treasure. It was a hazardous mission, but we were up to it. It was all rather Tolkien-esque.

A short while later, another kid who lived nearby came over with his soccer ball, hoping to catch a game with us. He was a little older than we were, only by a couple of years, but that's an awful lot when you're 7. When he saw us prancing around under the trees, he smirked and asked what we were doing digging holes and swinging our swords. When we explained our valiant quest to him, he laughed unkindly and suggested that soccer was a much better game than make-believe. My treasure-hunting companion and I stood motionless for a moment and looked at each other. Around us, the enchantment of the forest began to fade. The hundreds of miles of pine trees, the snow-capped mountains in the distance, the long winding rivers, and the fabulous creatures—all of it just disappeared. The steel of our swords became cheap, gray plastic, and the solid gold coins just garish yellow counters. The magic was gone. As it is with kids, the disappointment didn't last too long. Half an hour later, we were all playing soccer together on the sun-scorched lawn.

Nevertheless, that was the last time as a child that my imagination built a whole world. The stargate closed and all the awesome power of miraculous creation receded. Were it not for my later spiritual studies, esoteric knowledge, and disciplined practice, it would've been the *final* time.

I later began to seriously study spiritual philosophy and make it part of my day-to-day life. Anything and everything was a target for my input, from Nietzsche to Crowley, from Buddha to Castaneda, from Blavatsky to Christ. At some point during that ravenous period, on one particular day, I felt the distinctive quiver of magic that I thought had gone forever with my childhood. It was massively heartening and brought a deep sense of energized self-assurance, once I realized that it had never truly left me. I knew in that moment that the miracle of the spiritual path, and all the magic that goes with it, is available to everyone, all the time. It never goes away. Since then, I have always communicated to those conscious people that I engage with that one of the most awesome things about the unfoldment of the sacred journey is that it *re-magics* life.

In the practice of opening the portal of the imagination, it is wise to become conscious of what purposefully restricts it and how that can be undone. The chief culprit is belief. Consider that it is a child's fluidity of belief systems that enables the imagination to blossom so intensely. Up until the age of around 7, there has not yet been sufficient social conditioning to neutralize the potency of the imagination. The grievous unreality signal of social, political, and materialistic propaganda has not yet taken hold of the young mind. It is still free to perceive any way it wishes. In fact, a child does not require belief systems to operate effectively at all. Herein lies the secret of their power. So we have to consider what unhelpful belief programs we might have picked up and have probably been unconsciously running for years. This is where a healthy input of quality metaphysical philosophy, Zen perspectives, and mystical traditions can really help to clean house. As to selecting the most appropriate texts and teachings—this is necessarily left for readers to determine for themselves. The coursework is never standard. It is always customized to suit the individual's own tastes, challenges, and objectives.

My imagination was hampered throughout my 20s by the nagging doubt that consciousness was very much secondary to the physical. Although I understood at an intellectual level that this was not automatically always the case, the egoic skeptic in my head (which can be very useful at times) took some *serious* convincing. So I took some equally serious measures to formulate a range of authentic felt experiences that were irrefutably paradigm cracking. The old clockwork view of the world had to be upgraded, supplemented, and relaxed shortly thereafter. Rather than fall out with my ego over these matters, I made friends with it, listened to it, and communicated with it using its own preferred terminology. That meant a good slice of quantum physics, ethno-botanical research, and classical ascetic meditation practice. Though to some extent that process continues to this day, the doubt has gone. There is only knowing now. I am clear about what I know and clear on what I don't know. No belief required either way.

Finally, we come to the esoteric angle.

The imagination can be justly considered as a bridge to a higher order of reality. It augments our ordinary mind state by connecting it to the fourth density, a state of being where manifest energy is not of the thick and solid kind, like it is here. Form is fluid, changeable, and less substantial, yet it is intensely vivid, and fundamentally more dependable and real than it is in our accustomed third density state. One might conceive of the fourth density as a place where the imaginal may achieve immediate manifestation. Think of a banana in your hand, and it is in your hand. Think of being with the love of your life, and you are in their arms. Want to visit the Paris of the 1920s? No problem. The harebrained guidelines of time and space—the whole Newtonian-Cartesian physics modality thing—just stops being applicable anymore, thank you very much. It's like being in a lucid dream 24/7. Once you learn to control yourself, to properly navigate, and to become proficient with manifestation, the prospect of returning to the heavy meat of the third density is distinctly unappealing. Once someone has stepped through the stargate and shifted densities, she very rarely wants to go back. A balanced psyche is always therefore essential.

It is the same principle for those having a near-death experience (NDE), where the tunnel of light begins to shift the energetic density of their consciousness and releases it from the gravitation of the body. Form and density alter. There is a delicious *lightness* of being and the first real sensation of being absolutely liberated from the coarse machinery of cause and effect. It is one of the most exquisite feelings conceivable. For those who have spent time in the dense pain of some horrible disease, it is an especially welcome transition.

I first read about this potential portal of the imagination when I was about 18. I gathered books from the shelves of the mainstream bookstores and hunted down dusty old volumes from little independent bookshops in Somerset and Lancashire (this was way before the dawn of the Internet). Most of the books were a disappointment. There were no secret keys in them. None. Whenever I came across a metaphysical or new age book that focused on *visualization* techniques, I rolled my eyes. Ostensibly trustworthy books on contemporary shamanism ended a chapter on shapeshifting with a visualization exercise that read something like this: "Take a deep breath and close your eyes. Become silent. Imagine you are being drawn into the depths of the rain forest. You can hear the cacophony of animal calls; you can smell the trees and feel the humidity on your skin. You are home. Here, you can become the jaguar, whose spirit is within you. Breathe its spirit into your body. You rapidly morph into the powerful feline structure that feels so true to the land. You feel your agility, speed, vision, and instincts shift to supremely high levels. You are the jaguar. You move beneath the green canopy and see everything."

After reading the hundredth book that sprang passages like that on me, I stopped reading these sort of things altogether. I couldn't take it anymore. Though I appreciated that some people might like that sort of thing, I did not find them helpful in the slightest. What I realize now is that many of the texts were not delineating between the manifestation of the imagination in the third and fourth densities. They were conflating them. They were trying to perceive everything from only the third density. This is not possible. The dream cannot be changed from within the dream. Also, the language used gave zero concessions to the reason of the left brain, nor any overall spiritual context or metaphysical framework. For those works claiming to be handbooks of modern shamanism, this was transparently outrageous. They were poetic meditations on shamanism, at best. The unfoldment rarely requires guided symbolism. For good reason, experiential self-initiation is primary. You have to do it your own way. Where imaginal guidance is needed, it must be done in person.

To understand how to encourage the flow of consciousness from the imaginal realm, it is necessary to say a few words about the body's system of energy portals. Hindu philosophers called them *chakras* ("wheel" or "turning"). They are energy transformers. They are portals. There are seven primary portals, anchored in a straight line from the top of the skull, down to the base of the spine. They are not physical organs like the heart, liver, or kidneys. Their operation is more subtle than that. They overlay our physical body in a fourth density state and are designed to transfer energy between the 4D and the 3D. Though Indian, Chinese, and Tibetan practitioners each have their own differing ideas of how many portals there are, and what precisely they do, the principles are similar.

My personal formulation of the seven portals and their associated resonances is as follows:

1. The crown—knowing/transcendence.

2. The brow—insight/seeing.

3. The throat—expression/life-force.

4. The sternum—connection/sovereignty.

5. The solar plexus—will/purpose.

6. The sacral—gratification/flow.

7. The base—preservation/groundedness.

Activating the imagination depends on three things all happening at the same time:

1. *The central energy portal of the body being open* (located at the sternum). This particular portal is tuned for *connectivity*. It is the organic wireless modem for communicating with other consciousnesses, locations, objects, and realms. It can be stimulated through placing conscious attention on it, with the mind still, and intent unwavering. It takes practice. Unfortunately, this portal is rusted shut for many people and is only occasionally treated with psychic lubricant so it can swing open for brief, intense periods of emotional eruption, after which it is then usually slammed shut again. Developing a smooth energy flow is reliant on attaining a high degree of emotional intelligence.

2. *Mental programs, belief systems, and brain churn being switched off.* The imagination cannot deliver its payload from the fourth density if the pipe is clogged with stuff and nonsense. Lots of things have to be turned down, turned off, or thrown out altogether. The old neural pathways of behavioral routines, the prominence of self/personality, and the good old logic gates of yes/no have to be suspended. They are of no use here. Belief systems just serve to darken the purity of the imagination. It is like placing red tinted spectacles over your eyes. The actual colors of the world collapse down into just one frequency, and the *data* from all the other colors is lost. This is what belief systems do to the imagination. The fizz of brain static from the constant narration— by oneself of oneself—has to be totally turned off. In the classic days of Victorian occultism, wine was often used for

this purpose! Not advisable. For one thing, like any chemical prop, an over-dependence on any outside agency causes eventual weakness. The alchemist only attains mastery over his art when he can function without his powders, alembics, crucibles, and vessels. The flame is the only essential element—and that is always present in the alchemist himself.

3. *Surrender of personal circumstances for commitment to higher ascendance.* The flow of inspiration from the field is only really interested in opening for the purposes of growth. Though it can doubtless also bring technological breakthroughs and attractive works of art, they are, to some extent, merely peripheral consequences of a more profound deepening of consciousness. To place one's own self-interests of comfort, security, and the accumulation of resources to one side represents mindful intent to pledge one's will to the process of spiritual unfoldment. This can be *perceived* by the higher self and indeed the universe at large. One of the beautiful ironies of redirecting consciousness back into the core, as opposed to the outer shell, is that the material benefits of life tend to come more freely and abundantly. This flies in the face of the social logic we have been brought up to believe (you have to work a punishing schedule before you can reap the benefits). Make one slight modification to this idiom and it becomes more spiritually accurate: You have to work hard on yourself before you can reap the benefits.

With an integrated, disciplined, and lively imaginal mindscape, many of the insoluble problems of life begin to change their aspect. Previously ugly and insurmountable problems get less scary. Where once there was only an x-axis to move to the left or right of the problem, there is now a y-axis, which enables up and down movement. This adds a whole new dimension to analysis and resolution. As with philosophy, imagination gives *elevation*, but at a different density. It permits us to regard substantially more of our multi-dimensional life terrain, both internally and externally. The more we zoom out, the more we can appreciate the relationship between one thing and another, and how consequential each individual element is to the bigger picture. Self-determination and personal power increase. More things feel doable.

For the medieval laboratory alchemist, the enterprise of turning lead into gold was a means to an end. The deeper secret teaching was that in order for the procedure to actually work, a transmutation of the alchemist's own consciousness must also occur. Indeed, it is from the three-way interface between the universe itself, the human mind, and the physical form being focused upon that the real power emanates. Herein lies the wisdom.

We have heard the popular alchemical idiom that deals with the law of correspondence: "as above, so below." Inevitably, this conjures images of modern astrology with its aligning of archetypal behavioral patterns with celestial bodies. Yet there is another, far-less-heard part of this phrase, one that is particularly pertinent to the underlying principles of the unfoldment: "as within, so without." This is the first clue to indicate that the alchemist's journey leads to a revelatory piece of knowledge, one that we have already explored in a number of different ways in this book: *There is no separation between what is inside and what is outside.* The very consciousness that we "carry" around in our heads is in no way separate from the energies that flow through the wider world. It is only our sense of self that anchors us inside.

Physicist David Bohm felt that the ultimate nature of physical reality is not a collection of separate objects, but rather an undivided whole that is in perpetual dynamic flux. It is a vast ocean of shimmering energy. Once more, he was reinterpreting ancient spiritual and alchemical knowledge, and translating it into a modern quantum vocabulary. He said in his book with co-author F. David Peat, *Science, Order, and Creativity*: "[A]t a deeper level [matter and consciousness] are actually inseparable and interwoven.... Deep down, the consciousness of mankind is one." Bohm called this gigantic flow of energy and consciousness *the holomovement*.

Within this model of reality, neurophysiologist Karl Pribram suggests that our most fundamental notions about reality become suspect, for in a holographic universe even random events are based on holographic principles and therefore determined. Synchronicities or meaningful coincidences suddenly make sense, and everything in reality is seen as a metaphor, for even the most haphazard events express some underlying symmetry. As Pribram himself summarized, in an interview with Dr. Jeffrey Mishlove (for the television series *Thinking Allowed*): "The descriptions you get with spiritual experiences seem to parallel the descriptions of quantum physics."

We program the holomovement with our consciousness. Consciousness is the software behind the architecture. It follows, then, that if we shape the holomovement, and the holomovement constitutes all forms and events, then we are natural co-creators of the universe itself, alongside many other sentient beings. What we call the "soul" is the little unit of consciousness that we get to work with, a constantly evolving energy system that is both *here* and *there*. This is one of the great truths of mankind, long since shrouded in exoteric mythology—obscured, diluted, and exceedingly hard to lay one's hands upon. Yet there it is. Right in front of our eyes.

Moreover, within the grand holomovement of our reality, if we look hard enough, we can detect evidence of a super-soul, an awesome quality of consciousness with an ancient evolutionary path that seems to have existed from the beginning. It is the primary consciousness that holds the whole thing together. The elegant design of its fractal patterning is embedded into every manifest form, from the dazzling head of a sunflower to the stunning sophistication of DNA. The deeper we look, the more beautiful the design, yet it always follows a sequence of definite geometric principles. This super-soul is responsible for nurturing and guiding the substructure of reality and all the souls within it. It is the entity that authored the reality programming language itself. It is my understanding that it is directly from this ineffable source that we derive the universal impulse to explore the unfoldment of reality—to know it in ourselves, to embrace its movement, and to articulate it with our own creations.

Without real mindfulness of our own remarkable creative power, we simply serve as conduits for the programming instructions we get from elsewhere. And from whom do we get these instructions? Who makes the images? Can we trust them to always act from the highest and noblest intent? To unswervingly encode their images and symbols with the utmost integrity and growth? Suffice to say, it is prudent for us to take full ownership of the gift of imaginal power within ourselves.

It is in exploring the intimate relationship between individual consciousness and the flow of universal consciousness that we come to know that a human being is a rather more extraordinary and significant thing than we have been led to believe.

The imagination opens a channel from the 3D to the 4D. It brings field knowing and authorizes passage for the extraordinary to express itself into the ordinary. For true unfoldment, we have to *own* this channel. If we don't, then, by default, someone else will. We claim willful ownership simply in the same way that we own our courage, our humor, our love, and our insight. It is a natural component of our reality modeling apparatus. When the flesh realizes that its own condition is actually enhanced by allowing the imagination to flow, it stops getting in the way, and the imagination can enlighten everything we do. Mind and spirit coalesce. Quite organic. Quite genuine. Quite magical.

Resurgence

Unfoldment is a choice. It is an acknowledgment of our own sacred presence in the universe. To bring its truth into our everyday life, we must move our consciousness from personality, to thought, to self, to spirit. In so doing, we soften the boundaries of the inner and the outer. We get to shape the dream in more truthful and creative ways. We begin to see through the chimera of the distortion and recognize it for what it is: a small, objectionable dream within a vast, magnificent dream. It is all *our* dream. When we become lucid, we can change it.

The depth of our knowing parallels our living practice of unfoldment. The purer our experience, the truer our knowing. To get to the real essence of a thing, we first need to remove that which is inessential. We become lighter and lighter, less and less dense. Though we see the same things, our experiences are different. We go to the root. Through knowing polarization, we learn the art of integration. Through knowing the shadow, we comprehend the purpose of light. Through knowing separation, we attain the truth of wholeness.

Discipline allows us to move more gracefully through life. The discipline of the unfoldment is in nurturing a constant awareness that reality flows not through our self, but through our being. We realize that what we experience is what we are. When we know ourselves, the universe knows itself. When we learn, it learns. The only accountability is to our own sovereign essence, through which we contribute to the overall pattern of ascendant return.

The awakening of the unfoldment reaches into every part of our lives—not just into the big magical things, but into the little magical things, too. It changes *how we are* when we brush our teeth, when we buy bread, when we drive the car, when we talk to our loved ones, when we watch the trees swaying in the wind. In the little things, we see the one truth. We can then remember the majesty of what we are and the splendor of what we are doing.

Go deeply.

Index

About the Author

Neil Kramer is an English writer, philosopher, and spiritual teacher, specializing in the fields of consciousness, metaphysics, and mysticism. Neil has made a lifelong independent study of philosophy, mystical traditions, shamanism, religion, inner alchemy, and esoteric world history. He shares his path of transformation and empowerment in writings, interviews, and lectures, as well as giving one-on-one teachings and group workshops. Neil's work is regularly published on cutting-edge Websites, news portals, and popular media networks, as well as appearing on television in the U.S.A., UK, Canada, and Europe. Neil lives in Oregon, U.S.A.